JZ1251 .C574 2009

01341

Civiliza
and wo1
  200

Civilizational Dialogue and World Order

Culture and Religion in International Relations

Series Editors:
Yosef Lapid and Friedrich Kratochwil

Published by Palgrave Macmillan:

Dialogue among Civilizations: Some Exemplary Voices
By Fred Dallmayr

Religion in International Relations: The Return from Exile
Edited by Fabio Petito and Pavlos Hatzopoulos

Identity and Global Politics: Theoretical and Empirical Elaborations
Edited by Patricia M. Goff and Kevin C. Dunn

Reason, Culture, Religion: The Metaphysics of World Politics
By Ralph Pettman

Bringing Religion into International Relations
By Jonathan Fox and Shmuel Sandler

The Global Resurgence of Religion and the Transformation of International Relations: The Struggle for the Soul of the Twenty-First Century
By Scott M. Thomas

Religion, Social Practice, and Contested Hegemonies: Reconstructing the Public Sphere in Muslim Majority Societies
Edited by Armando Salvatore and Mark LeVine

Beyond Eurocentrism and Anarchy: Memories of International Order and Institutions
By Siba N. Grovogui

The Public Sphere: Liberal Modernity, Catholicism, Islam
By Armando Salvatore

Civilizational Identity: The Production and Reproduction of 'Civilizations' in International Relations
Edited by Martin Hall and Patrick Thaddeus Jackson

Civilizing Missions: International Religious Agencies in China
By Miwa Hirono

Civilizational Dialogue and World Order: The Other Politics of Cultures, Religions, and Civilizations in International Relations
Edited by Michális S. Michael and Fabio Petito

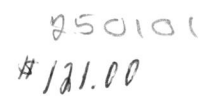

CIVILIZATIONAL DIALOGUE AND WORLD ORDER

THE OTHER POLITICS OF CULTURES, RELIGIONS, AND CIVILIZATIONS IN INTERNATIONAL RELATIONS

Edited by
Michális S. Michael and Fabio Petito

palgrave
macmillan

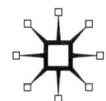

CIVILIZATIONAL DIALOGUE AND WORLD ORDER
Copyright © Michális S. Michael and Fabio Petito, 2009.

All rights reserved.

First published in 2009 by
PALGRAVE MACMILLAN®
in the United States—a division of St. Martin's Press LLC,
175 Fifth Avenue, New York, NY 10010.

Where this book is distributed in the UK, Europe and the rest of the world, this is by Palgrave Macmillan, a division of Macmillan Publishers Limited, registered in England, company number 785998, of Houndmills, Basingstoke, Hampshire RG21 6XS.

Palgrave Macmillan is the global academic imprint of the above companies and has companies and representatives throughout the world.

Palgrave® and Macmillan® are registered trademarks in the United States, the United Kingdom, Europe and other countries.

ISBN-13: 978–0–230–60820–7
ISBN-10: 0–230–60820–5

Library of Congress Cataloging-in-Publication Data is available from the Library of Congress.

A catalogue record of the book is available from the British Library.

Design by Newgen Imaging Systems (P) Ltd., Chennai, India.

First edition: May 2009

10 9 8 7 6 5 4 3 2 1

Printed in the United States of America.

Contents

Acknowledgments	vii
Notes on Contributors	ix

Introduction

1. Imperial Monologue or Civilizational Dialogue? 3
   Michális S. Michael and Fabio Petito

Part I   The Relevance of Civilizational Dialogue for World Order

2. Justice and Cross-Cultural Dialogue: From Theory to Practice 29
   Fred R. Dallmayr
3. Dialogue of Civilizations as an Alternative Model for World Order 47
   Fabio Petito
4. Dialogue among and within Faiths: Weaving a Culture of Peace 69
   Toh Swee-Hin (S. H. Toh)

Part II   Locating Civilizational Dialogue in International Relations

5. Civilizationism and the Political Debate on Globalization 93
   Raffaele Marchetti
6. Anti-Cosmopolitanism, the Cosmopolitan Harm Principle and Global Dialogue 111
   Richard Shapcott

Contents

7 Finding Appropriate Forms of Dialogue for
  Engaging with the Politics of Security   129
  Phillip Darby

Part III Civilizational Dialogue between Empire and Resistance in the Post-September 11 Context

8 Monologue of Empire versus Global Dialogue of
  Cultures: The Branding of "American Values"   147
  Manfred B. Steger

9 Terror, Counterterror, and Self Destruction:
  Living with Regimes of Narcissism and Despair   167
  Ashis Nandy

10 *Quo Vadis*, the Dialogue of Civilizations?
   September 11 and Muslim-West Relations   181
   Chandra Muzaffar

Part IV Cross-Cultural Dialogue in the Context of Civilizational Encounters

11 Openness and the Dialogue of
   Civilizations—a Chinese Example   201
   Zhang Longxi

12 From Tension to Dialogue? The Mediterranean between
   European Civilization and the Muslim World   217
   Armando Salvatore

13 History, Memory, and the Dialogue of Civilizations:
   The Case of Northeast Asia   239
   Michael T. Seigel

Bibliography   263
Index   283

Acknowledgments

Since the designation of 2001 as the UN Year of Dialogue among Civilizations and the events of September 11, dialogue has become a recurring and often controversial theme in international discourse. For its advocates, the dialogue of cultures, religions and civilizations offers one of the more promising contributions to public debate on how we diagnose the present and plan for the future... If dialogue is an idea whose time has come, it is necessary to develop a clearer understanding of the nature of dialogue.

With these words, La Trobe University's Centre for Dialogue convened on December 12–13, 2006 in Melbourne an international two-day conference entitled "The Politics of Empire and the Culture of Dialogue: Intellectual and Organisational Signposts for the Future." Attended by some of the world's leading scholars in this area, the workshop concluded with a call for serious reflection on the significance of a civilizational dialogue for the future of world order.

This book has its genesis in this workshop and is, to a large extent, a fitting outcome for a Center whose aim it is to further develop both the theory and practice of dialogue. In this regard we would like to thank all those at the Centre for Dialogue (notably Ben Zala, James Oaten, Christine Siokou, George Myconos) who made the 2006 workshop a success. A special thanks is, however, reserved for its director and our very good friend, Professor Joseph Camilleri. Without Professor Camilleri's contribution, we can unequivocally say that neither the workshop nor this book would have been possible.

We would also like to thank all those scholars who participated in the workshop and whose papers are not included in this publication: Professors Camilleri, Majid Tehranian (Director, Institute for Peace and Global Policy Research, Tokyo, Honolulu), Jon Goldberg-Hiller (University of Hawai'i), Wayne Hudson (Griffith University), Gary D. Bouma (Monash University), and Desmond Cahill (RMIT

University). We thank them for their hard work, their input, and the inspiration they provided.

We are also appreciative of the assistance from our publisher, Palgrave. We are particularly grateful to Yosef Lapid and Friedrich Kratochwil for their constant consideration and support of our work and also to Anthony Wahl who took on board this project and persevered with it despite our penchant for extensions. We are proud to feature our work in their series on "Culture and Religion in International Relations," which has contributed more than any other outlet to the expansion and advancement of this subfield of research.

It goes without saying that without the inputs from the contributing authors there would have been no book to edit. Their diligence and commitment made it possible. We would like to specially thank Armando Salvatore and Raffaele Marchetti for joining the project at a relatively later stage and finding time at such short notice to make their valuable contribution.

We would also like to acknowledge the generosity of the World Public Forum "Dialogue of Civilizations." Over the past five years, this forum has made it possible for many of the contributors to this volume to meet in a friendly atmosphere and to continue their dialogue on these issues.

MICHÁLIS S. MICHAEL
FABIO PETITO

Contributors

Fred R. Dallmayr is Packey J. Dee Professor of Philosophy and Political Science at the University of Notre Dame, where he has been teaching since 1978. He was a visiting professor at Hamburg University and at the New School, and a Fellow at Nuffield College in Oxford. His publications include, *Beyond Orientalism: Essays in Cross-Cultural Encounters* (1996); *Alternative Visions: Paths in the Global Village* (1998); *Dialogue Among Civilizations* (2002); *Peace Talks: Who Will Listen?* (2004); and *In Search of the Good Life: A Pedagogy for Troubled Times* (2007).

Phillip Darby is Director of the Institute of Postcolonial Studies and Principal Fellow in the Department of Politics, University of Melbourne. He has written in the fields of international relations, security studies, imperial history, and postcolonial studies. His most recent book is an edited collection, *Postcolonizing the International: Working to Change the Way We Are* (University of Hawai'i Press, 2006).

Raffaele Marchetti is Lecturer in International Relations at Libera Università Internazionale Degli Studi Sociali and John Cabot University (Rome). He also coordinates the Specific Targeted Research Project (STREP) "SHUR: Human Rights in Conflicts: The Role of Civil Society," funded by the European Commission's Sixth Framework Programme (FP6). His research interest revolves around international political theory and global politics. His most recent book is *Global Democracy: For and Against: Ethical Theory, Institutional Design, and Social Struggles* (Routledge, 2008).

Michális S. Michael is Research Fellow in the Centre for Dialogue and acting Director of the National Centre for Hellenic Studies and Research at La Trobe University. His research interest involves the multidisciplinary interfacing of conflict resolution, intercultural/

interreligious dialogue, international relations, and political sociology. Currently he heads two major projects, "Developing an Interfaith/Intercultural Network for Melbourne's Northern Region," and "Dialogue Diaspora: Locating Australia's Diaspora in Conflict Resolution." His most recent publication is a coedited book, *Asia-Pacific Geopolitics: Hegemony vs. Human Security* (Edward Elgar, 2007), and he is currently completing *Resolving the Cyprus Conflict: Negotiating History*.

Chandra Muzaffar holds the Noordin Sopiee Chair in Global Studies at the Centre for Policy Research and International Studies, Universiti Sains Malaysia. He is also the President of the International Movement for a Just World (JUST) and was the first director of the Center for Civilizational Dialogue at University Malaya. He has authored a number of books and articles on religion, human rights, Malaysian politics, and international relations. Recent publications include, *Rights, Religion and Reform—Enhancing Human Dignity through Spiritual and Moral Transformation*; *Subverting Greed—Religious Perspectives on the Global Economy*; *Muslims, Dialogue, Terror*; *Global Ethic or Global Hegemony?*; and *Hegemony: Justice, Peace*.

Ashis Nandy works in two opposite domains of social existence— human potentialities and human destructiveness. The oscillation between the two defines his work. His study of genocides in South Asia emphasizes not only human destructiveness but also resistance to organized violence and ethno-nationalism. His books include *Alternative Sciences*, *At the Edge of Psychology*, *The Intimate Enemy*, *The Illegitimacy of Nationalism*, *Creating a Nationality*, *The Tao of Cricket*, *The Savage Freud and Other Essays on Possible and Retrievable Selves*, *An Ambiguous Journey to the City*, *The Romance of the State*, *Time Warps, Time Treks*, and *Traditions, Tyranny and Utopias*.

Fabio Petito is Lecturer in International Relations at the University of Sussex and has taught in recent years at the ESCP-EAP in Paris and at "L'Orientale" University in Naples. He is coeditor of *Religion in International Relations: The Return from Exile* (Palgrave, 2003; Italian translation, 2006) and *The International Political Thought of Carl Schmitt: Terror, Liberal War and the Crisis of Global Order* (Routledge, 2007). Currently, he is working on a monograph entitled *The International Political Theory of Dialogue of Civilization*. He is a member of the International Coordinating Committee of the World Public Forum "Dialogue of Civilizations."

Armando Salvatore is Associate Professor of Sociology of Culture and Communication, School of Arab-Islamic and Mediterranean Studies, University of Naples "L'Orientale." His current research explores the sociological, political, and practical significance of religious traditions and secular formations in historical and comparative perspective. His recent publications include (authored, edited, and coedited) *The Public Sphere: Liberal Modernity, Catholicism, Islam* (2007); *Islam in Process: Historical and Civilizational Perspectives* (2006); *Religion, Social Practice, and Contested Hegemonies* (2005); and *Public Islam and the Common Good* (2004). He has been the editor of the *Yearbook of the Sociology of Islam* with Georg Stauth.

Michael T. Seigel is Research Fellow at the Nanzan University Institute for Social Ethics. An ordained Catholic priest, assigned to Japan since 1973, he completed his doctorate at Birmingham University (1993) on interreligious dialogue and Christian attitudes toward nature. He has had an interest in peace, Third World, and environmental issues since the late 1960s. His time in Japan has led him to an interest in understanding the background of the Second World War and of war in general, and also to an interest in reconciliation in post-conflict situations.

Richard Shapcott is Senior Lecturer in International Relations in the School of Political Science and International Studies at the University of Queensland, Australia. His main research focus is on cosmopolitanism in ethical and political theory and the philosophical hermeneutics of Hans Georg Gadamer. He has published *Justice, Community and Dialogue in International Relations* (Cambridge, 2001), in which he explored the idea of cosmopolitan dialogue between cultures based on Gadamer's work. He has recently completed work on *A Critical Introduction to International Ethics* for Polity Press and is currently working on the idea of drafting a cosmopolitan provision for national/state constitutions.

Manfred B. Steger is Professor of Global Studies and Director of the Globalism Research Center at the Royal Melbourne Institute of Technology. He is also a Senior Research Fellow at the Globalization Research Centre at the University of Hawai'i-Manoa. In addition to serving as an academic consultant on globalization for the US State Department, he is the author or editor of fifteen books on globalization and the history of political ideas, including *The Rise of the Global Imaginary: Political Ideologies from the French Revolution to the Global*

War on Terror (Oxford University Press, 2008); and *Globalization: A Very Short Introduction* (Oxford University Press, 2003; 2nd ed. 2009).

Toh Swee-Hin (S. H. Toh) is Professor and Director of the Multi-Faith Centre at Griffith University in Brisbane, Australia, and has taught in Australian and Canadian universities during 1980–2002. He has promoted education for a culture of peace, based on principles of nonviolence, justice, human rights, and sustainability, in the contexts of the North and South. A consultant to various UNESCO (United Nations Educational, Scientific and Cultural Organization)-related programs and current Convenor of the Peace Education Commission in IPRA (International Peace Research Association), he has participated in interfaith dialogue movements including the Parliament of the World's Religions and Religions for Peace. In 2000, he was awarded the UNESCO Prize for Peace Education.

Zhang Longxi is Chair Professor of Comparative Literature and Translation at the City University of Hong Kong. He has published widely in both Chinese and English, and is the author of *The Tao and the Logos: Literary Hermeneutics, East and West* (Duke University Press, 1992); *Mighty Opposites: From Dichotomies to Differences in the Comparative Study of China* (Stanford University Press, 1998); *Out of the Cultural Ghetto* (in Chinese, Commercial Press, Hong Kong, 2000); *Allegoresis: Reading Canonical Literature East and West* (Cornell University Press, 2006); *Ten Essays in Chinese-Western Cross-Cultural Studies* (Chinese, Fudan University Press, 2005); and *Unexpected Affinities: Reading across Cultures* (Toronto University Press, 2007).

Introduction

Chapter 1

Imperial Monologue or Civilizational Dialogue?

Michális S. Michael and Fabio Petito

On a brisk autumn afternoon as community activists congregated at the forecourt of the Darebin Town Hall for an interfaith dialogue, few would have noticed the auspicious monument towering over them. Erected in ostentatious Victorian grandeur, steeped in transient nationalist mystique, and draped by the names of young Anglo-Celtic men, the RSL (Returned and Services League of Australia) memorial honors those "who fought (and died)...for King and Empire" during "the Great War 1914–1918." Some 2400 years earlier, in another encounter of dialogue and empire, Athenian envoys advocated the pervasiveness of power and pragmatism against the besieged Melians' contestations for justice and neutrality.[1]

Partitioned by memory and history, what appear as two unrelated parables conveniently usher us into the foray that interfaces empire with dialogue. Since time immemorial, empire has been a metaphor for unadulterated power, whereas the philosophical inclination of dialogue lends itself as a conduit to peace. Until the end of the Cold War, both empire and dialogue were viewed through the prisms and the ideological apparatus of the bipolar confrontation. In the post-Cold War era this tension seems to have reached a different level of intensity with a distinctive civilizational connotation.

In this respect, September 11 exacerbated a deeper crisis of order that came to the fore with the collapse of the Cold War bipolar system, but was never far from the surface throughout the twentieth century in the dissolution of the forms and rules of international coexistence. It is, however, in the context of the post-Cold War debate on a future world order that "dialogue of civilizations" emerged as a discourse, often generic but increasingly professed as a political necessity to oppose the "monologue of Empire." More specifically, the global discourse of civilizational dialogue emerged against the background of two competing and powerful discourses, the "Clash of Civilizations" and the "Globalization of Liberalism."[2]

It is well-known that credit for the popularization of "dialogue of civilizations" belongs to Mohammad Khatami who, as President of Iran, used this formulation to secure the unanimous designation of 2001 as the United Nations (UN) Year of the "Dialogue among Civilizations."[3] In the same year, the tragic coincidence of September 11 catapulted to the fore of world consciousness the "civilizational debate" with even more urgency.

Civilizational Dialogue and the Western-Centric Matrix of International Relations

Since the developments discussed above, the idea of a dialogue of civilizations has been the subject of numerous conferences and international meetings, but it has received little attention by international relations and political theorists as a framework for the future of international relations—this is even more regretful when one considers that Khatami explicitly intended his proposal as "an alternative paradigm for international relations."[4]

Even after September 11, the idea of a dialogue of civilizations remained largely unexplored by the academic community despite frequently being used as a rhetorical antithesis to the popularized thesis of the clash of civilizations—often providing a convenient catchphrase to criticize Samuel P. Huntington or to refer to some sort of undefined normative political necessity to avoid a clash.[5]

True, academic reaction to the "clash of civilizations" thesis has been extensive, ranging from mainstream international relations to post-positivist approaches, through analytical philosophy to continental political theory, historical analysis, anthropological insights, literary criticism, and even theological arguments. However, such critique, particularly in Western literature, has rarely involved a substantial engagement with the idea of "dialogue of civilizations." Put differently, there appears to have been a "suspicious double movement" that, on one hand, reacts against the clash of civilizations thesis, whilst, on the other, remains indifferent to the idea of a dialogue of civilizations and its possibilities.

Of course, one could argue that such "doubling" is in fact nothing other than the analytical/normative rejection of civilization as a category in international relations. Put bluntly, if the idea of the clash of civilizations does not make any sense, why should that of dialogue? In other words, the use of civilization as a concept would belong to old-fashioned geopolitical arguments usually embedded in culturalist-orientalist frameworks and, therefore, is to be regarded as simplistic, theoretically flawed, and politically irresponsible.[6]

This argument, increasingly deployed against the dialogue of civilizations, has been authoritatively voiced by Amartya Sen, who has dubbed "civilization-based thinking" as deleterious not only when used in the theory of the clash but also in its well-meaning references to dialogue.[7] Such an argument cannot be cursorily dismissed and needs serious examination. However, it tells us little about the lack of Western academic attention to the issues, problems, and challenges that the idea of civilizational dialogue poses for the future of international relations and world order. Rather, we wish to argue that this dismissive intellectual attitude reveals something of the deeply entrenched Enlightenment (liberal, but not exclusively so) assumptions and Western-centric matrix of academic discourses on international relations and politics.[8] Both the issues of civilizations and the idea of a genuine mutually enriching dialogue with non-Western traditions seem to strike a sensitive point and activate a kind of almost instinctive defensive reflex amongst students of international relations and political theory in the West.

Such silence becomes more problematic given the plethora of initiatives and forums focussing on the dialogue of civilizations, cultures, and religions.[9] As we will see in subsequent chapters, such dialogical initiatives have proliferated during the past decade and increasingly resemble the genesis of a global social movement *in fieri*. This process is reminiscent of other major social movements such as the anti- or alter-globalization movement and the World Social Forum. What is striking, however, is the discrepancy between the richness of the intellectual formation of antiglobalization and the almost nonexistent academic reflection on the dialogue of civilizations.

The idea of civilizational dialogue seems also to reflect a recent emergence of dialogue as the central matter of reflection in philosophy and political theory.[10] Such dialogical approaches have critically analyzed the monological and logocentric (Western) assumptions of our philosophical thinking. In international relations, Richard Shapcott has argued that dialogical theory, inspired by Hans-Georg Gadamer's hermeneutics, would allow us to overcome the stalemate of the communitarian/cosmopolitan (liberal) divide and open up the way for a communitarian path to cosmopolitanism.[11] It is therefore not surprising that in the post-Cold War era, the philosopher who made the notion of dialogue central to his thinking, Gadamer, anticipated the idea of a civilizational dialogue:

> The human solidarity that I envisage is not a global uniformity but unity in diversity. We must learn to appreciate and tolerate pluralities, multiplicities, and cultural differences.... Unity in diversity, and not uniformity and hegemony—that is the heritage of Europe. Such unity-in-diversity has to be extended to the whole world—to include Japan, China, India, and also Muslim cultures. Every culture, every people has something distinctive to offer for the solidarity and welfare of humanity.[12]

In this light, Khatami's initiative becomes a call for a transformative dialogical journey in search of these "new global solidarities" capable of peacefully regulating the future multicultural and globalized international society. We could arguably see his contribution as one of several emanating from different parts of the Global South (or East) calling the West into a period of profound reflection; pointing to the need for a new global balance, not only between East and West, but also between the different traditions that constitute the European experience, some of which have been submerged since the Enlightenment and the industrial revolution.[13]

Against this backdrop, this volume takes up Khatami's and Gadamer's challenge in the hope of beginning to fill the glaring gap we have identified in Western scholarship. Inescapably, such an endeavor cannot but commence from the critical acknowledgment of the overwhelming political and ideological dominance of a US-centered Western and liberal world. The global predicament of the "imperial monologue" needs to be realistically brought into discussion for critical analysis and political contestation. It is against this monologue—and against, of course, the logic of the clash of civilizations—that a politics of dialogue of civilizations revolves. The search for a new "unity in diversity" is in fact needed today to defend the plurality of world politics against any imperial temptation, for, in the words of Gadamer "the hegemony or unchallengeable power of any one single nation...is dangerous for humanity. It would go against human freedom."[14]

Imperial Monologue and the Other (Dialogical) Politics of Cultures, Religions, and Civilizations

Empire has always been susceptible to human frailty and its fatalistic sense of insecurity. Promising stability and order in an otherwise anarchic world, for over three millennia, humanity has been dominated by the actions of a succession of imperial powers. So the end of the Cold War found the United States as the sole superpower capable of projecting its "ordering" power on a global scale.[15] Influential interests in the United States, interlinked with interests worldwide, seem intent on creating the "first global empire in history."[16] But as Fred R. Dallmayr notes, something broader seems to be at play:

> Ever since the demise of the Cold War, the world finds itself in a situation that is unprecedented in human history, in which the entire globe is under the sway of *one hegemonic framework*... None of the previous empires in history—neither the Roman, Spanish, and British empires nor the Chinese Middle Kingdom—had been able to extend their "civilizing mission" to the entire globe or humankind as a whole. Today all the countries and peoples in the world stand under a universal mandate or directive: to "develop" or to "modernize" and hence catch up with the civilizational standards established and exemplified by the West. "Globalization" involves to a large extent the spreading or dissemination of modern Western forms of life around the globe.[17]

Whilst Dallmayr's "hegemonic framework" bears a striking resemblance to other imperial models, it nevertheless requires the elaboration of substantially new analytical categories.[18] Leaving aside the issue of its analytical description, however, it has arguably been reinforced by the developments following September 11, which saw the emergence of an apparently unexpected fusion of realist and liberal/idealist arguments in what has been termed the American grand strategy's imperial temptation or ambition and variously described as "imperial liberalism" or "lite empire," and whose main idea could be well summarized as an attempt to remake the world in America's own image.[19]

American detestation of the "imperial" trademark is rather self-inflicted. Traditional definitions of empire find imperialism, in its classical sense, pertaining to the acquisition of territory, exploitation of resources, and subjugation of people.[20] Even prior to its imperial moment, Raymond Aron's qualifying dictum, that the "American empire...does not...resemble any other empire,"[21] reverberated some two decades later when US Secretary of Defense Donald Rumsfeld insisted that "we don't do empire."[22] Throughout the Cold War, the threat posed by Soviet expansionism was to overshadow any sustained engagement with the ambitions and possible consequences of American imperialism.

Until the end of the Cold War, imperial discourse was blurred by Ronald Reagan's characterization of the Soviet Union as the "Evil Empire"[23]—a precursor to George W. Bush's "axis of evil."[24] Postwar revival of the imperial project has centered on US foreign and security policy. In contrast to previous imperial projects, a US presence in international relations has been central to the postwar international landscape.[25] Always controversial, US hegemony has been captive to a Cold War mind-set, to which September 11 has provided a new lease of life.

September 11 and the ensuing "war on terror" rekindled debate about American power in the twenty-first century. Whilst some analysts argue that these events have accentuated US power by consolidating gains made during the 1990s,[26] others maintain that Washington's military, economic, and, in particular, political influence is in decline. Although the invasion and subsequent problems in Iraq have highlighted the military and economic costs associated with imperial overstretch, it is the political costs that are most debilitating.

Major civilizations are judged not merely by their military prowess or the wealth of their treasuries but also by the power of their ideas. In a malleable rendition of American power, Michael Cox reminds us that past empires were indelible because they did more than "repress and exploit," they also contributed to civilization.[27] Whilst there has always been a measure of "anti-Americanism" in the world generally, it is clearly on the rise in the Islamic world, many parts of Africa and Latin America, and even amongst traditional US allies. Both the Iraq war and the "war on terror" have severely eroded America's international credibility and legitimacy.

Furthermore, as Dallmayr suggests, imperial monologue appears to be inexplicably related to our era of globalization. Globalization intermingled with Liberalism is now represented as "the only game in town" and, more importantly, is projected as the only *rational* model available worldwide in the final consolidation of the linear progress of mankind. Coming to terms with the global is both necessary and instructive, yet the new epoch that is emerging is far too complex to be reduced to "globalization," or even to the "global" age. What we are witnessing is the interplay of two powerful forces at work: the homogenizing impact of financial, commercial, informational, demographic, and ecological flows on one hand, and the revitalization of cultural, religious, linguistic, and civilizational identities and allegiances on the other. This interplay of different and overlapping tendencies points to a new threshold in the evolution of human affairs. We could go so far as to argue that the "freezing effect" of the Cold War only delayed confronting the dilemma between universalism and pluralism that lies at the core of the key debates on the post–Cold War international order: unipolarity versus multipolarity, globalization versus fragmentation, cosmopolitanism versus communitarianism, and, to some extent, even Francis Fukuyama's "end of history" versus Huntington's "clash of civilizations."[28]

However, the empirical phenomenology that is behind this renewed visibility of the concept of civilization in geopolitical discourses is the return of cultural and religious identities as central factors in contemporary world politics. This is of course linked to the trends that many sociologists and philosophers have described as the "the end of modernity" or "de-secularization of the world"[29]—it is worthwhile recalling that the discourse of modernity was philosophically constructed as an opposite to tradition and traditional cultures[30]—but, for the purpose of our discussion, this has a more limited and specific meaning: the renewed centrality of cultural and religious identities in the discourses of post–Cold War world politics.[31] The resurgence of culture and religion in world politics is first of all an ideational change whose vectors are diffused throughout international/global society. What is happening, as Johann P. Arnason correctly pointed out—and in this regard Huntington's argument retains part of its validity—is that "civilizations, defined in a fundamentally *culturalist* sense, are reasserting themselves as *strategic frames of references*, not as direct protagonists of international politics."[32] And this is arguably part of that process of challenge to Western dominance, which has intensified from the Second World War and which Hedley Bull calls the "cultural revolt against the West."[33]

We should not forget that, as Enrique Dussel has argued, "modernity is not a phenomenon of Europe as an *independent* system, but of Europe as center."[34] The two world wars, the great depression, the Holocaust, and the advent of nuclear weapons suggest that the capacity of the modernist project to impose its logic on the global pattern of human affairs may have reached its limits. Though they assume different forms in different places at different times, these limits of modernity are not discrete, but are closely interconnected phenomena.[35]

Superimposed on the numerous connectivities (economic, technological, scientific, and even cultural) that we associate with modernity—and now with globality—are new layers built upon older traditions, loyalties, and belief systems, which are reasserting themselves with varying degrees of vigor and are injecting into the world system competing normative and institutional frameworks. From these multiple connectivities, a new consciousness of interdependence may be arising, side by side with a renewed sense of the need for a prolonged and extensive process of negotiation across two distinct but closely related international fault lines: North-South and Occident-Orient.

There is something of the violent legacy of the Enlightenment Project, which menacingly haunts the contemporary global predicament. Here, Alasdair C. MacIntyre's disquieting suggestions on the state of our moral predicament springs to mind:

> The notion of escaping from [particularity] into a realm of entirely universal maxims which belong to man as such, whether its eighteenth century Kantian form or in the presentation of some modern analytical moral philosophies, is an illusion and an illusion with painful consequences. When men and women identify what are their partial and particular causes too easily and too completely with the cause of some universal principle, they usually behave worse than they would otherwise do.[36]

Against the dangers and risks of a clash of civilizations haunting the world with war and carnage along cultural and religious fault lines, a different politics of (cultural, religious, and civilizational) identity, a politics of dialogue, is in our view urgently needed.[37] The overall political context of growing cultural misunderstanding and mistrust should be opposed by creating the conditions for widespread processes of "inter-civilizational mutual understanding" at multiple levels. The link between civilizational dialogue, mutual understanding, and peace is becoming more critical than ever. The politics of dialogue—*practically* entering into this inter-civilizational dialogical encounter—is also the only realistic response to the radical call for the rediscussion and renegotiation of the core Western-centric and liberal assumptions upon which the normative structure of international society is today based. This dialogical fusion, with also non-Western cultures and their non-liberal forms of politics, is really what has to be more persuasively and extensively explored and where, in our view, lies the key to the construction of a more peaceful and just world order.[38]

Structure of the Book

Within such a context, the current volume aspires to make sense of the questions and challenges that civilizational dialogue poses for the theory and practice of contemporary international relations and the prospects for a more peaceful and just world order. Given the broad ambition of setting a new research agenda, the chapters in this volume serve different purposes: some introduce and expand the idea of civilizational dialogue, others critically locate it within broader intellectual and political debates, while still others focus on specific civilizational encounters. Contributors approach their respective topics from a diversity of methodological, disciplinary, political, and civilizational perspectives. Viewed more broadly, however, all contributors attempt to address the antecedents and implications of the unresolved questions of the politics of cultures, religions, and civilizations in a post-Cold War setting. The volume is divided into four interrelated parts: (1) The Relevance of Civilizational Dialogue for World Order; (2) Locating and Analyzing Civilizational Dialogue in International Relations; (3) Civilizational Dialogue between Empire and Resistance in the Post-September 11 Context; and, (4) Cross-Cultural Dialogue in the Context of Civilizational Encounters. What follows is a critical presentation of the main arguments of each of the chapters and their respective contribution to the volume's overarching purpose.

Part I. The Relevance of Civilizational Dialogue for World Order

The first three chapters of the book provide a more robust theoretical and practical setting by considering the cultural, religious, and political differences of civilizational dialogue through a number of disciplinary perspectives—from philosophy and political theory, to international relations, and peace and religious studies. In doing so, they make a case for the relevance of the dialogue of cultures, religions, and civilizations for the future of world order. Specifically, they expand the theoretical horizons of civilizational dialogue by providing, respectively, a philosophical discussion of cross-cultural dialogue (Dallmayr), a political articulation of civilizational dialogue as an alternative model for world order (Fabio Petito), and an analysis of how interreligious dialogue can contribute to a culture of global peace (Toh Swee-Hin).

Dallmayr begins by reminding us why "dialogue" has emerged as an important notion both philosophically and politically. Philosophically, he notes that "dia-logue" means that reason or meaning is not the monopoly of one party but arises out of the intercourse or communication between parties or agents as shared logos. Viewed from this vantage point, the turn to dialogue can be seen as part of the "linguistic turn," which is a central feature of the philosophy of the twentieth century. Politically, the term has emerged into the limelight because it denotes the opposite of unilateralism and monologue, because it carries the connotation of collaboration and mutual respect—and thus offers a guidepost to interpersonal and intersocietal concord and peace. Dallmayr argues that since the basic aim of this dialogue is to achieve better understanding, mutual recognition, or a shared "good life" (in Aristotle's sense), it shows that politics cannot be identified simply with the struggle for power. Without being identical, politics is closely linked with ethics and questions of justice. This is a crucial issue today especially in cross-cultural or inter-civilizational relations.

In moving from theory to practice, Dallmayr distinguishes between three modalities of cross-cultural dialogue, namely, pragmatic-utilitarian communication, moral-universal discourse, and ethical-hermeneutical dialogue. Dallmayr's penchant is clearly situated with ethical-hermeneutical dialogue where partners seek to understand and appreciate each other's life stories and cultural backgrounds, including cultural and religious traditions, literary and artistic works, as well as existential agonies and aspirations. It is in this mode that, undoubtedly, Dallmayr believes that a "thick" cross-cultural dialogue can take place.

Petito argues that, though the idea of a "Dialogue of Civilizations" has provided an alternative to imperial skepticism in public discourses, very little attention has been devoted by students of international relations and political theory to clarify and articulate its possible meaning as a normative framework for the future of international relations. He maintains that whilst the "globalization of liberalism" and the "clash of civilizations" represent two different sets of discourses on the post-Cold War international order, they nevertheless share a practical/political commitment to an essentially Western-centric and liberal global order. In essence, they constitute two variants ("thick" and "thin") of the same denominator, namely, the overwhelming political and ideological dominance of a US-centered Western and liberal world.

Against this background, Petito sets out to delineate the contours of a dialogue of civilizations as an alternative model for world order. Such a theory articulates an argument for the moral basis of the contemporary globalized and multicultural international society that is not simply a *middle-ism* between a full-fledged "thick" cosmopolitanism and a minimal "thin" communitarian-based international ethics of coexistence. By rejecting the usefulness of the realist/idealist divide in international relations, Petito articulates the dialogue of civilizations as an argument for the normative structure of a peaceful, multicultural, and globalized international society organized around the notions of multipolarity, cross-cultural *jus gentium*, and a comprehensive idea(l) of peace.

In a similar vein and drawing on exemplars from various regions, Toh Swee-Hin presents a critical reflection of the contributions that faiths and spiritual traditions are making in constructing a culture of peace. Seeking to clarify how values, beliefs, and practices of diverse faiths and spirituality traditions have served peace-building (from dismantling a culture of war, to living with justice and compassion, promoting human rights, building intercultural respect, reconciliation, and solidarity, and living in harmony with the Earth for cultivating inner peace), he argues that the expanding movements of interfaith dialogue serve a critical role in forging solidarity among faiths and spirituality traditions that are essential in overcoming the multiple causes of peacelessness. While highlighting these hopeful signs, Toh is mindful of the transformation that all faiths need to undergo—including self-critical intra-faith dialogue, reinterpreting, revising, and discarding doctrines and perspectives that act as barriers to the building of a culture of peace. Finally, he suggests a number of key pedagogical principles that enhance the effectiveness of faith and spirituality education to create an actively nonviolent, just, compassionate, and sustainable "world order."

Part II. Locating and Analyzing Civilizational Dialogue in International Relations

The second part proposes a less "dialogically militant" approach to the idea and practice of civilizational dialogue in international relations.

It locates civilizational dialogue within the context of a number of significant contemporary debates in international relations, notably globalization (Raffaele Marchetti), the cosmopolitanism/communitarianism divide in international political theory (Shapcott), and the postcolonial preoccupation with the local and the personal (Phillip Darby). By critically analyzing this emerging political and theoretical discourse of civilizational dialogue, they offer a number of constructive engagements that help to clarify its content whilst discussing some of its possible weaknesses.

As part of a wider project that critically investigates the competing visions of global politics currently advanced in the context of globalization, Marchetti focuses on the discourse of dialogue of civilizations (or what he terms "civilizationism") as an ideal model—as a set of cultural resources that ground the different reading of human bonds. Marchetti compares the key features of this ideal model of global politics with three other alternative models of transnational political inclusion, which, in his view, constitute the main current political projects advanced by non-state actors in the global arena, namely, neoliberalism, cosmopolitanism, and alter-globalism. By doing so, he implicitly warns against what he believes are potentially conservative, elitist, and top-down tendencies of civilizational dialogue.

In the context of contemporary international political theorizing, the growing cosmopolitanism's association with liberalism has, in an era of geo-cultural contestation, arguably compromised its universalist appeal. In acknowledging this predicament, Shapcott insists that any defense of cosmopolitan ethics needs to address the issues arising from the attempt to enact a universal moral realm in a situation where universalism is either contested or lacking. Shapcott believes that the "do no harm" principle can be utilized to correct the depiction of cosmopolitanism as hostile to "pluralism." Such a commitment, he contends, by states and other political units invokes obligations beyond tolerance or coexistence. Because of the essentially contested nature of "harm," he argues that such a commitment requires a dialogue in order to assess the nature of harms being committed and to accommodate different understandings of what it means to harm and be harmed. In this context, dialogue becomes the principal means by which harms generated by misunderstandings and ignorance can be averted and by which differing conceptions of harm can be translated. Beyond the basic harms of deprivation of life and physical well-being, harms need to be assessed in a dialogical process whereby cross-cultural understandings can be achieved and consent to transborder practices can be sought. The recognition of the possibility of such harms further indicates the necessity of incorporating a dialogic ethic into the formulation of harm principles.

Drawing on a project situated between critical and human security with a decidedly postcolonial inflection, Darby privileges non-European experience and thought by working out from subaltern practices in the South Asian region and the struggles of Australia's indigenous peoples. While acknowledging that the need for alternative fora to enable dialogue and constructive exchange has become acute in an era of globalization, Darby is concerned that dialogue can easily be hauled into the service of the existing world order. A preoccupation with the global carries the risk of elevating processes over people. Knowledge about the global has its own colonizing practices that help shape the thinking of even those who oppose it. He also discerns difficulties associated with positing dialogue between cultures, religions, and civilizations. The search for commonalities and connections between such constructs works to discount the heterogeneity of human experience. It may also facilitate the reentry of the state—as for instance in the case of good governance. Rather, Darby opts for dialogue at a different level. Wary of the tendency to naturalize aggregated constructs, he focuses instead on the local and the personal. He suggests the feasibility of fundamental change by anchoring micro-dialogues in the everyday and taking what might be described as an indirect approach to "high politics."

Part III. Civilizational Dialogue in between Empire and Resistance in the Post-September 11 Context

The third section places the challenge of civilizational dialogue within the contemporary international context as shaped by the tension between Empire and Resistance: specifically, the hegemony of a US-centered Western and liberal world and the counter-hegemonic process of a "cultural revolt against the West," whereby cultures, religions, and civilizations become critical strategic frames of reference for political action. This political logic is critical in locating civilizational dialogue between the mutually reinforcing extremisms of American empire and international terrorism. All contributors—including two eminent non-Western voices— remain highly critical of the post-September 11 intensification of the "imperial monologue," in terms of American "public diplomacy"

(Manfred B. Steger) for a predominantly security-oriented strategy of counterterrorism (Ashis Nandy), and of a political strategy that overlooks the hegemonic relationship between the West and the rest (Chandra Muzaffar).

In exploring one critical aspect of "imperial globalism," Steger criticizes the ideological framework that underpins the propagation of "American values" as the "public diplomacy" strategy of winning hearts and minds around the world. In his review of the Bush administration, Steger maintains that US public policy is in essence an "imperial monologue" intent on spreading "American values" through marketing and "branding" drawn from advertising. The semiotic prominence of "American values" in the US government's monologic communicative strategy reveals its cultural rootedness in powerful diffusionist and orientalist models that rely on a deep-seated interpretation of "modernization" and "globalization" as civilizing processes originating in the West, which are to be diffused to "less developed" regions of the world. In order to move from an imperial monologue to a dialogue of cultures, Steger contends that educational and political alternatives to the dominant ideological model of globalization are required. Ultimately, the success of such alternatives rests on a strong commitment to cultural pluralism as well as on a conscious effort to highlight the contributions of all cultures to the creation of an increasingly global community of communities. From an institutional perspective, he suggests that the dialogic principles of the World Social Forum offer a useful first step in the pragmatic task of moving from a monologue of empire to a dialogue of culture.

For Nandy, the post-September 11 debate features two ways of looking at terror and culture. One way is to emphasize cultural stereotypes and how they hamper intercultural and interreligious amity; the other involves locating the problem in the worldview and theology of specific cultures. Whilst the first way—that of multiculturalism and intercultural dialogue—is seen as a soft option, it is the second that, in the short-term, appears as a viable basis for public policy and political action. Terror has always been an instrument of diplomacy and statecraft and, therefore, from this perspective the true antidote to terror can only be counterterror. But suicide bombers come prepared to die, and are therefore, personally, automatically immune to the fear of counterterrorism—something the globalized middle classes cannot handle. To the civilized modern citizen, such suicidal activism looks like the ultimate instance of savagery, apart from being utterly irrational and perhaps even psychotic. Yet, the key cultural-psychological feature of today's suicide bombers, despair, is not unknown to the moderns. The simple fact is that this new despair appears alien to the modern because it springs from cultures that have not only been defeated but have remained mostly invisible and inaudible. It is a desperation grounded not so much in defeat or economic deprivation but in invisibility and inaudibility.

As Nandy notes, for most of the world, all rights to diverse visions of the future are subverted by the globally dominant knowledge systems as instances of either romantic illusions or as brazen exercises in revivalism. The Southern world's future now is nothing other than an edited version of the contemporary North. What Europe and North America are today, the rest of the world will become tomorrow. Once the visions of the future are thus stolen, the resulting vacuum has to be filled by available forms of millennialism, some of them perfectly compatible with the various editions of fundamentalism floating around the global marketplace of ideas today. In the liminal world of the marginalized and the muted, he concludes, desperation and millennialism often define violence as a necessary means of exorcism.

In a similar vein, Muzaffar argues that by proposing a dialogue of civilizations, Khatami was articulating a practice that was deeply ingrained in Muslim history and philosophy. Whilst September 11 has in many ways distorted Islam, it has also catapulted to the forefront of world attention a fringe element that existed since the early days of Islam, reinforced to an extent by eighteenth-century Wahabi thinking, with its emphasis upon narrow doctrinal purity. In different ways, however, both visions of Islam are opposed to the global hegemony of the power elites in the West. Indeed, Muzaffar provocatively argues that it was this hegemony that was one of the principal reasons for the September 11 carnage. It is this hegemonic relationship between the West and the rest, with its roots deep in the colonial epoch, that constitutes the most formidable obstacle to civilizational dialogue. Since such a dialogue is based upon an unequal relationship between the dominant and the dominated, it negates mutual respect, which is an essential prerequisite for inter-civilizational understanding. Unless global hegemony is overcome, Muzaffar contends, there can be no concord among civilizations, and any dialogue between the West and the Muslim world, in particular, will appear naive, or worse, hypocritical.

Part IV. Cross-Cultural Dialogues in the Context of Civilizational Encounters

The final part looks at three case studies that explore the practices of cross-cultural dialogue in a long history of civilizational encounters. However, they do much more than that. They also contribute to the theory of civilizational dialogue, which is enriched by the specific insights embedded in the cultural and religious traditions involved in such civilizational encounters. This only reminds us of the need to move to concrete cross-cultural dialogues. Of course, dialogue is an open-ended, ongoing process that frequently involves difficulties, without guaranteeing any cross-cultural consensus. But the dialogical encounter with the cultural Other might well stretch our imagination by transforming and expanding its moral horizon. This is arguably what happens when the cultural concept of Chinese identity enters into a dialogue with the European notion of religious tolerance (Zhang Longxi); or the Muslim conception of power is aligned with the Aristotelian notion of *phrónesis* (Armando Salvatore). The final chapter draws on contemporary Japanese history in an attempt to affix historical memory as an essential focus of a dialogue of civilizations (Michael T. Seigel).

Zhang starts by depicting globalization as a conduit for either conflict or dialogue among civilizations. Requiring a truly global perspective, he notes that whilst religions and political ideologies are seen as different expressions of human life, neither has an exclusive claim to absolute truth. To accept our human finitude and be humble in front of some superior being is the core of religiosity, and that should be truly acknowledged by all faiths. Therefore, to de-emphasize the exclusive claims of one's own religion over other ones is a prerequisite for genuine dialogue and for the open-minded readiness to accept the humanity of others and the potential validity of their views. Tolerance of different religious beliefs has been a salient feature of Chinese culture, which is traditionally understood as the combination of "three teachings"—those of Confucianism, Taoism, and Buddhism. Despite the violence and conflicts that did exist in Chinese history, no war has ever been fought on religious grounds in China, and the cultural concept of identity—what it means to be Chinese—may offer helpful insights for the emerging dialogue of civilizations.

Salvatore's chapter can be located in the growing field of comparative civilizational analysis and is inspired by Rémi Brague's controversial idea of the "eccentric" origin of European identity. Overriding the typically "orientalist" ambiguities of the Western view of Islam, so often devalued as an oriental civilization incapable of sharing in the fruits of the progressive ethos of the West, Salvatore shows how the Muslim conception of power is aligned with classic notions of the balance between power and culture, and, in particular, with the Aristotelian notion of *phrónesis* (practical reason), and it is therefore more receptive to the idea of dialogue than the Western conception of power. While his approach may be clearly seen as an alternative to the idea of a clash of civilizations, it also offers a more realistic vision of the idea of civilizational dialogue between the Islamic and the Western civilizations.

If the purpose of dialogue is to promote reconciliation, or at least less hostile means of dealing with difference, then, Seigel insists, it needs to focus on the very issues that divide. Furthermore, if dialogue aspires to reach a genuine understanding of these differences and commonalities, then it needs to deal with historical memory. Seigel begins by explicating how dialogue on historical memory differs from other forms of dialogue, involving not only the correlation of facts but the intertwining of collective memories, narratives, and images. Through a comparison with the methods and experience of interreligious dialogue, Seigel highlights numerous factors associated with historical memory that make such dialogue particularly difficult. By focusing on Northeast Asia, and particularly on Japan's relations with its neighbors, he highlights the need for dialogue to make use of historical memory as a key component of civilizational dialogue.

In short, the book comes at a critical moment in civilizational debates. For its advocates, "dialogue of cultures, religions and civilizations" offers one of the more promising contributions to current public discussion about how we diagnose the present and plan for the future. Partly in response to the troubling trends of the contemporary period, the idea of dialogue continues to gather momentum. However, if the dialogical approach is to be seen as a viable response to the complex tensions and unresolved conflicts that presently beset humanity, such an approach will need to develop greater intellectual coherence. If this volume makes even a modest contribution in this direction, it will have amply served its purpose.

Notes

1. Written in pellucid narrative, Thucydides' Melian Dialogue (*History of the Peloponnesian War*, Book 5, Chapters 85–113) has become the *locus*

classicus for the perennial contest between *raison d'état* and ethical action, and the fulcrum by which great powers abandon their noble ideals in pursuit of narrow self-interest—a prime example of the philosophical clash between idealist and realist understanding of international relations.

2. For the most infamous articulations of these discourses, see, respectively, Samuel Huntington (1993) "The Clash of Civilizations?," *Foreign Affairs* 72, 22–49; and (1996) *The Clash of Civilizations and the Remaking of World Order* (London: Simon and Schuster); Francis Fukuyama (1989) "The End of History," *The National Interest* 16, 3–16; and (1992) *The End of History and the Last Man* (New York: Free Press).

3. Particularly significant was Khatami's 1998 interview to Christiane Amanpour of CNN and his 1999 speech at the European University Institute in Florence on the occasion of the first visit of a President of the Islamic Republic of Iran to a Western country since the Islamic Revolution of 1978. See Marc Lynch (2000) "The Dialogue of Civilizations and International Public Spheres," *Millennium: Journal of International Studies* 29 (2), 307–330. For official UN documentation, see UN General Assembly (1998), "United Nations Year of Dialogue among Civilizations," Resolution A/RES/53/22 (November 16).

4. Mohammad Khatami (2000), Address at the Dialogue among Civilizations Conference at the United Nations, New York, September 5, http://www.un.int/iran/dialogue/2000/articles/1.html, accessed August 1, 2008. As an implicit reminder, Khatami reiterated this point during his statement for the establishment of the Geneva-based Foundation for Dialogue Among Civilizations in 2007: "I would like, however, to emphasize that the main objective for this initiative of dialogue among cultures and civilizations is in fact to initiate a new paradigm in international relations.... This necessity will be clearer when we compare it with the other paradigms which currently form the basis of international relations. It is through a fundamental and structural critique of these paradigms that the raison d'être for this new paradigm is identified." Mohammad Khatami, "Vision of the Foundation for Dialogue Among Civilizations," http://www.dialoguefoundation.org/?Lang=en&Page=28, accessed August 1, 2008.

5. Exceptions include Fred Dallmayr (2002) *Dialogue among Civilizations: Some Exemplary Voices* (New York: Palgrave); Chandra Muzaffar (2005) *Global Ethic or Global Hegemony: Reflections on Religion, Human Dignity and Civilizational Interaction* (London: Asean Academic Press); Majid Tehranian and David W. Chappell (eds.) (2002) *Dialogue of Civilizations: A New Peace Agenda for a New Millennium* (London: I. B. Tauris); Fabio Petito (2007) "The Global Political Discourse of the Dialogue among Civilizations: Mohammad Khatami and Vaclav

Havel," *Global Change, Peace & Security* 19 (2), 103–126; Fred Dallmayr and Abbas Manoochehri (eds.) (2008) *Civilizational Dialogue and Political Thought: Tehran Papers* (Lanham, MD: Lexington Book); Joseph A. Camilleri (2004) "Citizenship in a Globalising World: The Role of Civilizational Dialogue," paper presented at the "Islamic-Western Dialogue on Governance Values: Rights and Religious Pluralism" Workshop, Canberra, February 15–18.

6. Contrary to this view, in contemporary social theory there is a growing interest in civilization both as an object of study and an analytical category. See for example the special issues by *Thesis Eleven* 62 (1) and *International Sociology* 16 (3), especially Shmuel N. Eisenstadt (2000) "The Civilizational Dimension in Sociological Analysis," *Thesis Eleven* 62 (1), 1–21; Edward A. Tiryakian (2001) "Introduction: The Civilization of Modernity and the Modernity of Civilizations," *International Sociology* 16 (3), 277–292; and Johann P. Arnason (2001) "Civilizational Patterns and Civilizing Processes," *International Sociology* 16 (3), 387–405. More broadly, in the field of "sociology of civilization," see S. N. Eisenstadt (2003) *Comparative Civilizations and Multiple Modernities* (Leiden: Brill); and Johann P. Arnason (2003) *Civilizations in Dispute: Historical Questions and Theoretical Tradition* (Leiden: Brill). For a new contribution to the analysis of civilization that relates to international relations theory, see Martin Hall and Patrick Thaddeus Jackson (eds.) (2007), *Civilizational Identity: The Production and Reproduction of "Civilizations" in International Relations* (New York: Palgrave).

7. Amartya Sen (2006) *Identity and Violence: The Illusion of Destiny* (New York: W. W. Norton). See also the conclusion of Elie Barnavi's essay (2006) *Les religions meurtrières* (Paris: Flammarion) entitled "Against the dialogue of civilizations" and the criticisms of dialogue of civilizations initiatives, with specific references to the Mediterranean, put forward by a EuroMeSCo (Euro-Mediterranean Study Commission) Report (2006), "Getting It Right: Inclusion within Diversity—Lessons of the Cartoons Crisis and Beyond" (European Commission MED-2005/109-063, November), on the grounds that they actually reinforce the Huntingtonian-culturalist approach.

8. For a classical statement on international relations as an America social science, see Stanley Hoffmann (1977) "An American Social Science: International Relations," *Dædalus* 3, 41–60. For a critique of the monological nature of contemporary political science and, in particular, political theory, see Fred Dallmayr (2004) "Beyond Monologue: For a Comparative Political Theory," *Perspectives on Politics* 2 (2), 249–257.

9. Some examples of these initiatives and organizations include: under the UN auspices, the Alliance of Civilizations, cosponsored by Spain and Turkey and launched in 2005, see http://unaoc.org/; UNESCO's

actions for the dialogue of civilizations, http://www.unesco.org/dialogue2001; ISESCO's (Islamic Educational, Scientific and Cultural Organization) programmes on dialogue of civilizations, www.isesco.org.ma; the World Public Forum "Dialogue of Civilizations" (a Russian-led initiative), http://www.dialogueofcivilizations.org; the Sant'Egidio community International Meetings "Peoples and Religions," http://www.santegidio.org/en/ecumenismo/uer/index.htm; and the Malaysian-based International Movement for a Just World (JUST), see www.just-international.org/, all pages accessed March 15, 2008.

10. For a classical hermeneutical approach to dialogue, see Hans-Georg Gadamer (1975) *Truth and Method* (New York: The Seabury Press), and also Charles Taylor (1989) *Sources of the Self: The Making of the Modern Identity* (Cambridge: Harvard University Press) and (1994) "The Politics of Recognition," in Amy Gutmann (ed.) *Multiculturalism: Examining the Politics of Recognition* (Princeton University Press), 25–74. For a different conceptualization of dialogue as communicative action inspired by the regulative idea of "ideal speech situations," see Jürgen Habermas (1984–1987, originally 1981), *The Theory of Communicative Action,* trans. Thomas McCarthy (Boston: Beacon Press).

11. See Richard Shapcott (2001) *Justice, Community and Dialogue in International Relations* (Cambridge: Cambridge University Press), and Stephen Mulhall and Adam Swift (1996) *Liberals and Communitarians*, rev. edn. (Oxford: Blackwell). For the centrality of the communitarian/cosmopolitan debate in international relations normative theories, see Chris Brown (1992) *International Relations Theory: New Normative Approaches* (Hemel Hempstead: Harvester Wheatsheaf).

12. Thomas Pantham (1992) "Some Dimensions of Universality of Philosophical Hermeneutics: A Conversation with Hans–Georg Gadamer," *Journal of Indian Council of Philosophical Research* 9, 132.

13. For this point we are indebted to Joseph Camilleri.

14. Pantham, "...A Conversation with Hans–Georg Gadamer," 132.

15. For a straightforward account of this viewpoint, see Zbigniev Brzezinski (1997) *The Grand Chessboard: American Primacy and Its Geostrategic Imperatives* (New York: Basic Books).

16. It has been argued that, like consumerism and capitalism, the US Empire has become a necessity for the American way of life. See, for example, William Appleman Williams (1980) *Empire as a Way of Life* (New York: Oxford University Press), ix.

17. Fred Dallmayr, *Alternative Visions*, 1 (emphasis added).

18. For an attempt to reformulate a new theory of imperialism, see Michael Hardt and Antonio Negri (2000) *Empire* (Cambridge, MA: Harvard University Press). For a critique of Hardt/Negri's thesis

that the United States is not the centre of this new imperialist project, see Danilo Zolo (2007) "The re-emerging notion of Empire and the influence of Carl Schmitt's thought," in L. Odysseos and F. Petito (eds.), *The International Political Thought of Carl Schmitt: Terror, Liberal War and the Crisis of Global Order* (London: Routledge), 154–165. For a discussion in international relations, see Tarak Barkawi and Mark Laffey (2002) "Retrieving the Imperial: Empire and International Relations," *Millennium: Journal of International Studies* 31 (1), 109–127; see also replies by Alex Callinicos (2002) "The Actuality of Imperialism," *Millennium: Journal of International Studies* 31 (2), 319–326; Martin Shaw (2002) "Post-Imperial and Quasi-Imperial: State and Empire in a Global Era," *Millennium* 31 (2), 327–336; and R. B. J. Walker (2002) "On the Immanence/Imminence of Empire," *Millennium* 31 (2), 337–345.

19. See *The National Security Strategy of the United States 2002*, http://www.whitehouse.gov/nsc/nss.html, accessed March 15, 2007; Jedediah Purdy (2003) "Liberal Empire: Assessing the Arguments," *Ethics and International Affairs* 17 (12), 51–64; Michael Ignatieff (2003) "Empire Lite," *Prospect* 83, 36–43; Michael Cox (2003) "Empire's Back in Town: or America's Imperial Temptation—Again," *Millennium* 23 (1), 1–27; John G. Ikenberry (2002) "America's Imperial Ambition," *Foreign Affairs* 81 (5), 44–60. An example of this is the so-called "coercive democracy-promotion" doctrine that fuses the liberal/idealist theme of promoting democracy with the realist emphasis on deployment of military means.

20. For the US's imperial reluctance, see Michael Cox (2005) "Empire by denial: the strange case of the United States," *International Affairs* 81 (1), 15–30. For a historical survey that has the United States as an "invited empire," see Gier Lundestad (1986) "Empire by Invitation? The United States and Western Europe, 1945–1952," *Journal of Peace Research* 23 (3), 263–277.

21. Raymond Aron (1973) *Imperial Republic* (London: Weidenfeld and Nicholson), 279.

22. In similar language, George W. Bush during a campaign speech outlining his vision of US foreign policy reiterated that "America has never been an empire. We may be the only great power in history that had the chance, and refused—preferring greatness to power and justice to glory." Governor George W. Bush, "A Distinctly American Internationalism," Ronald Reagan Presidential Library, Simi Valley, California, November 19, 1999 http://www.globalsecurity.org/wmd/library/news/usa/1999/991119-bush-foreignpolicy.htm, accessed March 21, 2008.

23. Full text of Ronald Reagan's "evil speech" (June 8, 1982), http://www.pbs.org/wgbh/amex/reagan/filmmore/reference/primary/evil.html, accessed July 14, 2008.

24. See US President's State of the Union Address delivered on January 29, 2002, http://www.whitehouse.gov/news/releases/2002/01/20020129-11.html, accessed September 10, 2007.
25. In this context, Arthur M. Schlesinger maintains that history cannot deny the imperial role of the United States in designing and constructing the postwar liberal world. Arthur M. Schlesinger (1986) *The Cycle of American History* (Boston: Houghton Mifflin), 141.
26. Robert Kagan (1998) "The Benevolent Empire," *Foreign Policy*, 34.
27. Michael Cox (2004) "Empire by Denial? Debating US Power," *Security Dialogue* 35 (2), 233–234.
28. For a critical discussion of the multipolarity-unipolarity debate, see Kenneth Waltz (2000) "Structural Realism after the Cold War," *International Security* 25 (1), 5–41. For the cosmopolitanism/communitarianism divide in international relations theory, see Chris Brown (1992) *International Relations Theory: New Normative Approaches* (New York: Columbia University Press). In addition to Fukuyama and Huntington, see also Ian Clark (1997) *Globalization and Fragmentation: International Relations in the Twentieth Century* (Oxford University Press).
29. See for example, Peter Berger (ed.) (1999) *The Desecularization of the World: Resurgent Religion and World Politics* (Grand Rapids, WI: Wm. B. Eerdmans/Ethics and Public Policy Center).
30. See for example, Jürgen Habermas (1987) *The Philosophical Discourse of Modernity: Twelve Lectures*, trans. Frederick G. Lawrence (Cambridge, MA: MIT Press).
31. For the now widely accepted subfield, see Yosef Lapid and Friedrich Kratochwil (eds.) (1996) *The Return of Culture and Identity in International Relations Theory* (London: Lynne Rienner). The focus on culture and identity in international relations theory during the 1990s has been supplemented by a growing number of works devoted to religion, a dimension about which international relations theory had conspicuously remained silent. The Palgrave Series on "Culture and Religion in International Relations," in which this work appears, has been critical in expanding this subfield. See for example, Fabio Petito and Pavlos Hatzopoulos (eds.) (2004) *Religion in International Relations: The Return from Exile* (New York: Palgrave); Jonathan Fox and Shmuel Sandler (2004), *Bringing Religion into International Relations* (New York: Palgrave Macmillan); Scott Thomas (2005) *The Global Resurgence of Religion and the Transformation of International Relations* (New York: Palgrave).
32. Arnason, *Civilizations in Dispute*, 11 (our emphasis).
33. Hedley Bull (1984) "The Revolt Against the West," in H. Bull and Adam Watson (eds.), *The Expansion of International Society* (Oxford: Clarendon Press), 217–228.

34. Enrique Dussel (1998) "Beyond Eurocentrism: The World System and the Limits of Modernity," in Frederic Jameson and Masao Miyoshi (eds.), *The Cultures of Globalization* (Durham: Duke University Press), 3–31, and quote 4.
35. Here we borrow from a new line of inquiry that is developed in detail in Joseph A. Camilleri and Jim Falk *Worlds in Transition: Evolving Governance across a Stressed Planet* (Edward Elgar, forthcoming).
36. Alasdair C. MacIntyre (1985) *After Virtue*, 2nd edn. (London: Duckworth), 221.
37. For examples of works that discuss the "new wars" and the terrorist attacks as a post-Cold War form of politics of identity, see Mark Juergensmeyer (2000) *Terror in the Mind of God: The Global Rise of Religious Violence* (Berkeley, CA: University of California Press); and Mary Kaldor (1999) *New and Old Wars: Organised Violence in a Global Era* (Cambridge: Polity Press). For a critique of their views, see Petito and Hatzopoulos (2003).
38. For an interesting attempt in this direction, see Richard Falk (2004) "A Worldwide Religious Resurgence in an Era of Globalization and Apocalyptic Terrorism," in Petito and Pavlos Hatzopoulos (2003), 181–208; and, Amitai Etzioni (2004) *From Empire to Community: A New Approach to International Relations* (New York: Palgrave).

PART I

THE RELEVANCE OF CIVILIZATIONAL DIALOGUE FOR WORLD ORDER

Chapter 2

Justice and Cross-Cultural Dialogue: From Theory to Practice

Fred R. Dallmayr

Today, nothing seems more urgently needed than the emergence of something like a global "public sphere" that, as a part of global civil society, would serve as a kind of public tribunal before which political leaders—from would-be emperors to petty dictators—would be held at least morally and ethically accountable. At a time when many "leaders" seem ready to go "berserk" and when our world is overshadowed by warfare, terror wars, and indiscriminate killings, some restraint on ferocity needs to be imposed—which, in the absence of a global superstate (beset by its own problems), can only come from the alertness and vigilance of responsible people around the world.

In the present context, I want to reflect in some detail on the promises and possibilities opened up by this perspective.[1] In particular, I want to explore some of the paths leading from the institutional setting—and the "dialogue" pursued in that setting—to broader ramifications in the global arena. Differently stated, I want to investigate certain parallels that exist between dialogue, or certain forms of dialogue, and various international or cross-cultural interactions, and thus sketch a transition "from theory to practice." Specifically, I want to do three things. First, I want to talk about the meaning and contemporary relevance of dialogue, both from a theoretical-philosophical and a political angle. Next, I want to highlight the different forms or modalities of dialogue and communicative interaction as they are found in actual intersocietal practices. By way of conclusion, I wish to put the spotlight on the relation between dialogue and political power, in an effort to show how dialogue can be an antidote to political domination as well as political or economic injustices and hence a resource for the promotion of global justice.

Why Dialogue?

An initial question that may be asked is, why dialogue? Alternatively, to put it another way, what is the meaning of a commitment to a "dialogue" among civilizations and, ultimately, among peoples? By common agreement, the meaning of a term is best grasped by its juxtaposition to counter-terms that limit or circumscribe it. The relevant counter-term here is "monologue," that is, a situation where only one voice is allowed to talk or where one voice drowns out all others—including perhaps its own inner voice or conscience. Transferred to the political context, monologue corresponds to a policy of unilateralism or to a situation where a hegemonic or imperial power reduces all other agents to irrelevance and silence. Silhouetted against this background, dialogue denotes the communicative interaction between two, several, or many interlocutors where no party can claim to have the first or the last word. Politically, this translates into a policy of multilateralism or multilateral cooperation, which is the opposite of any absolutism or empire. This rejection of absolutism and empire is, in turn, a precondition of just peace.

Perhaps a brief glance at etymology may clarify things. As we know, the term *"dialogue"* derives from ancient Greek and is composed of two words: *"dia"* and *"lógos."* Without going into needless subtleties, we can say that *"lógos"* in Greek means something like reason, meaning, and (more simply) language and word. On the other hand, *"dia"* signifies "moving through" or "moving between." Hence, etymologically, dialogue entails that reason or meaning is not the monopoly of one party but arises out of the communicative intercourse between parties or interlocutors. Put differently, in this context *"lógos"* is a shared *lógos*, the truth a shared truth that depends crucially on the participation of several or many people or agents. This means, in turn, that dialogue is intrinsically at odds with any kind of cognitive absolutism (or a claim to "apodiotic" truth)—which does not in any way signal a lapse into relativism or arbitrary randomness. The latter decay can only happen if dialogue is equated with empty chatter or chitchat where participants only "pass the time of day." What protects dialogue from this decay is its constitutive *"lógos"*: without claiming any monopoly, all the participants are oriented toward meaning and truth. They do this by remaining carefully attentive to the issue at hand, that is, by jointly seeking to explore or clarify a pressing problem or dilemma. In the political arena, the most pressing issue is justice and just peace.

If this is the general sense of dialogue, we can ask: are we not faced here with a perennial issue? So, why does the recent call for cross-cultural dialogue have special significance in our time? The simple answer—but one which requires a great deal of unpacking—is that dialogue has been egregiously neglected in modern Western history (and perhaps in the world as a whole). This statement is prone to give rise to misunderstanding. I do not mean to say that Western history and Western thought have always been entirely neglectful of the dialogical dimension. This claim, unfortunately, has of late gained prominence and has been disseminated under such labels as "logocentrism" and "egocentrism" (without any adequate clarification of the terms "logos" and "ego"). In my view, classical Western thought—and even a part of medieval thought—pays tribute to dialogue in exemplary ways. Significantly, Plato's works are written in dialogue form; Aristotle's writings reflect a teacher-pupil interaction, and Cicero pays tribute to both Plato and Aristotle in all his texts. To some extent, the dialogical spirit persisted in the European Middle Ages—a period marked by learned disputations and encounters on a high level of erudition. (Cross-culturally one may also point here to the teacher-student interaction—the *guru-shishya-parampara*—in the Indian tradition, and to the many question-and-answer passages in Confucius' *Analects*.)

A slow movement away from dialogue, however, occurred in the late Middle Ages with the rise of nominalism and scientific empiricism. With this development, a type of knowledge steadily gained center stage, which was no longer based on probabilities and open to dialogical give-and-take, but which aimed to be certain or apodictic, and hence binding on everyone. Without neglecting the role of the community of scientists, one can say that modern science, especially mathematical science, is inherently monological and oriented toward the goal of universal agreement regarding its findings. This bent of modern science was reinforced by dominant tendencies in modern philosophy, especially by the rationalism of Descartes, with its focus on the centrality of the "ego" or singular "I." His well-known formula *"ego cogito ergo sum"* ("I think therefore I am") implied that reality can be known by the thinking individual alone—without any need to refer or to communicate with other people. Seen from this perspective, the "logos" is not basically a shared logos or reason, but one that can be possessed and cultivated by the individual scientist or philosopher alone. In different variations, the Cartesian formula has tended to dominate Western thought until the end of the nineteenth century (a story that, in its complexity, cannot be recapitulated here).

As it happened, philosophical developments were paralleled by trends in modern politics, which, likewise, pointed away from dialogical engagement and in the direction of unilateral autonomy. Most prominent among these trends was the rise of the modern nation-state endowed with a radical autonomy labelled "state sovereignty." To be sure, throughout history, political communities have always claimed some kind of autonomy—but in a limited or circumscribed sense. In ancient Greece, city states were surely independent or autonomous from each other—but without denying their embeddedness in a larger Hellenic civilization. Similarly, during the European Middle Ages, national kingdoms or principalities were often fiercely competing with each other—but rarely to the point of rupturing or negating their participation in a larger imperial structure held together by Christian faith. It was only the fragmentation of Christianity in early modernity, and the association of different Christian confessions with independent kingdoms or states, that ruptured the earlier community and gave way to more radical conceptions of autonomy or sovereignty. To be sure, fragmentation was never complete, and efforts were continuously made to reaffirm some kind of unity—under the auspices of a shared enlightened humanism, an advanced industrial civilization, and the like.[2] Yet, with the eruption of two world wars, initially instigated by European nation-states, the fragility of these attempts was made glaringly evident during the twentieth century. These events also demonstrated the pitfall of radical autonomy. Linked with violent aggression, state sovereignty is liable to destroy not only others but, in the end, also itself.

The same twentieth century, however, also brought signs of change—and again this happened in both the philosophical and political domains. In the former domain, the twentieth century is noteworthy particularly for its incipient move from monologue and the Cartesian *cogito* to language and communication—a move frequently captured by the label "linguistic turn." This turn, in due course, led to a reappraisal and reaffirmation of dialogue, coupled with the renewed realization that reason and truth cannot be an individual possession but is necessarily to be shared with others. In this sharing, language plays a crucial role (where language needs to be taken in a broad sense as comprising a multitude of verbal and nonverbal modes of communication). The philosopher Ludwig Wittgenstein is famous for arguing that truth and meaning only make sense within the confines of a given language game—an argument that has been interpreted in many ways (and not always with sufficient attention to the "*lógos*" of language). The basic building blocks for a theory of dialogue, during the same period, were provided by a number of other European thinkers. Thus, Martin Buber developed his interactive view of human life ("I and Thou"), while Gabriel Marcel formulated a notion of human existence strongly rooted in language and shared embodiment. Perhaps philosophically most significant and influential was Martin Heidegger's portrayal of human existence (Dasein) not as an isolated ego but as a mode of being, which is necessarily linked with others through language and care. Proceeding on this basis, his student Gadamer articulated a conception of meaning and interpretive understanding based entirely on dialogue and communicative understanding. On a more formal or formalistic level, other theorists of the same period proposed various new conceptual models, such as those of "communicative rationality," "discourse theory," and the like.[3]

Paralleling these developments, the twentieth century witnessed innovative initiatives in the political arena; initiatives designed to correct, at least in part, the excesses of radical state autonomy. Thus, largely in response to the ravages of the great wars, efforts were made to establish, at least, the rudiments of shared international structures: First the League of Nations and later the United Nations with its complex array of affiliated agencies. These initiatives on the global level were seconded and supplemented by attempts at regional collaboration and unification. The most prominent example of regional reorganization was the formation of the European Union (EU). A process that initially started by a nucleus of a few states and expanded gradually to comprise the majority of West and East European countries. Significantly, the formation of the EU involved not only the unification of economic markets but extended deeply into political, legal, and cultural domains. Although very well known and widely discussed, the EU is only one example of regional cooperation. On a more limited scale, similar initiatives can be found in Asia, Africa, and Latin America. Likewise, within the confines of Islamic civilization, the idea of the *umma* (community of all Muslims) has gained renewed appeal as a corrective to the antagonism of separate (and often artificially created) nation-states. To be sure, the sketched trend is not universally followed or effective; some countries—especially hegemonic—tenaciously cling to the old ways of unilateralism. Supported by exceptional wealth and military power, traditional state sovereignty in these cases tendentionally is expanded into a super-Leviathan claiming radical autonomy and blanket immunity from accountability for state actions.

Modes of Cross-Cultural Dialogue

Having sketched some of the reasons for the recent rise to prominence of dialogue, it now seems appropriate to move from general theoretical and historical considerations to actual practice, that is, to the ways in which dialogue is concretely practiced in intersocietal and cross-cultural relations. In this respect, I like to distinguish between at least three modalities, namely, a *pragmatic-utilitarian*, a *moral-universal*, and an *ethical-hermeneutical* form of dialogue or communicative interaction. This tripartition is an adaptation, but it is also a significant modification of a scheme that was first proposed by Jürgen Habermas in an essay distinguishing the different types of (what he called) "practical reason."[4] The main difference between my approach and the Habermasian scheme has to do with the status of moral-universal discourse—a discourse to which he grants absolute priority whilst I treat as an intermediary modality needing to be deepened and supplemented by ethical understanding.

The tripartition I propose represents, in a way, an ethical ascent in the sense of a progressive move away from unilateralism and monologue in the direction of growing mutual respect and recognition. The first modality, pragmatic-utilitarian communication, still hovers close to the domain of monologue. Each partner in such communication seeks to advance primarily his or her own interests, his or her own goals and agendas, against those of others. Sometimes the impression that prevails is that one is simply witnessing an exchange of monologues. What saves pragmatic communication from this kind of exchange (or non-exchange) is the element of bargaining; each party, in seeking to advance the interests of the party, needs to take into account the perceived interests of others—if only in order to better counter, circumvent, frustrate, or negate the others' interests. For this reason, even a narrowly pragmatic approach needs the medium of dialogue (however closely circumscribed). This kind of communication forms the core and foundation of modern economics and "rational choice theory," that is, the theory according to which each partner seeks to maximize gains or profits while minimizing losses or expenditures. The narrow curtailment of dialogue in this interaction is demonstrated by the fact that rational choice can be, and frequently is, formalized in a strategic "game" scenario where each participant, without further attentiveness, pursues their own strategies on the assumption of the opponents' best possible strategies.

Beyond the economic domain, pragmatic communication also plays a large role in modern international or intersocietal political relations. Here, the legacy of the modern nation-state and state sovereignty still exacts its tribute both in the practice of state actors and the conceptions of mainstream scholars. Thus, the so-called "realist school" of international politics—the dominant Western perspective in this area—takes it for granted that all politics outside the domestic arena is interstate competition where each state actor single-mindedly pursues the "national interest" (often identified with national security) and assumes that other state actors do the same. The difference between the "realist" scenario and the scenario envisaged by game theory—a difference recognized by most realists—is that interstate politics occurs in variable historical and cultural contexts whose components cannot be neatly formalized or predicted. Hence, a measure of real-life dialogue is accepted as important by most proponents of this perspective. Evidence of pragmatic communication can be found in nearly all traditional interstate interactions, such as trade negotiations, disarmament negotiations, settlements of border disputes, and the like. The most prominent example of such communication, carried forward in continuous, day-to-day interactions, is traditional diplomacy (where the skill of a diplomat can probably be measured by the extent of his/her dialogical skill).

In proceeding to the second modality, moral-universal discourse, we move beyond the level of a narrowly construed self-interest, but only up to a point. The aim of such communicative discourse is to establish general, potentially universal rules of the game or norms of conduct that are binding on all participants in a given interaction. In order to establish and, at least in principle, follow such norms, participants must be able to transcend their immediate self-interests and cultivate a higher interest in general or universal rules. To be sure, in cultivating this higher perspective, participants do not simply abandon their particular interests. On the contrary, general rules or norms are established precisely for the purpose of allowing participants to pursue their goals with minimal mutual interference or obstruction. For this reason, rules or norms must be sufficiently abstract in order not to thwart or unduly restrict individual initiatives. One speaks here of "rule-governed freedom," and most modern legal or constitutional systems seek to advance this conception. Of course, rules and norms do not exist by themselves but require some form of communicative endorsement—although this feature gained prominence only in modernity. Philosophically, moral-universal discourse can look back to a long and venerable tradition—stretching from Kantian moral philosophy and modern natural law all the way back to Stoic cosmopolitanism.

Moving again from theory to practice, it is not hard to find rudiments of moral-universal discourse in the international and intersocietal arenas. Thus, basic norms of potentially universal significance can be found in the rules of international law—a legal system whose development can be traced from the ancient *ius gentium*, through the golden age of Spanish jurisprudence, to the rise of modern international law (inaugurated by Hugo Grotius and others).[5] Again, rules and norms in this area do not exist by themselves but rely on communicative endorsement. As it happens, the central norms of international law have, in late modernity, been endorsed or ratified by a large majority of governments and peoples around the world. Among these rules we find the norms governing warfare (both *ius ad bellum* and *ius in bello*); the norms dealing with war crimes and crimes against humanity; the Geneva Conventions concerning the treatment of prisoners of war; the Universal Declaration of Human Rights; and many others. It is inherent in the definition of norms that actual behavior is measured against them, hence, norms have (what is called) a mandatory or prescriptive, in Kant's language a "categorically binding," character. This fact has to be remembered in our time when norms, especially international ones, are often sacrificed on the altar of particular (national) interests. Thus, it is mandatory that the rules of the Geneva Conventions be followed in all armed conflicts, no matter what terminology particular governments choose to adapt. Likewise, launching an aggressive war is, and will remain, a crime against humanity, and so is the wanton killing of civilian populations. In all these instances, the collective conscience of humanity has reached a certain level, below which they do not dare regress.

To be sure, appealing to the conscience of humanity means to move a step beyond the level of the rules of the game or the legal norms of conduct. As everyday experience indicates, rules or norms do not by themselves assure their observance. If resort to force is to be avoided (or minimized), the only alternative is to cultivate and strengthen the conscience of people, that is, the genuine awareness of the ethical quality of all human relations and interactions. This leads me to the third modality mentioned earlier: ethical-hermeneutical dialogue. "Ethical" here refers to the "ethos" or shared sense of humanity prevailing among peoples (or groups of people); "hermeneutical" points to the effort to gain better understanding among participants and thereby enhance mutual respect and recognition. In such a dialogue, partners seek to understand and appreciate each other's life stories and cultural backgrounds, including religious or spiritual traditions, storehouses of literary and artistic expressions, as well as existential agonies and aspirations. In contrast to the abstract and formal character of general rules and legal norms, ethical-hermeneutical dialogue enters into the "thick" fabric of lived experiences and historical sedimentation. The effort here is not so much as to ascend above particular life stories to reach the "bird's eye" view of rule governance, but rather to render concrete life-worlds mutually accessible as a touchstone of ethical sensibility. In the language of classical philosophy (from Aristotle and Alfarabi to Confucius and Mencius), dialogue here is oriented toward the "good life"—not in the sense of an abstract "ought" but as the pursuit of an aspiration implicit in all life-forms (though able to take very different expressions in different cultures).

Since dialogue at this level speaks to deeper human motivations—leaving behind narrow self-interests—this is really the kind of communication that is most likely to mold human conduct in the direction of justice and just peace. Hence, there is an urgent need in our time to foster this mode of interaction not only on the domestic but also the global level. Fortunately—albeit on a limited scale—cross-cultural dialogue in this sense is already practiced today in a variety of forms. Examples would be interfaith dialogues; the Parliament of the World's Religions; the World Social Forum bringing together a multitude of nongovernmental organizations and grassroots movements; and the embryonic World Public Forum seeking to generate something like a public arena or global "public sphere" where the pressing political issues troubling the globe could be discussed from the vantage of justice and ethical obligations. A role that is by no means negligible is also played by exchange programs of scholars and students, grassroots diplomacy programs, and the like. Needless to say, much more needs to be done to make cross-cultural ethics a meaningful antidote or a corrective measure to hegemonic ambitious and the tradition of political unilateralism.

Dialogue and Power

At this point, the following question is liable to be raised, especially by political "realists": what good is dialogue in confrontation with power and domination? How can dialogue possibly serve as an antidote to the strategies of the powerful? Here, one has to agree, at least initially, that the former is no match for the latter, that power, at least at a first glance, holds the "trump card". From this fact, "realists" draw the conclusion that power can only be corrected by power, and hence all the efforts of the powerless (or less powerful) should be directed at matching, and even outstripping, the power wielded by the powerful. But the result of this can easily be foreseen: the competition for power will lead to a steady burgeoning of power, which will finally culminate in a super-Leviathan (which will be of little or no benefit to the powerless). In this context, it is good to remember the comment by Hannah Arendt on the role of violence: "The practice of violence, like all action, changes the world; but the most probable change is to a more violent world."[6]

There is another consideration that realists might usefully ponder. Power cannot maintain itself solely through power, especially through the power of the armed force. Here the insight of the great diplomat, Abbé Talleyrand, is relevant when he observed that "[T]here are many things one can do with bayonets, except sit on them."[7] This means that power, in the sense of coercive force, may be useful for conquest, but it is completely inadequate for maintaining a regime over time. If a ruler wished to rely on coercive force alone, a soldier or police officer would have to be assigned to every citizen in order to insure obedience—but then who would police the soldier or police officer? This indicates that every ruler or regime has to rely to a great extent on the approval or good will of the citizens, that is, on their sense that the regime is not entirely out of step with their pragmatic, moral, and ethical sensibilities. This need to "keep in step" is usually called legitimacy; and one can now add that without a general sense of legitimacy, power, as coercive force, is in the long run powerless. Such legitimacy, in turn, is fostered by open communication in its different modes—which brings us back to the role of dialogue as a corrective to, and restraint on, power.

I would like to add, however, that dialogue can itself be structured in such a way as to include a critique of power and domination. This happens in what I like to call an "agonal" or agonistic dialogue or contestation. In such an agonal situation, participants seek not only to understand and appreciate each other's life-forms but also to convey to each other grievances, that is, experiences of exploitation, domination, and persecution, experiences having to do with past or persisting injustices and sufferings. Hence, dialogue here serves directly the goal of restoration of justice or just peace. Great care must be taken in this context to preserve the dialogical dimension of the encounter. In the absence of such care, there is great danger that the encounter deteriorates into a sheer power play and that the goal of justice is replaced by the desire for revenge and retribution. For this reason, I prefer to treat this mode as a subcategory of ethical-hermeneutical dialogue—in order to make sure that the accent is not placed purely on power, and also not on the desire to return injustice by turning victims into victimizers. Seen as an ethical engagement, agonistic contestation is not an end in itself but an instrument in the service of healing and reconciliation.

Turning our attention to the contemporary global arena, we can find several examples of agonal dialogue put into practice. I am referring to the great commissions of inquiry established in various parts of the world at the end of ethnic conflicts and/or political dictatorships: the so-called "truth and justice" or "truth and reconciliation" commissions. The purpose of these commissions has been basically twofold: first, to establish a record of past criminal actions and injustices through archival research and the interviewing of large numbers of witnesses; and second, to initiate and foster a process of social healing so as to prevent the future recurrence of victimization or unjust domination. The two aims are obviously in tension: while, in the first goal, agonistic contestation and confrontation assume centre stage, the second goal seeks to reduce agonistics for the sake of mutual respect and understanding. Hence, great skill and wisdom are required to preserve the commissions from derailment.

By way of illustration, let me cite Bishop Desmond Tutu, who served as president of the Truth and Reconciliation Commission of South Africa, who in his book *God Has a Dream: A Vision of Hope for Our Time* declared that:

> I saw the power of the gospel when I was serving as chairperson of the Truth and Reconciliation Commission in South Africa.... The Commission gave perpetrators of political crimes the opportunity to appeal for amnesty by telling the truth of their actions and an opportunity to ask for forgiveness.... As we listened to accounts of truly monstrous deeds of torture and cruelty, it would have been easy to

dismiss the perpetrators as monsters because their deeds were truly monstrous. But we are reminded that God's love is not cut off from anyone.[8]

From Theory to Practice

The series of international institutions, conventions, and commissions mentioned above reveal that the notion of an international legal and ethical order is not merely a "nice idea," but has taken roots in many domains of contemporary international life. For many centuries, philosophers and religious thinkers had speculated about the feasibility of a world parliament or a global "league of nations"; but today we have institutions that instantiate or at least approximate the content of these speculations in real-life contexts. Here we encounter another objection raised by political "realists," that is, people wedded to the primacy of power: the objection that theories or theorizing are pointless exercises with little or no relevance for practical political life. In a particularly emphatic manner, this objection takes aim at the supposedly abstract and hopelessly "impractical" character of normative or ethical theorizing. During the nineteenth and twentieth centuries the distance between normative theory and factual reality, or between "ought" and "is," was erected into a first-order philosophical maxim: every attempt to bridge the distance between norm and fact, or to move from one to the other, was (and continues to be) denounced as a serious mental lapse (labelled "naturalistic fallacy").

No doubt, the relationship between norm and fact—or more broadly, between theory and practice—is complex and cannot be reduced to a simple linear derivation. Fortunately, the philosopher Immanuel Kant has helped us in this matter with an essay he wrote in 1793, titled "On the Common Saying: 'This May be True in Theory, but it does not Apply in Practice.'" In his essay, Kant took exception to some arguments advanced by a prominent contemporary, the philosopher Moses Mendelssohn. Although himself a child of the Enlightenment, Mendelssohn disagreed with one of the most cherished beliefs of Enlightenment thinkers: the belief in the continuous moral progress of humankind. In his view, enlightened thought was able to generate fine and high-sounding theories or principles—theories that were perhaps beneficial to some individuals here and there, but were of no use to the practical life of humanity at large. For Mendelssohn, it was sheer fantasy to say "that the whole of mankind here on earth must continually progress and become more perfect through the ages." The only thing one could say about human history with some degree of certainty was that, taken as a whole, humanity keeps "moving slowly back and forth" and that, whenever it takes a few steps forward, "it soon relapses twice as quickly into its former state." Seen from this angle, human history thus resembles the fate of Sisyphus, whose practical labors were constantly thwarted or came to naught—no matter how high the ideals or theories animating the struggle.[9]

From Kant's perspective, Mendelssohn's skeptical line of reasoning was unacceptable because it vitiated both the meaning of theory or philosophy and the integrity of practical life. Basically, the skeptic's argument was predicated on a Manichean view that erects a gulf between norm and fact, between thinking and doing. For Kant (still imbued with some classical teachings), this kind of Manicheism was misleading because it distorted the character of both moral reasoning and practical conduct. Although famous for postulating—in his own moral theory—a series of "categorical imperatives" binding on human conduct, these imperatives were by no means akin to arbitrary or despotic commands imposed from an external source. Rather, these commands derived from reflection on human "nature" and on its inherent dispositions and capabilities, including the potentiality for moral improvement. In Kantian terminology, human beings are able, through the use of reason, to legislate norms for their own conduct, and hence to subject themselves not to an external despot but to their own better judgment and insight. Seen in this light, theoretically formulated norms and practical conduct are no longer opposites but are closely connected or linked. As in a democratic regime (properly constructed), rulers and the ruled are not at loggerheads, but are united in the enterprise of self-rule. To be skeptical about this possibility is to be skeptical about human life itself.

This point was forcefully put forward in Kant's essay on theory and practice. "I may be permitted to assume," he writes, "that, since the human race is constantly progressing in cultural matters (in keeping with its natural purpose), it is also engaged in progressive improvement in relation to the moral end of its existence." Although this progressive movement may at times be interrupted, it will "never be broken off." As Kant submits, Mendelssohn himself must have been imbued with a belief of this kind, seeing that he was indefatigable in trying to teach and educate the younger generation. "The worthy Mendelssohn," we read, "must himself have reckoned on this [improvement], since he zealously endeavored to promote the enlightenment and welfare of the nation to which he belonged. For he could not himself reasonably hope to do this unless others after him continued upon the same path." Hence, moral skepticism—although a shield against an empty utopianism—offers no excuse from the hard work of education and self-transformation. At this point, Kant articulates one of his most important guideposts, valid for all times: the counsel that, irrespective of empirical obstacles or periodic setbacks, the task of ethical improvement (of both the individual and humanity at large) constitutes a moral duty (*Pflicht*) that cannot be shirked. "It is quite irrelevant," he writes,

> whether any empirical evidence suggests that these plans, which are founded only on hope, may be unsuccessful. For the idea that something which has hitherto been unsuccessful will therefore never be successful does not justify anyone in abandoning even a pragmatic or technical aim.... This applies even more to moral aims which, so long as it is not demonstrably impossible to fulfil them, amount to duties.[10]

This means that the path from theory to practice cannot be arbitrarily disrupted without moral blemish.

It is largely in the field of international politics that concrete experience may lead to frustration and skepticism. In Kant's words: "Nowhere does human nature appear less admirable than in the relationships which exist between peoples. No state is for a moment secure from the others in its independence and its possessions." At another point, he speaks eloquently of "the distress produced by the constant wars in which the states try to subjugate or engulf each other"—a distress greatly increased in our time by global wars, "terror wars," and ethnic cleansings. For Kant, there is one redeeming feature, however, in this distress. Namely, that the calamities and miseries endured by peoples may prompt them, at long last, with or against their express will, to form a peaceful "cosmopolitan constitution" or at least a "lawful federation under a commonly accepted international right." Thus, calamities endured in real life can provide a cue or incentive to human reasoning to reflect on the source of misfortunes and possible ways of correcting or avoiding them. Once the light of reflection illuminates the scene, however, the practical enactment of corrective measures is no longer an optional task but an ethical duty whose fulfilment—with the help of "divine providence"—is within reach. In Kant's words again:

> The very conflict of inclinations, which is the source of all evil, gives reason a free hand to master them all; it thus gives predominance not to evil, which destroys itself, but to good, which continues to maintain itself once it has been established.

Hence, theoretical moral insight and practical conduct can eventually be seen in harmony—contradicting the common saying: "This may be true in theory, but it does not apply in practice."[11]

In his subsequent writings, Kant always remained faithful to the notion of a possible harmony between moral insight and practice—or at least the notion that, despite enormous obstacles and constant setbacks, it was possible to reconcile the two through moral efforts. It may be true, as some have asserted, that reconciliation for Kant always was unidirectional, or moved in one direction, from theory to practice (where other thinkers might prefer a more reciprocal, especially dialogical relationship). Yet, Kantian "moralism" always remained tempered by common sense and human sensibility. One of his most famous political tracts is titled "Perpetual Peace: A Philosophical Sketch" (of 1796). Here, Kant made explicit room from human inclinations, commercial interests, and ambitions—but without abandoning the notion of a cosmopolitan duty. "The peoples of the earth," we read, "have entered in varying degrees into a universal community, and it has developed to the point where violation of rights in *one* part of the world is felt everywhere." Hence, through travels, commercial interactions, and improved communications, people have entered into a condition of "cosmopolitan right" (we might call it a "global civil society"). Thus, Kant adds in a famous formulation:

> Nature guarantees perpetual peace by the actual mechanism of human inclinations. And while the likelihood of its being attained is not sufficient to enable us to *prophesy* the future theoretically, it is enough for practical purposes. It makes it our duty to work our way towards this goal, which is more than an empty chimera.[12]

To these lines, one can add the equally famous statement from the conclusion of *The Metaphysics of Morals* (of 1797):

> By working towards this end, we may hope to terminate the disastrous practice of war, which up till now has been the main object to

which all states, without exception, have accommodated their internal institutions. And even if the fulfilment of this pacific intention were forever to remain a pious hope, we should still not be deceiving ourselves if we made it our maxim to work unceasingly towards it, for it is our duty to do so.[13]

In light of Kant's arguments, it becomes clear that the current call for dialogue does not reflect an empty "pipe" dream, but responds, or corresponds, to deep-seated human needs or aspirations in our time, and it means to move humanity a few steps closer to the accomplishment of a basic moral aim shared by people around the world: the aim of perpetual peace.

Notes

1. For a number of reasons one such example is the recent creation of the Centre for Dialogue at La Trobe University in Melbourne. Institutionally the Center provides a forum where intellectuals and social scientists from around the world can meet and discuss pressing issues in a spirit of goodwill and mutual sympathy. In this context, the Center supplies an important venue or meeting place for international conferences and symposia.
2. Reference should also be made in this context to such unifying efforts as the Holy Alliance, the Concert of Europe, and balance of power. In the background of national rivalries, there was also something called "*Jus Publicum Europaeum*," or European public law, which limited the excesses of nationalist ambitions. On the latter, especially see Carl Schmitt (2003) *The Nomos of the Earth in the International Law of the Jus Publicum Europaeum*, trans. G. L. Ulmen (New York: Telos Press).
3. Compare in this context, Ludwig Wittgenstein (1968) *Philosophical Investigations*, trans. G. E. M. Anscombe (Oxford: Blackwell); Martin Buber (1986) *I and Thou*, trans. Ronald G. Smith (New York: Scribner); Galbriel Marcel (1962) *Homo Viator: Introduction to a Metaphysics of Hope*, trans. Emma Craufurd (New York: Harper and Row); Martin Heidegger (1962) *Being and Time*, trans. John Macquarrie and Edward Robinson (New York: Harper and Row), and (1971) *The Way to Language*, trans. Peter D. Hertz (San Francisco: Harper and Row); Hans-Georg Gadamer (1989) *Truth and Method*, 2nd rev. ed., trans. Joel Weinsheimer and Donald G. Marshall (New York: Crossroad); Jürgen Habermas (1979) *Communication and the Evolution of Society*, trans. Thomas McCarthy (Boston, MA: Beacon Press); David Howarth et al., (eds.) (2000) *Discourse Theory and Political Analysis* (Manchester: Manchester University Press).

4. See Jürgen Habermas (1994), "On the Pragmatic, the Ethical, and the Moral Employments of Practical Reason," in *Justification and Application: Remarks on Discourse Ethics*, trans. Ciaran P. Cronin (Cambridge, MA: MIT Press), 1–17.
5. Compare, in this respect, Fred Dallmayr (2004) "The Law of Peoples: Civilizing Humanity," in *Peace Talks—Who Will Listen?* (Notre Dame, IN: University of Notre Dame Press), 42–43.
6. See Hannah Arendt (1972) "On Violence," in *Crises of the Republic* (New York: Harcourt Brace Jovanovich), 177.
7. J. F. Bernard, *Talleyrand: A Biography* (New York: Putnam, 1973), 205.
8. Bishop Desmond Tutu (with Douglas Adams) (2004) *God Has a Dream: A Vision of Hope for Our Time* (New York: Doubleday), 58.
9. For this argument, see Moses Mendelssohn (1783) *Jerusalem, oder über religiöse Macht und Judentum* (Berlin: Maurer), par. 2, 44–47. Mendelssohn's argument was directed chiefly against Gotthold Ephraim Lessing (1729–1781), who had defended a theory of human moral advancement in his (1780) *Die Erziehung des Menschengeschlechts* (Berlin: Voss and Sohn).
10. Immanuel Kant (1970) "On the Common Saying: 'This May be True in Theory, but it does not Apply in Practice,'" in Hans Reiss (ed.) *Kant's Political Writings*, trans. H. B. Nisbet (Cambridge: Cambridge University Press), 88–89.
11. Kant, "On the Common Saying," 90–92.
12. Immanuel Kant, "Perpetual Peace: A Philosophical Sketch," in *Kant's Political Writings*, 107–108, 114. As Kant adds in an Appendix (116): "There can be no conflict between politics, as an applied [practical] branch of right, and morality, as a theoretical branch of right (i.e., between theory and practice)." In recent times, some political "realists" cast doubts on the emergence of a global civil society and its ethical role in tempering warfare between states. For a critique of this kind of realism, see Fred Dallmayr (2007) "Global Civil Society Debunked? A Response to David Chandler," *Globalizations*, vol. 4, 301–303.
13. Kant, "The Metaphysics of Morals," in *Kant's Political Writings*, 174.

CHAPTER 3

DIALOGUE OF CIVILIZATIONS AS AN ALTERNATIVE MODEL FOR WORLD ORDER

Fabio Petito

On November 4, 1998, the General Assembly of the United Nations unanimously adopted a resolution proposed by the President of the Islamic Republic of Iran, Mohammad Khatami, which designated 2001 as the Year of the "Dialogue among Civilizations." In the same year, on September 11, the shadow of a future clash of civilizations came looming down with incredible velocity, leaving in its wake an atmosphere of fear, mistrust, and war. At the dawn of the third millennium, this coincidence increasingly appears as a sign of the times, a symbolic indication of the historical epoch we are entering.

More than fifteen years after the end of the Cold War, the overwhelming political and ideological dominance of a US-centered Western and liberal world seemed well-entrenched, but the promises of a peaceful "New World Order" had clearly not been fulfilled. On the contrary, international society has been drawn into a *crescendo* of instability, wars, and political violence. Against such a background and within the context of a widespread public debate on the future of the world order, the call for a "dialogue of civilizations" has emerged as a set of ideas, which are often generic but increasingly perceived as a political necessity all over the world to somehow contribute to a more peaceful and just world order. Since then, the idea of a dialogue of civilizations has been the subject of many public conferences and international meetings, but it has received scant attention from international relations and political theorists in clarifying and articulating its potentiality as an alternative framework for the future world order. This is even more regretful when one notes that Khatami had explicitly put forward this vision with such an aim in mind.[1]

Against this background of academic indifference, I will take the suggestion of Khatami seriously and outline an argument for a normative structure of contemporary multicultural and globalized international society inspired by the political discourse of dialogue of civilizations. In the same way that modern political theory did not emerge from (and within) a vacuum, but in response to the political problems and inquiries of the day (think of the key founding texts of the modern theory of the state), the great issues of today's politics, arguably *in primis* its global predicament of a crisis of order combined with a growing worldwide political manifestation of cultural pluralism, are calling for an adequate international political theory of world order, that is, a theory for the normative structure of a multicultural and globalized international society.

Dialogue of Civilizations as a Global Political Discourse: Against the Background of the "End of History" and the "Clash of Civilizations"

As I have already argued, the idea of a dialogue of civilizations emerged in the 1990s as a global political discourse against the background of two competing and powerful discourses, the "Clash of Civilizations" and the "Globalization of Liberalism/End of History."[2] From this perspective, the idea of a dialogue of civilizations constitutes a third political reaction to the end of the Cold War that, while not a synthesis of the two above-mentioned discourses, could not be set and framed, except against the background of these two intellectually and politically powerful theses.

However, from the outset, a crucial distinction needs to be underlined. The political discourse of a dialogue of civilizations has yet to be conceptualized in the realm of the theoretical reflection on international relations, very broadly conceived, in the way that the "end of history" and the "clash of civilizations" have been. As a first step in this direction, a preliminary analysis of the dialogue of civilizations as a global political discourse may well explore in more detail the comparisons and contrasts with the above mentioned two theses.[3] In a simplified and schematic way familiar to international relations mainstream scholarship—which this chapter indirectly aims to criticize—it can be argued that dialogue of civilizations shares *analytically* some essential assumptions with the thesis of the clash of civilizations, while *normatively* it is closer to the approach endorsed by the end of history. In contrast to the analytical and empirical argument that finds the globalization of liberalism as the last stage of the modernization and secularization of the world, dialogue of civilizations stresses the global resurgence of cultural and religious pluralism in world politics, and identifies the quest for cultural authenticity as the main contemporary political issue effecting the relationships between the Western and non-Western world. But, whereupon Huntington saw the clash of civilizations scenario as mainly a social-scientific *prediction* grounded in a *primordialist* worldview of politics, the political discourse of dialogue of civilizations considers it as a dangerous *possibility* (or political construction) resulting from wrong policies that need to be opposed.[4]

From a normative perspective, it is self-evident that the proposal for a dialogue of civilizations is formulated as a reaction to the clash of civilizations thesis. Put simply, the former is primarily designed to prevent the latter. The reason why, from rather convergent empirical considerations, the political discourse of dialogue of civilizations derives at a different conclusion from that of Huntington's is due to their differing notions of (international) politics. Where Huntington subscribes to a *realist* political framework, dialogue is committed to an *idealist* notion of politics that is implicit in the end-of-history thesis.

In the first case, struggle for power is perceived as an unavoidable necessity of politics, which condemns international politics to the realm of conflict *recurrence and repetition* that can only be, partially, mitigated by a *consequentialist* ethics of statecraft based on non-interference. In the second case, both an idealist commitment to politics as a search for *justice as fairness* and a liberal emphasis on cooperation and nonmilitary issues prevail, and, as a consequence, international politics is perceived as a realm where *progress*, however difficult, is nonetheless possible on the base of an ethics of *ends*.

These two distinctions—normative/analytical and realist/idealist—that are essential to mainstream approaches in international relations are, however, part of the theoretical problems that a full-fledged international political theory of dialogue of civilizations will have to confront. It is important to stress that such preliminary comparative reading does not suggest that dialogue of civilizations, as an argument for the normative basis of contemporary international society, can be interpreted as a *via media* theoretical position between "the clash of civilizations" and "the end of history." Rather, if attention is shifted from theory to practice, the radical distance between dialogue of civilizations and the other two theses becomes apparent. In particular, while the two envision, respectively, a "thin" or "thick"[5] but essentially Western-centric and mainly liberal—international society, the political discourse of dialogue of civilizations calls for the reopening and rediscussion of the core Western-centric and liberal assumptions upon which the normative structure of the contemporary international society is based.

From this perspective, the idea of a dialogue of civilizations represents a powerful normative challenge to the contemporary political orthodoxy implicit in the above political discourses. In other words, as Amitai Etzioni has convincingly argued:

> both the end-of-history and the clash-of-civilizations arguments approach the non-Western parts of the world as if they have little, if anything, to offer to the conception of a good society—at least to its political and economic design—or to the evolving new global architecture.[6]

Within this horizon, three major theoretical and political lines of arguments emerge as prerequisites to any normative structure of contemporary international society that wishes to be sensitive to the call for a dialogue of civilizations.[7]

First, if the normative structure of future global coexistence is to be genuinely universal, then it cannot solely be liberal and Western-centric. Genuine universality requires a sharp awareness of the presence of different cultures and civilizations in world affairs; in many ways it must also spring from there. A fundamental void looms when this normative structure reflects the tenets of cosmopolitan liberalism, a political tradition that excludes the centrality of cultural and religious identity in the everyday practices of "really existing communities."[8]

Second any reflection on a principled world order based on dialogue of civilizations must acknowledge something like a fundamental, ethical, and political crisis linked to the present liberal Western civilization and its expansion, and recognize that dialogue civilizations seem to enshrine the promise of an answer, or rather to chart a path toward an answer as, in Khatami's words, every dialogue, based on a presumption of the worth of the Other, "provides grounds for human creativity to flourish."[9] Furthermore, as the Indian postcolonial theorist Ashis Nandy has interestingly argued, such an opening also calls for a reengagement with the disowned or repressed traditions that make up the European experience for "any alternative form of dialogue between cultures cannot but attempt to rediscover the subjugated West and make it an ally."[10]

Finally, the present international situation places on all of us a moral obligation to pursue an active politics of inter-civilizational understanding by engaging in a concrete practice of cross-cultural dialogue. It cannot be ignored that since September 11, the shadow of a "clash of civilizations" came looming down on the world with incredible velocity, leaving in its wake an atmosphere of fear and war. Not only that: the search for a new normative order, that is, unity in diversity, is needed even more today to defend the plurality of world politics against any imperial temptation. In the words of Gadamer "the hegemony or unchallengeable power of any one single nation...is dangerous for humanity. It would go against human freedom."[11] With this context in mind, a politics of understanding would already be a great achievement. Nevertheless, to effectively face this challenge at its roots, we need to find an exit from the strict grid of choices imposed by the contemporary Western-centric and liberal global order and move toward the construction of a multicultural and peaceful world order.

Dialogue of Civilizations as International Political Theory

There is no blueprint for the construction of a multicultural and peaceful world order. It is my contention, however, that for such a new normative structure to emerge, an adequate theory of world order inspired by the political discourse of dialogue of civilizations is an essential element. Such an international political theory of dialogue of civilizations needs to articulate an intellectual strategy that problematizes the contemporary predominant cosmopolitan preference predicated on the idea of "world unity"—visible in Fukuyama's thesis but also in other streams of post-89 international theorizing[12]— and gives a renewed centrality to the issue of cultural and political pluralism. Integral to this theoretical recentering is a critique of the "wishful thinking" approach and its underlying philosophy of history, with its absolute faith in progress and in the unlimited perfectibility of human nature typical of cosmopolitan-liberal political theorizing. This brings into question what, in international relations theory, is normally referred to as Idealism, with its emphasis on the idea of world government and its commitment to anthropological optimism and a philosophy of history.[13] From this perspective, an international political theory of dialogue of civilizations would clearly be anti-idealist.

This would be a paradoxical conclusion, however, since one of the major arguments of the supporters of dialogue of civilizations is a normative (idealist-like) critique of the realist discourse of power politics. Such criticism is unsurprisingly mirrored by the realist accusation against the idea of dialogue of civilizations and concerns the idealist and wishful thinking nature of its discourse. The argument is that dialogue of civilizations might well be normatively worthwhile and even conceptually possible, but ultimately it remains an unrealistic utopia (or worse, a rhetorical *escamotage* in the hands of dangerous illiberal politicians) when projected into the realm of real-world politics where power and interest are sovereign. This argument reproduces, of course, the classical realist critique to the idealist worldview of international politics, according to which any attempt to construct a world order based on ethical and normative considerations is doomed since it fails to engage with the "real nature" of international relations as power politics.[14] From this perspective, the international political theory of dialogue of civilizations could not but be located in the anti-realist camp.

In the discussion that follows, I want to address this apparent contradiction. As I have already anticipated, the realist/idealist opposition, essential to mainstream approaches in international relations, is in fact part of the theoretical problem that a comprehensive international political theory of dialogue of civilizations needs to address. By rejecting the usefulness of the realist/idealist divide, I will delineate, more clearly, the contours of dialogue of civilizations as an argument for the contemporary normative structure of a peaceful and multicultural global order around the notions of multipolarity, cross-cultural *jus gentium*, and a comprehensive idea(l) of peace. To the discussion of these three dimensions, I now turn.

Multipolarity as the Spatial Order of Dialogue of Civilizations

As has been argued, the political discourse of dialogue of civilizations represents a radical critique of the political and ideological dominance of a US-centered Western and liberal world. At the core of this discourse, one finds a clear normative resistance against the idea of a unipolar world order, often accompanied by the conviction that we are gradually, but ineluctably, moving toward a multipolar world. The question then arises whether such an international political theory of dialogue of civilizations should endorse the idea of a multipolar world order.

This is an awkward question, since polarity is clearly associated with a realist (and neorealist) approach to international politics and with a conceptualization of the international arena as a system of forces to be brought into equilibrium (the stability of the system) by the well known mechanism of the balance of power.[15] The emphasis here is overwhelmingly on material sources and great power status, the rest (the ideational/normative dimension) being fundamentally irrelevant.

It should be noted, however, that a widespread debate has been ranging throughout the post-Cold War period about whether the end of the bipolar international system would lead to unipolarity or multipolarity. While there have been different positions on the nature of the post-89 international system in terms of distribution of power—and the predictive assessments of the evolution of the polarity of the system have been even more diverging—it is fair to say that the view that we are living in a "unipolar era" is today less popular than it was in the early 1990s, and the predictions that the twenty-first century will see the emergence of a genuine multipolar structure are increasingly common.[16] This view is arguably the result of the recent security and political developments and in particular the "quagmire" of the war in Iraq, but it is also based on less contingent medium/long-term economic evidence and estimations, which suggest the fast progression of the (relative) economic decline of America in favor of the new Asian fast-growing economies of China and India.[17]

My point here is that the increasing consensus on the empirical trend of worldwide decentralization of power away from what Huntington has defined as the "lonely superpower,"[18] toward other major regional powers (China, India, EU, Japan, Russia, Brazil, Iran, and others), may well be more conducive to the emergence of a pluralistic world order. This is why even critical scholars such as Chantal Mouffe and Danilo Zolo have recently focused on the idea of a balance of regional spaces and argued for a multipolar world order in the context of their critique of the American unipolar/imperial project.[19]

Mouffe has argued that the central problem that the current unipolar world, under the unchallenged hegemony of the United States, is facing is the impossibility for antagonisms to find legitimate forms of expression. Under such conditions, antagonisms, when they do emerge, tend to take extreme forms. In order to create the channels for the legitimate expression of dissent, we need to envisage, Mouffe suggests, a pluralistic multipolar world order constructed around a certain number of "greater spaces" and genuine cultural poles. Along similar lines, Zolo argues that to confront the United States' dangerous imperial tendencies,

> the project of a peaceful world needs a neo-regionalist revival of the idea of *Großraum* [greater space], together with a reinforcement of multilateral negotiation between states as a normative source and a democratic legitimization of the processes of regional integration.[20]

These arguments for a multipolar world order, however, require a degree of caution, for, as Zolo has correctly sensed, "before this kind of order can be achieved complex economic, technological, cultural and religious conditions must be met that make a dialogue between the world's major civilizations possible."[21] The risk is that without a process of dialogue of civilizations at different levels, as an overarching framework of reference, this multicivilizational world order would look very much like the model of multipolar multicivilizational order put forward by Huntington as the antidote to what he sees as the greatest threat to world peace, the clashes of civilizations.[22] This is an important point, as this part of Huntington's argument—absent in his original *Foreign Affairs*' article—has gone largely unnoticed (the reason also being that it is sketched in the last few pages of a book of more than 300 pages—an unbalance that arguably confirms the impression that the book is really about the clash rather than how to avoid it).

Huntington argues that the only way to avoid the clash of civilizations is to envisage a multipolar multicivilizational order organized around what he calls "the core states of civilizations [which would be the] sources of order within civilizations and, through negotiations with other core states, between civilizations."[23] He then adds that "a world in which core states play a leading or dominating role is a sphere-of-influence world" and that "a core state can perform its ordering function because member-states perceive it a cultural kin."[24] Such a framework seems strikingly similar to the arguments advanced by Mouffe and Zolo, the idea being the construction of a planetary balance of power around macro-regions defined along civilizational lines.

The problem with such a model of order is that its constructed only on the grounds of a material structure of power, which might well represent the spatial orientation of the global order but does not make for the normative structure of such an order. It is true that Huntington sketches very briefly (in less than a page) three rules for a possible normative structure of his multipolar multi-civilizational order: the *abstention* rule (core states should abstain from intervention in conflicts in other civilizations); the *joint mediation* rule (core states should negotiate to contain or halt fault-line wars among states or groups from their civilizations); and, finally, the *commonalities* rule (peoples in all civilizations should search for and attempt to expand the values, institutions, and practices they have in common with peoples of other civilizations).[25] These rules, however, reveal even more neatly the "realist" assumptions of the model as they, in essence, amount to nothing but a minimalist ethics of non-interference—the commonalities rule pointing perhaps to some "thin" minimal communal denominator of universal morality, but in fact being the perfect exemplification of that rhetorical technique, which consists in vaguely referring to some kind of undefined normative necessity of an opposite aspiration to the clash. The result of the Huntingtonian construction is, therefore, a worrying system of forces of civilizational macro-regional great powers ready for collision—the clash of civilizations—and the only possible hope is to make the stability of the system attainable through the mechanism of the balance of power. However, the "realist" emphasis, shared by Huntington on the centrality of fear, insecurity, and threats in an anarchic environment, seems simply to make the clash of civilizations unavoidable—and its occurrence as merely a matter of time.

This is why Zolo correctly cautions about the apparent self-evident force of this multipolar model and points to the necessity of immersing it in a broader and real process of dialogue between the world's major civilizations. I will add some further comments on this aspect in the final section of this chapter. This leads me to the need for what I have called an active politics of dialogue of civilizations, that is, to practically enter into this inter-civilizational dialogical encounter to create, in Gadamer's words, these "new normative and common solidarities that let practical reason speak again" in a way that is appropriate to the new global predicament.[26] It is my contention that practical reason should speak today in the form of a new cross-cultural *jus gentium* providing the normative structure appropriate to the contemporary multicultural and globalized international society.

A New Cross-Cultural Jus Gentium as the Normative Order of Dialogue of Civilizations

As Bull has argued, the emergence of a "multicultural international society" imperatively requires a *new normative structure* since "we have...to recognise that the nascent cosmopolitan culture of today, like the international society which it helps to sustain, is weighted in favor of the dominant cultures of the West."[27] The political discourse of dialogue of civilizations calls for the reopening and redefining of the core Western-centric and liberal assumptions upon which the normative structure of the contemporary international society is based.

The discussion of *jus gentium* has recently been reinvigorated by John Rawls' *The Law of Peoples*.[28] This is a welcome development as it has contributed to advancing a debate on the philosophical basis of international law that has unfortunately been severely limited by the legal positivism predominant in the theory and practice of international law. More importantly, as Dallmayr outlined,

> in times of historical change and upheaval, the law of peoples (*jus gentium*) has tended to serve as a go-between or mediating agent between local or city law and rational philosopher's law, an agent able to stretch the former's parochialism while harnessing the latter's aloofness. It is in this sense that...[Giambattista] Vico speaks of "natural law of peoples" (*jus natural gentium*), distinguishing it from mere custom and philosophers' precepts.[29]

The mediating role of the *jus (naturale) gentium* seems to confirm the usefulness of reinvigorating a discussion of this concept as a response to the crisis of global order whose solution, I would argue, revolves precisely around the dilemma between universalism and pluralism.

Commenting on Rawls' "quasi-Kantian tenor," Dallmayr suggests that his approach should be "integrated and 'sublated' (*aufgehoben*) in a more densely textured cross-cultural *jus gentium*."[30] Interestingly, he contends that this requires a shift from the level of universal moral theorizing predominant among liberal-cosmopolitan supporters to a political plane, or what he calls a global political *praxis* that can address "the neglect of relevant differences among peoples and cultures and also the sidelining of motivational disposition which might foster moral conduct."[31]

Echoing Václav Havel's critique of a technology of world order and the need for a genuine universality grounded in the social ethics and practices of "really existing communities," Dallmayr's point reprises the first line of argument I identified as a prerequisite to any forward-looking reflection on the normative structure of contemporary international society that wishes to be sensitive to the call for a dialogue of civilizations. From this perspective, what is at stake in this cross-cultural encounter is the very legitimacy and, as a consequence, legal effectiveness of a future *jus gentium* in a context whereby, on one hand, international law is increasingly perceived—for reasons that are understandable and worrying at the same time—as the ideological component of new imperialist strategies and, on the other hand, as even Michael Walzer has argued, the legal positivist interpretations of the UN Charter, which "have constructed a paper world, which fails at crucial points to correspond to the world the rest of us still live in."[32]

However, drawing on the second insight identified as essential for an international political theory of dialogue of civilizations, a dialogically constituted cross-cultural *jus gentium* seems to enshrine the promise of not only a more genuine but also of a "better" common ground. Whether in the empirically grounded (though daring) statement of Bhikhu Parekh, according to whom, "since each culture is inherently limited, a dialogue between them is mutually beneficial"; or in Taylor's more cautious presumption of worth, which involves, in his own words, "something like an act of faith" about a world where different cultures complement each other, the argument here is that, in Khatami's words, every dialogue, based on a presumption of the worth of the Other, "provides grounds for human creativity to flourish."[33] This is particularly challenging for the "Orientalist mindset" of superiority of the West, but it also provides a hope for those Westerners perceiving a fundamental ethical and political crisis in their liberal societies.

Dialogue is an open-ended process, which frequently involves difficulties, and there is no guarantee that it can produce a cross-cultural consensus. With reference to the case of human rights, unquestionably an essential element of any future *jus gentium* and arguably a realm where the idea of a world dialogical consensus has been making way in recent times, Taylor has asked, for example, how their conceptualization might be transformed through an understanding of the Theravada Buddhist search for selflessness, for self-giving, and dana (generosity), or through the Hindu notion of nonviolence, or by resting on the Islamic themes of the mercy and compassion of God.[34] Similarly, Etzioni has called for a "new normative global synthesis" between the West's preoccupation with autonomy and the East's preoccupation with social order.[35] Perhaps the dialogical encounter with the cultural Other, by stretching our imagination, might bring about a cross-cultural human rights regime, on one hand, which is more adequate to the multicultural nature of contemporary international society and, on the other, which is transformed and expanded in terms of its moral horizon beyond (and more profound than) the Western emphasis on rights-talk with its implicit set of liberal assumptions on the nature of subjectivity.

In addition, the third dimension integral to any international political theory of dialogue of civilizations, peace through inter-civilizational mutual understanding, bears some implications for the idea of a new cross-cultural *jus gentium*—which I will deal with more extensively in the final section of this chapter. But before turning to that, I should add that the very logic of the argument I have been making for a cross-cultural *jus gentium* as a *praxis* of dialogue disqualifies me, in a sense and in that context, from saying more on the content of this cross-cultural *jus gentium ă venir*. This remains the exclusive mission of the dialogue among scholars as well as practitioners who are personally engaged in this intercultural dialogue academically and in various public *fora*. Here, however, I would like to mention that there is a thriving and well-established field of comparative philosophical study as well as a growing set of works in the young and flourishing field of comparative political theory whose aim is precisely to contribute to this global political intercultural dialogue.[36]

Peace as the Critical Horizon/Aim of Dialogue of Civilizations

As I have already argued, the present international situation imposes on all of us a moral obligation to pursue a politics of inter-civilizational understanding; to engage in an intercultural dialogue is today crucial for peace, as it cannot be ignored that since September 11, in the very year designated by the United Nations as the "Year of Dialogue of Civilizations," global political violence and conflicts have reached a critical new level, both quantitatively and qualitatively, and the shadow of a future clash of civilizations has been hammering down on the world and, very worryingly, in the collective psychologies of its peoples.

This overall political context of growing cultural misunderstanding and mistrust, which prompted Edward Said to speak of a real danger of a clash of ignorance, should be opposed by creating the conditions for widespread processes of "inter-civilizational mutual understanding" at multiple levels. In this respect, the link between civilizational dialogue, mutual understanding, and peace is, fortunately, becoming more widely acknowledged. The ideal of "building bridges of mutual understanding" in order to learn (or relearn) how to live together among different cultural communities—what Andrea Riccardi has called in his last book the art of "con-vivere"[37]—is also critical for the global order in a more specific sense; it provides the key for the combination of the spatial orientation of multipolarity and of the normative order of a cross-cultural *jus gentium*. To explain this point, I want to return for a moment to the Huntingtonian model of multipolar, multicivilizational order discussed above.

The popularity of Huntington's thesis no doubt has to do with bringing to center stage the post-89 debate on the future of international relations, the political resurgence of religion, and the emergence of a multicultural international society. In other words, it could be said that Huntington has framed post-89 international politics as a multicultural fact. In this respect, its proposal of multipolar multicivilizational order is indeed an acknowledgment of the centrality of the growing multicultural nature of international society, but, and here lies the problem, it is based on the opposite logic to the dialogical multiculturalism that I have defended.

In Huntington's view, the multicultural nature of the world has, on one hand, internationally to be almost confined within a civilizational cage following the "good fences make good neighbours" principle, and, on the other hand, it has domestically to be contrasted through strict immigration policy and a new integrationist approach, as Huntington has argued in his most recent book with reference to the growing presence of Latinos in the United States and what, as he argues, could be its weakening effect on American national identity.[38] In sum, his argument is not about building bridges of mutual understanding, but, rather, walls of containment and separation.

The international political theory of dialogue of civilizations envisages "bridges," not "walls," to link multipolarity with a cross-cultural *jus gentium*. In particular, here the emphasis is not on the geographical-territorial dimension of civilizations but rather on the normative one, that is, on civilizations as the great cultural and religious social traditions of the world. This implies, for example, that the neo-regionalist revival that Zolo and Mouffe favor as a way of constructing a multipolar spatial ordering does not need to take shape along civilizational-culturalist lines. Rather it cannot be dismembered from reinforcing a politics of multiculturalism "at home and abroad."[39] To illustrate this point, I refer to a case of contemporary relevance to European regional integration and the relationship between Europe and the Muslim world: the hotly debated issue of the EU enlargement to Turkey.

From such a perspective, the framing of Turkey's EU-accession discursive strategy, by the current Turkish Prime Minister Recep Tayyip Erdoğan, as a "bridge" between Asia and Europe or as a new "alliance of civilizations" is to be welcomed and supported.[40] My argument is, in fact, that multiculturally constituted processes of regional integration are more conducive to a peaceful global order as they act as a preventive antidote to the possible negative politicization of cultural differences on a global scale. A similar additional point can be made to support the creation of multicultural forms of regional cooperation and integration, which are, anyway, arguably justifiable on functionalist grounds to respond to the common challenges brought about by the processes of globalization. Initiatives of regionalization involving, for example, member-states from a plurality of existing regional political organizations can further contribute to the dilution of the risks of a multipolarization along enclosed civilizational lines.[41]

Regionalization processes can be multiple and overlapping insofar as collective identities and political circumstances allow. For example, from such a perspective, initiatives of Mediterranean regionalization involving European and Arab countries are to be encouraged as a way of fostering bridges of communication and mutual understanding between the European Union and the Arab League and can also constitute laboratories for the praxis of inter-civilizational dialogue necessary for the emergence of a new cross-cultural *jus gentium*. Finally, multiculturalism "abroad" is likely to facilitate "living together" at home and *vice versa*, a fact that cannot be overlooked in our era of global communication. I would, for example, anticipate a reciprocally beneficial relationship between the integration of the growing Muslim presence in Europe, arguably the greatest challenge facing the future identity of Europe, and a peaceful relationship between Europe and the Muslim world in the Mediterranean and in the Middle East.

An active politics of dialogue of civilizations may represent an essential mechanism of connection between multipolarity and a new cross-cultural *jus gentium*, both as a way to mitigate the risk of a "culturalist enclosure" in the former and to dialogically inscribe plurality in the latter. If this is so, however, the driving idea, the polar star of dialogue of civilizations as international political theory, is a comprehensive and politically realistic idea(l) of peace. I can only suggest a few lines of thought to shed light on this comprehensive and realistic idea(l) of peace, which I think should be the object of a separate study.[42]

A realistic idea(l) of peace points to the need for creatively accommodating into a broader normative vision the realities of interests and power represented, in this case, by the condition of multipolarity. But more importantly, the ideal of peace needs also to be comprehensive. Contrary to an abstract emphasis on legal-positivistic engineering of the cosmopolitan "legal pacifism," which expands on the Kelsenian maxim of "peace through law," and the ethnocentric and problematic emphasis by the so-called "democratic peace theory" on the liberal-democratic model *as conditio sine qua non* for international peace,[43] a comprehensive reconceptualization of peace should explore the mutually constitutive and reinforcing relationships, at various concrete levels, among peace, justice, and reconciliation, as the visionary words of John Paul II, "there is no Peace without Justice and no Justice without Reconciliation" suggest and the remarkable concrete experience of the "Truth and Reconciliation Commission" in South Africa proved.[44] It is my view that such a comprehensive reconceptualization might effectively inform real-world bottom-up initiatives of conflict-resolution, prevention, and post-conflict reconstruction and may indeed have greater chances of politically realistic success than the top-down abstract approach of proceduralism and liberal rule of law.

Dialogue of civilizations is at the very heart of such three-dimensional interplay, and more cross-cultural work needs to be done to explore these relationships in theory and practice.[45] At a time when a great deal of thinking has been devoted to justifying and making sense of the doctrine of "preventive war," I reunite with Riccardi in arguing that now is instead the time for a strategy of "preventive peace."[46]

Sketching Dialogue of Civilizations as an Alternative Model for World Order

This investigation began by suggesting that the global political discourse of dialogue of civilizations emerged as an alternative political reaction to the end of the Cold War against the background of the clash of civilizations and the globalization of liberalism. In the cases of two outspoken supporters of this political discourse, Khatami and Havel, an awareness of the inadequacies and problems of these two alternative visions of world order is accompanied by a moral *élan* for fostering universality while recognizing and valuing plurality. The postmodern need for transcendence (Havel) and the Sufi-inspired mysticism of unity (Khatami) ground, respectively, what are indeed two impressive dialogical visions for the future of world order. But they also manifest the necessity for more work to be done by international and political theorists for a translation and accommodation of these visions into the language and concepts of international political theorizing.

Moving from these reflections, therefore, I have attempted to bring these visions into the realm of academic reflection on the nature of contemporary global politics and the future of world order. The alternative model of world order inspired by dialogue of civilizations has multipolarity as its spatial orientation and a new cross-cultural *jus gentium* as its normative order. An active politics of dialogue of civilizations represents the combination mechanism of connection between multipolarity and the new cross-cultural *jus gentium*, both as a way to mitigate the risk of a "culturalist enclosure" in the former and to dialogically inscribe plurality in the latter. Concretely, this neo-regionalist, multipolar, and cross-cultural model of greater spaces is different from the Huntingtonian model of multipolar, multicivilizational order as: (1) it is not shaped by civilizational-culturalist lines but by a dialogical multiculturalism; (2) its conflicts and disputes are neutralized by a "thick" dialogically constituted normative order (a new cross-cultural *jus gentium*) based on a "genuine" and "enriched" universality; and (3) it is committed to a widespread process of "inter-civilizational mutual understanding" at multiple levels.

Such an outline of dialogue of civilizations as an alternative model for world order is of course still very general. Many other contextual conditions and considerations should be brought into the discussion to provide a more developed model responding to the present international situation. This is not the place to deepen such a discussion.

Seven years after the designation of the UN Year of the Dialogue among Civilizations and the events of September 11, in a time of great international tensions and political turmoil, critics have increasingly labeled the idea of inter-civilizational dialogue as idealistic, abstract, rhetorical, and even politically dangerous. At the same time, there exists a critical mass of activism and commitment—at different levels—to the idea and practice of dialogue of civilizations, cultures, and religions. In other words, it seems to me that a critical juncture has been reached; the global political discourse of dialogue of civilizations needs to move beyond general and rhetorical statements and assume a clearer and concrete political agenda if it wants to be taken seriously and not be cursorily dismissed or relegated to the margins.

The idea of dialogue of civilizations as an alternative model for world order might provide this global movement with a more intelligible and effective political synthesis, which can contribute to the necessary conceptual and political upgrade of such an idea. But perhaps more important is the need for new heterodox alliances: the promotion of common initiatives (cultural, social, communicative, and political) to build new transversal practices of solidarity, and cooperation and mobilization involving groups from different cultural backgrounds and religious affiliations acting together on the basis of common political aspirations. This practice of dialogue of civilizations carries the hope that we may learn how to live together in our increasingly multicultural and globalized international society. Dialogue of civilizations as international political theory hopes to be a small contribution to this great dream.

Notes

1. For the lack of academic attention paid to the issues, problems, and challenges that the idea of dialogue of civilizations poses for the future of international relations and world order, see the introduction to this volume.
2. For this argument with specific reference to the visions of global dialogue put forward by Khatami and Havel, see Fabio Petito (2007) "The Global Political Discourse of Dialogue among Civilizations: Mohammad Khatami and Vaclav Havel," *Global Change, Peace & Security* 19 (2), 103–125. For the most renowned academic articulations of these discourses, see, respectively, Samuel Huntington (1996) *The Clash of Civilizations and the Remaking of World Order* (London: Simon and Schuster); and Francis Fukuyama (1992) *The End of History and the Last Man* (New York: Free Press).
3. For a comparison of Huntington and Fukuyama, see Stanley Kurtz (2002) "The Future of History," *Policy Review* 112, 43–58.
4. Here I draw on Hasenclever and Rittberger's categorization, within the context of peace studies, of three theoretical perspectives on the impact of faith on political conflict, namely, primordialism (with which they associate Huntington), instrumentalism (associated to the rational-actor approach that misses the role of identity), and what

is called moderate constructivism (associated to various dialogue strategies for conflict resolution). See Andreas Hasenclever and Volker Rittberger (2003) "Does Religion Make a Difference? Theoretical Approaches to the Impact of Faith on Political Conflict," in Fabio Petito and Pavlos Hatzopoulos (eds.), *Religion in International Relations: The Return from Exile* (New York: Palgrave), 107–145.
5. The "thick" and "thin" distinction is borrowed from Michael Walzer (1994) *Thick and Thin: Moral Argument at Home and Abroad* (Notre Dame, IN: University of Notre Dame Press).
6. Amitai Etzioni (2004) *From Empire to Community: A New Approach to International Relations* (New York: Palgrave), 26.
7. See Petito, "The Global Political Discourse."
8. Jean Bethke Elshtain (1999) "Really Existing Communities," *Review of International Studies* 25 (1), 141–146.
9. Mohammad Khatami, speech at the UN General Assembly, New York, September 21, 1998, www.parstimes.com/history/khatami_speech_un.html (accessed August 1, 2008).
10. Ashis Nandy (1998) "Defining a New Cosmopolitanism: Towards a Dialogue of Asian Civilizations," in Kuan-Hsing Chen (ed.), *Trajectories: Inter-Asia Cultural Studies* (London: Routledge), 146.
11. Thomas Pantham (1992) "Some Dimensions of Universality of Philosophical Hermeneutics: A Conversation with Hans–Georg Gadamer," *Journal of Indian Council of Philosophical Research* 9, 132.
12. This includes, for example, Wendt's constructivism. See Alex Wendt (2003) "Why a World State is Inevitable," *European Journal of International Relations* 9 (4), 491–542 and Fabio Petito (2007) "Against World Unity: Carl Schmitt and the Western-centric and Liberal Global Order," in Louiza Odysseos and Fabio Petito (eds.), *The International Political Thought of Carl Schmitt: Terror, Liberal War and the Crisis of Global Order* (London: Routledge), 166–183.
13. For a classical discussion of the three approaches in international relations (realism, idealism, and rationalism), see Martin Wight (1991) *International Theory: The Three Traditions* (Leicester: Leicester University Press).
14. Here the *locus classicus* for the so-called realist critique of idealism is E. H. Carr (2001) *The Twenty Years' Crisis. An Introduction to the Study of International Relations, 1919–1939*, ed. Michael Cox (Basingstoke: Palgrave).
15. For the classical realist and neorealist view, see, respectively, Hans Morgenthau (1948) *Politics among Nations* (New York: Knopf) and Kenneth Waltz (1979) *Theory of International Politics* (Reading: Addison-Wesley).
16. This debate has mainly taken place in some of the leading mainstream US journals, such as *International Security*, *Foreign Policy*, and *The National Interest*, as a sort of "analytical" controversy, moulded in

the social-scientific and positivist language of American international relations. In this context, the different prescriptive views take normally the form of concluding policy implications for American Grand Strategy, and the positions vary from a primacy stance (hard unilateralism) to a liberal-internationalist multilateralism. For arguments focussing on unipolarity, see Charles Krauthammer (1991) "The Unipolar Moment," *Foreign Affairs* no. 1: 23–33; William C. Wohlforth (1999) "The Stability of a Unipolar World," *International Security* 24 (1), 5–41; and for multipolarity, see Christopher Layne (1993) "The Unipolar Illusion: Why New Great Powers Will Rise," *International Security* 17 (4): 5–51; and Kenneth Waltz (2000) "Structural Realism after the Cold War," *International Security* 25 (1), 5–41. For a debate on the ascendancy and decline of US hegemony, see Paul Kennedy (1987) *The Rise and Fall of Great Powers: Economic Change and Military Conflict from 1500 to 2000* (New York: Random House).

17. If at the end of the Second World War, the United States accounted for half of the world's economic output, today it is estimated to account for less than one-third; and as per current projections, it is estimated that by 2020 it will be about 20 percent. See, for example, Angus Maddison (2003) *The World Economy: Historical Statistics* (Paris: OECD Development Centre Studies). This does not necessarily imply that the US economy will cease to be the main engine of world economic growth (I owe this point to Jason Abbot).

18. Samuel P. Huntington (1999) "The Lonely Superpower," *Foreign Affairs* 78 (2), 35–49.

19. Chantal Mouffe (2007), "Carl Schmitt's Warnings on the Dangers of a Multipolar World" and Danilo Zolo, "The Contemporary Use of the Notion of 'Empire'" in Odysseos and Petito (eds.), *The International Political Thought of Carl Schmitt*, respectively, 147–153 and 154–165.

20. Zolo, "The Contemporary Use," 7.

21. Ibid., 13.

22. Huntington, *The Clash of Civilizations*.

23. Ibid., 156.

24. Ibid.

25. Ibid., 316 and 320.

26. Pantham "Some Dimensions of Universality of Philosophical Hermeneutics," 132.

27. Hedley Bull (1977) *The Anarchical Society: A Study of Order in World Politics* (London: Macmillan), 305.

28. John Rawls (1999) *The Law of Peoples—with "The Idea of Public Reason Revisited"* (Cambridge, MA: Harvard University Press).

29. Fred Dallmayr (2004) *Peace Talks—Who will Listen?* (Notre Dame, IN: Notre Dame University Press), 47.

30. Ibid., 59–60.
31. Ibid., 15.
32. Michael Walzer (2000) *Just and Unjust War: A Moral Argument with Historical Illustrations*, 3rd ed. (New York: Basic Books), xix.
33. Bhikhu Parekh (2000) *Rethinking Multiculturalism: Cultural Diversity and Political Theory* (Basingstoke: Macmillan Palgrave), 337; Taylor, "The Politics of Recognition," 66 and 73.
34. Taylor, "Conditions for an Unforced Consensus on Human Rights."
35. Etzioni, *From Empire to Community*.
36. See for example, Gerald James Larson and Eliot Deutsch (eds.) (1988) *Interpreting Across Boundaries: New Essays in Comparative Philosophy* (Princeton: Princeton University Press); P. T. Raju (1997) *Introduction to Comparative Philosophy* (Delhi: Motilal Banarsidass). For Comparative Political Theory, see the overview in Fred Dallmayr (2004) "Beyond Monologue: For a Comparative Political Theory," *Perspectives on Politics* 2 (2), 249–257.
37. Andrea Riccardi (2006) *Convivere* (Bari: Edizioni Laterza). For an English translation (by Francesca Simmons) of its Introduction, see http://www.resetdoc.org/EN/Coexistence.php (accessed June 1, 2007).
38. Huntington, *Who Are We*.
39. "At home and abroad" stands for "domestically and internationally" and is an expression taken from the title of Michael Walzer's book *Thick and Thin: Moral Argument at Home and Abroad*.
40. For the UN Alliance of Civilizations initiative, see http://unaoc.org/ (accessed August 1, 2008).
41. This is a sort of open-regionalism, which could represent the basis for a truly decentralized and multilateral structure of global governance. In this context, however, the system of global governance, to borrow an effective image of Zolo, should operate a transition "from the logic of the Leviathan to that of the thousands fragile chains of Lilliput," Zolo, *Cosmopolis*, 154.
42. Regretfully, the research on the concept and practice of peace has been generally neglected since the end of the Cold War, perhaps in concomitance with a certain liberal illusion that peace had become politically unproblematic. Some ideas that I have found interesting and could be further explored in a multidisciplinary way for a theoretical and practical reconceptualization of peace, along what I would call a comprehensive and realistic notion, can be found in, for international relations and security studies, Ole Wæver, "Peace and Security: Two Concepts and Their Relationship," in Stefano Guzzini and Dietrich Jung (eds.) (2004) *Contemporary Security Analysis and Copenhagen Peace Research* (London: Routledge), 94–116, and Michael Howard (2000) *The Invention of Peace: Reflections on War and International Order* (London: Profile Books); in the context of political

theory and philosophy, Dallmayr, *Peace Talks*, and Danilo Zolo, "Towards a Weak Pacifism," in *Cosmopolis*, ch. 5 and "Universalismo imperiale e pacifismo 'secessionista,'" *La rivista del Manifesto* 32, (2002), 47–52, also available online www.juragentium.unifi.it/it/surveys/wlgo/secpacif.htm (accessed June 2, 2007); in the context of theology and religious studies, Miroslav Volf (2000) "Forgiveness, Reconciliation, and Justice: A Theological Contribution to a More Peaceful Social Environment," *Millennium: Journal of International Studies* (29) 3, 861–877; see also Andrea Riccardi (2004) *La pace preventiva. Speranze e ragioni in un mondo di conflitti* (Cinisello Balsamo, Edizioni San Paolo), Michael T. Seigel, "History, Memory, and the Dialogue of Civilizations," chapter 13 in this book, and a collection of John Paul II's (2005) speeches and writings on peace, *Non uccidere in nome di Dio*, ed. Natale Benazzi (Casale Monferrato: Edizioni Piemme). A recent initiative to fill this void has been the 2008 *Millennium: Journal of International Studies* Special Issue on "Peace in International Relations" 36 (3).

43. For the approaches that Danilo Zolo critically label in his volume *Cosmopolis* as "legal pacifism," see Noberto Bobbio (1979) *Il problema della guerra e le vie della pace* (Bologna: Il Mulino), and Hans Kelsen (1944) *Peace Through Law* (Chapel Hill: The University of North Carolina Press). For the democratic peace theory, see Michael W. Doyle (1997) *Ways of War and Peace* (New York: W. W. Norton).

44. See for example. Volf, "Forgiveness, Reconciliation, and Justice." See also Pope John Paul II, "There is No Peace without Justice and No Justice without Forgiveness," Message for the celebration of the World Day for Peace, January 1, 2002, extracts in John Paul II, *Non uccidere in nome di Dio* and available online at http://www.vatican.net/holy_father/john_paul_ii/messages/peace/documents/hf_jp-ii_mes_20011211_xxxv-world-day-for-peace_en.html (accessed January 15, 2007). For the "Truth and Reconciliation Commission" in South Africa, see, Desmond Tutu (2004) *God Has a Dream: A Vision of Hope for Our Time* (New York: Doubleday).

45. For an initial effort in this direction, which addresses the overlooked role of historical memories and reconciliation, see Seigel's chapter 13 in this book.

46. Riccardi, *La pace preventiva*.

Chapter 4

Dialogue among and within Faiths: Weaving a Culture of Peace

Toh Swee-Hin (S. H. Toh)

The present world order is marked by the realities of economic marginalization and the suffering of many amidst the affluence of a minority of elites. The end of the Cold War has not delivered the promised peace dividends, as violent conflicts (accentuated by post-September 11) continue to rage and destroy lives and the habitat worldwide. Human right violations still abound, including discriminations or even genocidal violence on the basis of culture, ethnicity, and faith identities. The ecological crisis can no longer be denied, and a deep sense of inner peacelessness reveals itself in symptoms of alienation and anxieties. However, amidst such pessimism, there is a growing awareness amongst a diversity of groups about overcoming the pervasive culture of violence.

This chapter presents a critical reflection on the contributions of one increasingly visible sector in building a culture of peace at the local, national, and global levels of life, namely, faiths and spirituality traditions. Exemplars from various societies and regions will be drawn upon to clarify how values, beliefs, and practices of diverse faiths and spirituality traditions have catalyzed peace-building amidst conflicts and violence. It will argue that the movement of interfaith dialogue serves a critical role in forging solidarity amongst faiths and spirituality traditions that is essential in inspiring people, communities, and organizations to find common ground in building a better and peaceful world for all.

While highlighting these optimistic aspects, the chapter is also conscious of the transformational challenges that all faiths need to face, namely, to critically revise doctrines and perspectives that act as barriers to the building of a culture of peace. Finally, a number of key pedagogical principles will be suggested to enhance the effectiveness of faith and spirituality education in creating an actively nonviolent, just, compassionate, and sustainable "world order."

Interfaith Dialogue: A Survey of Principles and Practices

In essence, interfaith dialogue seeks to promote understanding, respect, and reconciliation amongst the diversity of faiths and religions in the world. From the Christian-Muslim dialogue between St. Francis of Assisi and the Sultan of Cairo, to King Asoka of India's policy of acceptance and mutual interfaith learning, the twentieth century has witnessed a blossoming of international interfaith movements and organizations. Locally, regionally, and globally, diverse faith communities have engaged in dialogue not only to gain a deeper understanding of each other's traditions, but most importantly, also to critically engage participants in revealing common values and principles that would lead to collaboration for a more peaceful world.[1]

A useful framework for conceptualizing interfaith dialogue is provided by Johannes B. Banawiratma's five dimensions: (1) a dialogue of life, whereby people of different faiths, in open spirit, live and share with each other; (2) a dialogue of ethical critical reflection to understand social-economic conditions; (3) a dialogue of sharing religious experiences and spiritual richness; (4) a theological dialogue that aims to deepen understanding amongst the religious traditions; and, (5) a dialogue of interfaith action to promote social and environmental justice.[2]

Globally, the accomplishments of interfaith dialogue are reflected in the growth of various networks and coalitions, such as the Religions for Peace, the Parliament of the World's Religions, and the United Religions Initiative. Their frequent gatherings have shown that it is possible to establish mutual respect and understanding, as well as collaborate in tackling common societal and global problems. For example, the Parliament of the Worlds' Religions has provided much impetus to the Declaration of a Global Ethic for building a humane and just global order, based on the basic commitments of nonviolence, a just economic order, tolerance, truthfulness, equal rights, and partnership between men and women.[3] In its 8th World Assembly, the Religions for Peace issued its Kyoto Declaration on Confronting Violence and Advancing Shared Security that called on all faiths to "transform conflicts, build peace, struggle for justice, and advance sustainable development."[4] By drawing on John Paul Lederach's "moral imagination,"[5] the United Religions Initiative is also promoting peace-building in various countries such as Uganda, Ethiopia, India, and the Philippines.[6] Led by Indonesia, Australia, New Zealand, and the Philippines, an intergovernmental interfaith initiative has also brought delegations of several Asia-Pacific nations for annual regional conferences in Yogyakarta (2004), Cebu (2006), Waitangi (2007), and Phnom Penh (2008). These meetings affirmed the importance of interfaith dialogue and cooperation in promoting "regional peace and security," "social and economic development," "human dignity," "social and economic justice," "minority empowerment," and "reconciliation among conflicting groups in society" as well as the crucial role of education and media in enhancing interfaith understanding and cooperation.[7]

Faith institutions have also implemented various programs and projects in interfaith understanding, such as the Vatican's Pontifical Council for Interreligious Dialogue, the World Council of Churches' Office on Interreligious Relations, the International Jewish Committee on Interreligious Consultations, the World's Muslim League's Office for Interreligious Affairs, initiatives of several Buddhist orders and temples (e.g., International Network of Engaged Buddhists, Pure Land Learning College, Dharma Drum, Fo Guang Shan), United Sikhs, World Alliance of Reformed Churches, the Baha'i Faith, and the Brahma Kumaris World Spiritual Organization. At local, national, regional, and international levels, many interfaith centers and organizations (e.g., Temple of Understanding, World Congress of Faiths, and International Interfaith Centre) have emerged and are promoting dialogue and understanding amongst diverse faiths and spirituality traditions. In 2002, the Multi-Faith Centre at Griffith University in Brisbane, Australia, was established that integrates education, research, and advocacy in local, national, and global interfaith dialogue.[8]

However, if interfaith dialogue is to be authentic, it must include several principles, including an openness to learn a sense of humility and a willingness to be self-critical. Such principles require that each faith reinterpret their beliefs in light of contemporary societal changes and challenge any tendencies toward extremism and intolerance. As many faith leaders have emphasized, intra-faith dialogue needs to complement interfaith dialogue. Importantly, interfaith dialogue needs to involve not only leaders but also ordinary people from all sectors of society. Finally, the role of education in promoting interfaith dialogue is vital, so that children and young people, as prospective future leaders and individuals, are committed to a culture of respect, harmony, justice, and nonviolence.

Building a Culture of Peace

As noted earlier, despite a sense of despair over the state of peacelessness confronting humanity, there are growing signs of hope as conflicts and violence are challenged on a daily basis by a network of peoples, communities, and movements that are working toward creating a culture of peace.[9]

In this vast peace-building project, it is evident that faiths and spirituality traditions act as inspirational sources for values and principles, guiding the transformation of a culture of violence to a culture of peace.[10] Despite various inimical expressions, religion potentially can make a constructive contribution toward "humane governance."[11]

In 1994, UNESCO (United Nations Educational, Scientific and Cultural Organization) sponsored an interfaith conference that issued a Declaration on the Role of Religions in the Promotion of a Culture of Peace. However, such values and principles need to be revived as many believers may be entrapped by a culture of competitive materialism and egocentric attachments, (such as greed, power, and so on). Simultaneously, all faiths need to engage in intra-faith dialogue, to query and transform doctrines and perspectives that act as barriers to a culture of peace. As Charles Kimball warned, it is possible for religion to become "evil."[12]

It is also vital to acknowledge the role that education plays in interfaith dialogue as well as in building a culture of peace.[13] Without education, interfaith dialogue and peace-building cannot be effective or sustainable. How can participants enter into authentic interfaith dialogue unless they have been educated on the basic beliefs of each other's faiths? How can individuals and communities build peace unless the realities of violence and conflicts are critically understood?

Furthermore, weaving a culture of peace is a multidimensional and holistic endeavor. In addition to peace as the absence of war, peace also implies justice, human rights, environmental care, and intercultural respect. As reflected in the declarations of global interfaith movements, faiths are called to acknowledge and to overcome violence in all its forms and at all levels. Hence, a holistic paradigm of a culture of peace encompasses the interrelated themes of dismantling a culture of war, living with justice and compassion, promoting human rights and responsibilities, building intercultural respect, reconciliation, and solidarity, living in harmony with the Earth, and cultivating inner peace.

Dismantling the Culture of War

Despite the removal of Cold War tensions and the nuclear arms race, the world is still suffering from the symptoms of a culture of war. Millions have died in conflicts or have become refugees. Wars, terrorism, counterterrorism, armed intervention, and military occupation are grim reminders of the violence that nations and groups readily resort to. Horizontal proliferation in nuclear weapons, as well as other weapons of mass destruction, is a major global concern.[14]

Clearly there is a need for peace education that focuses on nonviolent resolution of armed conflicts and disputes. As successive generations of peace builders stress the need for conflicts to be settled through negotiation, the role of the UN and other multilateral agencies need to be fully supported and strengthened.[15] While the participation of governments and official bodies is necessary, the inspirational role of civil society peacemakers in critical education and empowerment of ordinary citizens in the peace-building process has been recognized.[16] Another dimension of disarmament education and advocacy lies in the campaign to abolish the arms trade, which fuels the engines of wars at the expense of basic human needs. The historic treaty banning land mines also crystallizes how ordinary citizens can mobilize together with state agencies to enhance the safety of innumerable peoples worldwide.

But the culture of war is not restricted to the "macro" level, it is also to be found in the more "micro" sectors of society. Domestic violence, gun ownership, a vigilante mentality at interpersonal, familial, institutional, and community levels have also been challenged by educational campaigns and programs. The role of the media, sport, entertainment, and other cultural and social agencies, including even the toy industry, are demystified for their explicit and indirect support of a culture of war and physical violence. In many formal schooling systems, the integration of nonviolence principles in policies, programs, curricula, and teaching-learning environments has expanded in recent decades (e.g., conflict resolution, peer mediation, non-bullying, and violence-prevention).[17]

In interfaith dialogue, education as a means to dismantle a culture of war resonates with the core values of diverse faiths and spirituality traditions. Believers are guided to build peace in their daily lives and communities, and to resolve conflicts through nonviolent means, such as negotiation and mediation. A number of traditions explicitly endorse *ahimsa* or non-killing, and therefore encourage active nonviolence as a way of life. There are now many inspiring exemplars of local initiatives in which different faiths are collaborating to overcome long-standing armed conflicts, such as the Bishops-Ulama Forum and the Silsilah Christian-Muslim Dialogue Movement in Mindanao, Philippines.[18] Local Christian-Muslim communities have been able to establish zones for peace and have committed to grassroots development projects that benefit everyone regardless of culture or faith. When Christian-Muslim violence erupted in Maluku, Indonesia, the Baku Bae movement helped to mediate the conflict through dialogue, led by faith leaders, to rebuild social capital and trust.[19] Facilitated by the Catholic Community of Sant'Egidio, faith leaders brokered the peacetalks that ended the deadly internal violence in Mozambique.[20] In the Middle East, many Muslim, Jewish, and Christian faith leaders have continued, despite the ongoing spiral of violence, to work for reconciliation and a peaceful settlement.[21] Northern Ireland and Yugoslavia also illustrate useful case studies where interfaith efforts have contributed toward the peace process. In a significant compilation, Douglas Johnston and Cynthia Sampson demonstrated that religion can be a "potent force in encouraging the peaceful resolution of conflict."[22]

Through interfaith dialogue, many have also contributed to campaigns for nuclear disarmament and arms disarmament and to nonviolent strategies to deal with terrorist acts such as the events of September 11. In the conferences of the Parliament of the World's Religions (Barcelona, 2004) and Religions for Peace (Kyoto, 2006), these global movements appealed to their followers to overcome religiously motivated violence and to speak out against violent extremist tendencies within their faith communities. The Decade to Overcome Violence, as per the declaration of the World Council of Churches, is yet another example of an ecumenical contribution to raise awareness of the ubiquitous problem of militarization. Dedicated Christians for nonviolence, such as John Dear and David Loy, and many engaged Buddhists, such as Thich Nhat Hanh and Sulak Sivaraksa, have demystified the militaristic ideology underpinning "terrorism" and the global "war against terrorism."[23] In Indonesia, Azyumardi Azra considers the rise of Islamic radicalism and extremism as mainly a political, rather than a religious, phenomenon that require social, economic, and political solutions.[24]

Whilst acknowledging the positive contribution by interfaith dialogue in dismantling the culture of war, there is also a major challenge confronting many faith leaders and their communities. Namely, the doctrine of a "just war" and "jihad," whereby war and violence under certain conditions are seen as justifiable.[25] Dialogue on this issue is understandably complex and difficult, but this is urgent if an active nonviolent dimension in each faith is to be promoted. In this capacity, many faiths are educating their followers to resort to nonviolent resolutions of their conflicts. However, such a process will need to go beyond theological platitudes that simply endorse "peace." Rather, churches, temples, mosques, and synagogues all need to implement education and training programs in active nonviolence.

Living with Justice and Compassion

Over the past centuries, the world economic order has been shaped by industrialization and rapid exploration of natural and human resources under the paradigm of "modernization"—now referred to as "globalization." The prevailing framework of development views economic growth through a *laisser-fair* free-market prism with its "trickle down" effect and an aid, investment, and trade regime that seeks to integrate the South in the global marketplace. Such globalization is controlled by the powerful nation-states, transnational corporations, and international financial and trade agencies.[26]

However, such modernization and corporate-led globalization have accentuated structural violence against the poor majorities. Whilst a small number of newly industrializing nations have gained a measure of prosperity, others have suffered major setbacks and economic crises. Within many South societies, there is tremendous deterioration in wealth and income, reflecting conditions of structural violence where economic and social injustices, combined with repressive political regimes, further marginalize the rural and urban poor.[27]

Confronting the challenges of world poverty, a critical paradigm of development focuses on the causes of inequality as well as on the international structures. As the erstwhile UN Secretary-General, Kofi Annan, stated: "true peace is far more than the absence of war. It is a phenomenon that encompasses economic development and social justice."[28] According to the ILO (International Labor Organization)-sponsored World Commission on the Social Dimensions of Globalization, a Fair Globalization called for globalization that is "fair, inclusive, democratically governed, and provides opportunities and tangible benefits for all countries and peoples."[29]

To tackle this situation, non government organizations (NGOs), civil society organizations, global advocate networks, and some governments have advocated for an alternative people-centered development paradigm. As reflected in the "globalization from below" movement, known as the World Social Forum, such alternative development prioritizes the basic needs and rights of all citizens and rethinks the goals of high-consumerist technologically advanced progress.[30] From rural to urban contexts, the poor and solidarity groups are empowering themselves through self-reliant, equity-led, and sustainable projects. Worldwide, there is an intensifying campaign to persuade states and banks to cancel the crippling debts of the South nations. In many societies of the North, a whole spectrum of NGOs dealing in aid and development have emerged promoting links of solidarity with the people, which essentially are engaging in the grassroots development of the South. They advocate changes in aid, trade, and other foreign policies of their governments, corporations, and international financial institutions, in order to reverse North-South inequities.[31] Alternative economic indicators that integrate equity, justice, and other indicators (e.g., sustainability, Genuine Progress Index, and Gross National Happiness) are now emerging.

Engaging with human suffering is another key challenge/responsibility for the interfaith dialogue movement. In many civilizations and faiths, compassion is an ethical principle that guides all interrelationships. Unlike pity, compassion is an authentic expression of solidarity promising to alleviate/transform the conditions of suffering—including being self-critical and admitting complicity.

A prominent exemplar of faith-based advocacy in overcoming structural violence is the Catholic-based liberation theology movement that originated from the impoverished slums of Latin America. Facilitated by models of critical education, or conscientization, popularized by the Brazilian educator Paulo Freire,[32] Christian communities worldwide have empowered marginalized people to speak out against injustices and to advocate for a participatory, sharing, and just society. Many Christians have been moved by the church's social teachings to promote campaigns for fair trade, people-centered aid, and freedom from debt that reflect a "spirituality of resistance."[33]

In a parallel manner, critical interpretations of the Buddha's teachings in contemporary social and economic contexts have led to the formation of an engaged Buddhist movement. Leading voices in the International Network of Engaged Buddhists, such as Thich Nhat Hanh and Sulak Sivaraksa, have emphasized that Buddhist principles of freeing oneself from attachments (greed, egotism, power) imply rejecting excessive consumerist needs and the desire for unlimited growth in favor of simpler lifestyles and the compassionate sharing of local and global resources for the well-being of all peoples and species.[34]

While acknowledging this critical role of faith-based advocacy for social and global justice, it is equally important to note that, within faith institutions, different interpretations of faith doctrines support the dominant development/globalization paradigm. Thus, not all Christian denominations share the conviction of transforming structural violence, while a number of Buddhist orders restrict their involvement to charity and relief work.

Promoting Human Rights and Responsibilities

Since the proclamation of the Universal Declaration on Human Rights, one of the major challenges facing the building of a culture of peace is the fulfilment of all human rights (political, economic, social, cultural) for all peoples at individual, community, national, and international levels. Despite some progress in implementation, through legal and social institutions and practices, human rights violations continue to cause great suffering. While governments readily ratify international conventions and covenants, too often vested interests and social-economic inequalities pose major obstacles to the building of a culture of human rights. As international human rights NGOs (such as Human Rights Watch, Amnesty International, and Corpwatch) have noted, geostrategic and economic stakes of powerful North governments and private corporations can also bolster human rights violations under repressive regimes. In the post-September 11 era, concomitant with the proliferation of the "war against terror," North/Western societies have witnessed diminished respect for the human rights of their own citizens through antiterrorist legislations and racial or faith profiling.

Though human rights remain a complex issue, sufficient conceptualization affirms some of the key principles and themes that underpin efforts to build a culture of human rights consistent with a culture of peace. To begin, given the indivisibility and interrelatedness of all rights, it is essential to avoid the earlier emphasis on individual civil and political rights and neglect social, economic, cultural, and communal rights. While sensitive to cultural diversity, the universality of human rights should be upheld so that cultural beliefs and practices are not used as a rationale to violate human rights (e.g., violence against women). In relating human rights with building a culture of peace, the human rights of specific marginalized sectors (e.g., women, children, people with disabilities, indigenous peoples, refugees, etc.) must also be promoted. Due to patriarchal social systems and previous gender-biased development models, inequalities between men and women remain grave in many societies. Facilitated by the historic Convention on the Rights of the Child, critical education and action have been undertaken to defend children against exploitation, marginalization, and violence (economic, sexual, cultural, social, and domestic). As clarified below, indigenous peoples also continue to face enormous challenges, including poor implementation of the recently ratified International Declaration on the Rights of Indigenous Peoples. In recent years, countries such as Australia have tarnished their earlier positive record by embarking on regressive policies that constitute violation of the human rights of refugees and asylum seekers.[35]

While the concept of human rights is not necessarily explicitly found in faith doctrines, the spirit underlying human rights is reflected in the principle of dignity, values, and norms of good conduct and human relationships taught by faith prophets and founders.[36] As faith institutions join the human rights community to clarify the meaning of human rights embedded in all civilizations, it will assist us in overcoming resistances to a universal conception of human rights achieved through participatory and equitable consensus rather than a concept that is determined by only one group or civilization.[37] In an interesting proposal, Abdullahi Ahmed An-Na'im seeks to "explore the possibilities of cultural reinterpretation and reconstruction through internal cultural discourse and cross-cultural dialogue as a means to embracing the universal legitimacy of human rights."[38]

The relationship between human rights and faith are understandably controversial, in particular when it comes to upholding the principle of universality. Clearly, interfaith dialogue needs to clarify faith values, norms, and practices that prevent the full realization of human rights within faith communities.

Building Intercultural Respect, Reconciliation, and Solidarity

Another key theme in building a culture of peace lies in the conflicts between different cultures and identity groups. While such conflicts have occurred throughout history, they are increasingly becoming the major faultlines of conflict. Much debate occurred over Huntington's "clash of civilizations" thesis, in which he especially warns about an escalating conflict between the West and the Islamic world. As a number of critical analysts have argued, Huntington's framework fails to acknowledge the complexities of civilizations and the dynamic interrelationships between power structures that cut across faith and civilizational lines.

Rather than a "clash of civilizations," there is a "clash of extremisms" (or "fundamentalisms") that struggle to maintain/attain power.[39] Often, it is not cultural differences alone that result in conflict. It is vital to critically understand the political, economic, and cultural causes underpinning conflicts that engage ethnic and religious groups and communities, which include competition for resources, territories, and power.

A number of countries have instead opted for a "dialogue of civilizations"—which culminated in the UN Year of Dialogue among Civilizations (2001) and the UN High Level Group Report on the Alliance of Civilizations (2006). This is not to deny, however, that religious or faith identity can play a negative role, and therefore needs to be seriously addressed, such as when certain beliefs and interpretations of doctrines are used to "justify" violent or extremist means.[40]

In culturally diverse societies, there is a need to promote values, attitudes, and policies that enhance mutual respect, understanding, and nondiscrimination. In recent decades, the growth of ethnic and religious intolerance and prejudices have led to violent conflicts in different parts of the Asia-Pacific region. Since September 11 and the subsequent "war on terror," people of Arab and/or Muslim background have also suffered racist attacks and profiling, which need to be challenged and overcome.

Therefore, a vital strategy toward building a culture of peace is promoting active harmony between cultural groups within and between nations. A peaceful world is not feasible without the ability of all groups to live nonviolently in unity amidst diversity. In many multicultural societies, formal school curricula and institutional environments have integrated principles, values, and strategies of intercultural and multicultural education. What constitutes national "history" must be inclusive of all groups and subcultures. However, it is crucial to avoid superficial frameworks of multiculturalism that merely "celebrate" cultural differences without promoting critical understanding of the causes of intercultural disharmony (e.g., racism, discrimination, structural injustices, and historical oppression).[41] There is also a need to respond constructively to the growing globalization-led forces pushing for "cultural homogenization" worldwide, as reflected in foods, clothing, music, and communication. Alongside a healthy assertion of one's own cultural identity, critical multicultural education also encourages an informed openness to critically learn from other cultures.

Living in Harmony with the Earth

Except for a minority of voices, most people and, increasingly, governments acknowledge the very serious ecological crisis confronting humanity. Whether it is pollution, soil degradation, depletion of nonrenewable resources, exhaustion of fisheries, deforestation, or climate change, the impact of environmental destruction has extended to virtually every corner of the planet. From the perspective of a culture of peace, the environmental crisis represents the violence that humanity is inflicting on the planet. Clearly, a major cause of such environmental destruction stems from an unsustainable paradigm of striving for an "unlimited" economic growth, profit maximization, rapid depletion of resources, and a lifestyle norm of excessive consumerism. Each person, country, and society has a responsibility to lighten their ecological footprint by, among other remedies, rejecting overconsumerism and shifting toward renewable sources of energy. However, relatively much more effort is justifiably expected from the industrialized North societies that have left eco-footprints much larger than those left by the South.

The challenges of living in harmony with the earth are therefore substantive, demanding the willingness of all peoples, institutions, and nations to accept the ethics of intergenerational responsibility. But "sustainable development" needs to go beyond individual and state actions that include the decision to recycle, limit greenhouse gases emission, ensure efficient energy use, or save species from extinction. Education must encourage all consumers to opt for sustainable growth, which rejects over-materialist and overconsumerist lifestyles in favor of voluntary simplicity.[42] In addition, local and global "green justice" needs to be promoted, so that environmentalist agendas and North-South relationships simultaneously enable people to meet their basic needs and rights free from structural violence and environmental destruction. If "sustainable development" is conditioned to serve the unchanged goals of growth-centered globalization, the roots of the ecological crisis will remain unshaken.

Turning to interfaith dialogue, there has been an accelerated growth of awareness and commitment among many faith leaders, believers, and institutions on living in harmony with the earth. The wisdom of indigenous peoples clearly holds lessons for rethinking about modernist "progress."[43] Increasingly, religious institutions and leaders have spoken out for "green theology" and eco-spirituality, and inspired their communities to practice their faith inclusive of reverence for the earth.[44] Christian environmentalists such as Thomas Berry and Sean McDonagh emphasize that "stewardship" is a more authentic expression of Christ's message than "dominion," while Pope John Paul II enunciated the theme of "ecological conversion," or a conversion to ecological awareness and action.[45] The Holy Qur'an teaches its followers to care for all creatures, not just humanity. In Buddhism, all parts of the universe are interdependent, and hence loving-kindness and compassion need to be extended to all beings and the earth. In Thailand, Buddhist monks have led a movement to ordain trees in the remaining forests as a way to stop further logging. As Gary Gardner usefully summarizes, religions have the capacity and the "assets" to "inspire" "progress" in directions away from further ecological destruction and toward a more sustainable development. It can do so by instilling in people a sense of spiritual vision and meaning to protect the earth; harnessing the moral capital and authority of faith leaders; making use of the influence of a number of adherents; utilizing their substantial physical and financial resources; and exercising their capacity in generating social capital for advocacy.[46] Patricia Mische shares similar views and refers to more than a hundred ecological declarations that faith institutions and leaders have cosponsored (e.g., Earth Charter, Assisi Declaration, World Council of Churches' statement on the integrity of creation, Earth Covenant).[47]

By linking the theme of "living with justice and compassion" with the theme of "living in harmony with the earth," interfaith dialogue can become an integrating force. The values and principles of faiths should motivate people to consume moderately and live simpler lifestyles, which in turn will create conditions for a just world where there is sustainable progress and everyone can meet their basic needs in dignity.

Cultivating Inner Peace

The five previous themes of building a culture of peace have focused mainly on visible relationships and structures of human life and our interrelationships with nature and the planet. But there is a growing consensus that the inner dimensions and sources of peaceful values and practices should not be ignored. Especially in industrialized societies marked by an ever frenetic pace and commodification of life, serious symptoms of inner peacelessness are evident in the increasing levels of anxieties, addictions, depression, and alienation, for which chemicals are often prescribed as "cures." The opportunities and space for quiet contemplation and equilibrium are markedly reduced. There is an alarming increase in the rate of suicides, indicating that increased material affluence may not necessarily yield greater "happiness."

As the prophets, saints, and sages of diverse faiths and spirituality traditions have counselled, each human being has a need and responsibility to cultivate a deeper sense of inner peace. For thousands of years, there existed many methods of meditation and contemplation that helped people to develop inner equilibrium and tranquility. The growth of spirituality that accompanies this deepening of inner peace is seen as an intrinsic goal of life. There is also a basic assumption that core values and key principles of diverse cultures and faiths provide guidance and inspiration for developing a culture of inner peace. As reflected in the holy texts, doctrines, oral wisdom, and body of practices across many faiths, including indigenous spiritualities, it is through the constant cultivation and renewal of such roots of inner peace that individuals can grow spiritually. In the Buddhist and other spiritual traditions, for example, we are reminded to overcome attachments to such vices as greed, power, fame, and other addictions that cause conflicts and even violence. As Lao Tzu teaches us,

> There is no greater sin than desire,
> No greater curse than discontent,
> No greater misfortune than wanting something for oneself.
> Therefore he who knows that enough is enough will always have enough.
> Tao Te Ching—Lao Tzu—Chapter 46[48]

A similar message is given by the German Christian theologian, Dietrich Bonhoeffer, who noted that,

> earthly possessions dazzle our eyes and delude us into thinking that they can provide security and freedom from anxiety. Yet all the time they are the very source of all anxiety. If our hearts are set on them, our reward is an anxiety whose burden is intolerable.[49]

At the same time, peace education cautions us against cultivating inner peace in a self-centered way. Is it possible to be contented with a sense of inner peace while ignoring the multiple and pervasive realities of peacelessness and suffering in our societies and our world? Or, even more important, is it possible to be contented with a sense of inner peace while avoiding a self-critical assessment of our potential, or actual, complicity in causing outer conflict and violence? Therefore, it is vital for educators to link the cultivation of inner peace with a strong responsibility to the building of outer peace.

Furthermore, there are many voices arguing that, in cultivating inner peace, people from diverse traditions, faiths, and cultures become better prepared ethically, emotionally, and spiritually to work for outer or societal peace. For example, as mentioned earlier, Basic Christian or Ecclesial Community members are motivated to deeply embrace Christian values and principles so as to experience authentic inner transformation while engaging in critical social analysis that challenge them to work for more peaceful and just communities. David Tacey revisions a Christian spirituality of healing and reconnection,[50] while feminist eco-spirituality also emphasizes the link between spiritual meaning and personal/political praxis.[51]

Similarly, in engaged Buddhist visioning, while the central principles and purposes of prayer and meditation practices toward self-enlightenment remain vital, cultivation does not remain alienated from societal events, especially those promoting peacelessness.[52] A search for inner peace is guided by Buddhist principles of nonattachment to things and power, moderation in lifestyle, and compassion for all beings. In Islam, the greater "jihad" is to struggle for inner purification.[53] But at the same time, a Muslim is expected to strongly promote the principle of social justice and to care for the well-being of all other members of society and, by extension, the whole world.

Educational Principles and Strategies

In seeking to build a culture of peace, I have suggested a holistic paradigm of six possible and interrelated themes for intra- and interfaith dialogue. Necessarily complex, and requiring the resolution of the tension between faith traditions and the more secular discourses in peace-building, this multidimensional project will demand commitment, courage, and, above all, patience. It calls for a process of education, which then empowers and, hopefully, leads to transformation. Education, however, is not solely about "content." Equally important is the process, or pedagogical strategy. Drawing on the work of peace educators in diverse contexts, four principles for effective pedagogy may be articulated:

1. The first principle can be described as holism, whereby a holistic framework is used to clarify possible interrelationships between, and among, different problems of peacelessness, conflict, and violence, in terms of causes and resolutions. Holism integrates various levels and modes of education for peace and interfaith dialogue (e.g., formal, nonformal, children to adults, social, economic, and cultural groups) since they complement, sustain, and support each other.
2. The second principle is about educating for a culture of peace and interfaith dialogue, and emphasizes the crucial role of values in shaping learners' understanding of realities and their actions in the world. In this regard, peace education shares many common values with faith traditions, whether they are compassion, justice, equity, gender-fairness, caring for life, sharing, reconciliation, integrity, hope, and active nonviolence. Commitment to nonviolence needs to be active, not passive, so that we are motivated to transform a culture of violence. Hope is vital to avoid being overwhelmed by the enormity of conflicts rendering us powerless.
3. A third important pedagogical principle rests on the value and strategy of dialogue. It would be a contradiction if educating for peace and interfaith dialogue becomes an exercise in "banking," as teachers assume the role of authoritarian "experts" and learners become passive recipients of peace knowledge. A dialogical strategy, however, cultivates a more horizontal teacher-learner relationship that both educates and learns. The realities

and voices of learners yield essential inputs into the learning process, and the learners have opportunities for critical reflection leading to transformation.
4. A fourth vital principle in educating for interfaith dialogue toward a culture of peace is critical empowerment—or what Freire has called conscientization. While dialogical, participatory, and nonbanking pedagogies and methodologies are crucial, they are not sufficient. Peace education must move not just our minds but also our hearts and spirits into personal and social action for peace-building.

Concluding Reflection

The world in which we now live is a complex and fragmented place, full of tragedies, sorrows, pain, and destruction. Yet, it is also full of many human beings and communities engaged in joyful, courageous, patient, and hopeful struggles to build a more peaceful world. In considering the twin discourses of "the politics of empire" and "the culture of dialogue," this chapter has sought to show how critical dialogue within and among faiths can help build a culture of peace. Hopeful and inspiring signposts can be found in many societies and regions, as well as through regional and international networks and movements. However, it is also vital to be mindful of the challenges posed by tensions between faith-based traditions and secular discourses, which have also built up a body of knowledge in peace-building. Through dialogue undertaken in its authentic spirit, these tensions can be transcended. In turn, the common project facing humanity, of building and sustaining a holistically peaceful world for future generations, will, in my view, be even more successful.

Notes

1. Marcus Braybrooke (1998) *Faith and Interfaith in a Global Age* (Oxford: Braybrooke).
2. Johannes B. Banawiratma (2002) "Contextual Theology and the Dialogical Building Blocks of Democracy," in Alan Race and Ingrid Shafer (eds.) *Religions in Dialogue: From Theocracy to Democracy* (Aldershot: Ashgate), 51–62.
3. Parliament of the World's Religions (1993) *Declaration Toward a Global Ethic* (Chicago: Parliament of the World's Religions).

4. Religions for Peace (2006) *The Kyoto Declaration on Confronting Violence and Advancing Shared Security* (Religions for Peace, Eighth World Assembly, August).
5. John Paul Lederach (2004) *The Moral Imagination* (Oxford: Oxford University Press).
6. Marites G. Africa (2007) "Re-membering…re-newing…re-visioning Peace: Reflections on the Challenges to Peace-building in Ethiopia and Northern Uganda" (Reflections on the United Religions Initiative Moral Imagination Field Visits to Uganda and Ethiopia, July) (Quezon City: The Peacemakers Circle Foundation).
7. *Cebu Dialogue on Regional Interfaith Cooperation for Peace, Development and Human Dignity* March 14–16, 2006, Shangri-La Mactan Island Resort, Cebu, Declaration of the Cebu Dialogue on Regional Interfaith Cooperation for Peace, Development and Human Dignity, http://www.dfa.gov.ph/news/pr/pr2006/mar/pr192.pdf, (accessed July 4, 2007). The Third Asia-Pacific Regional Interfaith Dialogue, Waitangi, Bay of Islands, May 29–31, 2007. Waitangi Declaration Third Regional Interfaith Dialogue Action Plan, http://www.mfat.govt.nz/Foreign-Relations/1-Global-Issues/Security/0-Waitangi-Interfaith/0-Waitangi-Declaration.php. Phnom Penh Dialogue 2008. Interfaith Cooperation for Peace and Harmony, *April 3–6, 2008,* http://assembly.uca.org.au/resources/news/ppdialogue.
8. For details of the Centre and its activities visit its Web site, http://www.griffith.edu.au/centres/mfc/, (accessed March 22, 2008).
9. See European Centre for Conflict Prevention (1999) *People Building Peace* (Utrecht: ECCP with IFOR and Coexistence Initiative of State of the World Forum); and William Fisher and Tomas Ponniah (eds.) (2003) *Another World is Possible* (London: Zed Books).
10. See David R. Smock (ed.) (2002) *Interfaith Dialogue and Peacebuilding* (Washington, DC: US Institute of Peace); Patricia M. Mische and Melissa Merkling (eds.) (2001) *Toward a Global Civilization? The Contribution of Religions* (New York: Peter Lang); David W. Chappell (ed.) (1999) *Buddhist Peacework: Creating Cultures of Peace* (Boston: Wisdom Publications with Boston Research Center for the 21st Century); Harold Coward and Gordon S. Smith (2003) *Religion and Peacebuilding* (Albany: SUNY); Mohammad Abu-Nimer (2003) *Nonviolence and Peacebuilding in Islam: Theory and Practice* (Gainesville: University Press of Florida); Daniel L. Smith-Christopher (ed.) (1998) *Subverting Hatred: The Challenge of Nonviolence in Religious Traditions* (Maryknoll: Orbis Books).
11. Richard Falk (2001) "The Religious Foundations of Humane Global Governance," in Mische/Merkling (2001), 41–59.
12. Charles Kimball (2003) *When Religion Becomes Evil* (New York: Harper Collins).

13. Toh Swee-Hin (ed.) (2000) "Education for a Culture of Peace." Special Issue, *International Journal of Curriculum & Instruction* 2 (1).
14. Helen Caldicott (2002) *The New Nuclear Danger* (New York: New Press); Robert Hutchinson (2004) *Weapons of Mass Destruction* (London: Cassell).
15. John Darby and Robert MacGinty (eds.) (2003) *Contemporary Peacemaking: Conflict, Violence and Peace Processes* (New York: Palgrave MacMillan); David Carment and Albrecht Schnabel (eds.) (2003) *Conflict Prevention—Path to Peace or Grand Illusion* (Tokyo: United Nations University Press).
16. Ed Garcia (ed.) (1994) *Pilgrim Voices: Citizens as Peacemakers* (Quezon City: International Alert, GZO Peace Institute, and Ateneo Center for Social Policy and Public Affairs).
17. Linda Lantieri and Janet Patti (1996) *Waging Peace in our Schools* (Boston: Beacon).
18. Sebastiano D'Ambra (2006) "Silsilah Dialogue: A Movement for Muslims and Christians and People of other Faiths," in S. H. Toh and V. F. Cawagas (eds.) *Cultivating Wisdom, Harvesting Peace* (Brisbane: Multi-Faith Centre, Griffith University), 187–192.
19. People Building Peace (n.d.) "Dialogue Spices Peace: Baku Bae in Indonesia," www.peacebuildingpeace.org/thestories/article.php?typ=theme&id=153&pid=34 (accessed March 23, 2008).
20. Andrea Bartoli (2001) "Catholic Peacemaking: The Experience of the Community of Sant'Egidio" (Sant'Egidio Community and Columbia University) presented at a US Institute of Peace workshop, Washington, DC, February 5.
21. See Mohammad Abu-Nimer (2006) "Viewpoint: Interfaith Dialogue in Israel-Palestine" *Middle East Times* (February 1), www.metimes.com/storynew.php?sStoryID=20060201-052002-2710; also Interfaith Encounter Organization, www.interfaith-encounter.org; and Sulha Peace Project, www.appricom.com/sulha/index.asp.
22. Douglas Johnston and Cynthia Sampson (eds.) (1994) *Religion, the Missing Dimension of Statecraft* (Oxford: Oxford University Press). Also see the inspiring stories of sixteen faith peacemakers in conflict resolution in diverse regions in David Little (ed.) (2007) *Peacemakers in Action: Profiles of Religion in Conflict Resolution* (Cambridge: Cambridge University Press).
23. See John Dear (2004) *The Question of Jesus* (New York: Image Books); Thich Nhat Hanh (2005) *Calming the Fearful Mind: A Zen Response to Terrorism* (Berkeley: Parallax); Sulak Sivaraksa (2005) *Socially Engaged Buddhism* (Delhi: B. R. Publishing); David R. Loy (2003) *The Great Awakening: A Buddhist Social Theory* (Boston: Wisdom).
24. Azyumardi Azra (2006) *Indonesia, Islam, and Democracy: Dynamics in a Global Context* (Jakarta: Solstice Publishing).

25. Daniel L. Smith-Christopher (ed.) (1998) *Subverting Hatred: The Challenge of Nonviolence in Religious Traditions* (Maryknoll: Orbis Books).
26. Wayne Elwood (2001) *The No-nonsense Guide to Globalization* (Oxford: New Internationalist).
27. Sarah Anderson (ed.) (2000) *Views from the South* (Oakland, CA: Food First); David Korten (1999) *The Post Corporate World* (West Hartfort, CT: Kumarian). Simultaneously, North and South elites disproportionately benefit from regimes of trade, investment, debt, structural adjustment, and even aid, while such "progress" has also resulted in rising inequalities within rich societies and a plethora of social "consumerist" ills, aptly labelled as "affluenza." See Clive Hamilton and Richard Denniss (2005) *Affluenza: When too much is Never Enough* (Crows Nest, NSW: Allen and Unwin).
28. UN Secretary-General Kofi Annan (1999) "Message on the occasion of the launch of the International Year of the Culture of Peace, Paris, September 14, 1999."
29. World Commission on the Social Dimension of Globalization (2004) *A Fair Globalization—Creating Opportunities for All* (Geneva: ILO).
30. Jeremy Brecher, Tim Costello, and Brandon Smith (2002) *Globalization from Below* (Cambridge: South End); William F. Fisher and Tomas Ponniah (eds.) *Another World is Possible* (London: Zed Books).
31. Tom Mertes (ed.) (2004) *A Movement of Movements: Is Another World Really Possible?* (London: Verso); and Walden Bello (2004) *De-Globalization: Ideas for a New World Economy* (London: Zed).
32. Paulo Freire (1985) *The Politics of Education* (New York: MacMillan).
33. Konrad Raiser (2003) "Spirituality of Resistance." Paper presented at the World Council of Churches Internal Encounter of Churches, Agencies and other Partners on the World Bank and IMF, Geneva, September 12.
34. Ken Jones (2003) *The New Social Face of Buddhism* (Boston: Wisdom Publications); Sulak Sivaraksa (2005) *Socially Engaged Buddhism* (Delhi: B. R. Publishing).
35. Frank Brennan (2003) *Tampering with Asylum: A Universal Humanitarian Problem* (Sta. Lucia: University of Queensland Press).
36. Irene Bloom, J. Paul Martin, and Wayne L. Proudfoot (eds.) (1998) *Religious Diversity and Human Rights* (New York: Columbia University Press).
37. Abdullahi Ahmed An-Na'im (ed.) (1992) *Human Rights in Cross-cultural Perspectives: A Quest for Consensus* (Philadelphia: University of Pennsylvania Press).
38. Abdullahi Ahmed An-Na'im (1990) cited in Abdullahi Ahmed An-Na'im (ed.) (1992) *Human Rights in Cross-Cultural Perspectives* (Philadelphia: University of Pennsylvania Press), 3.

39. Tariq Ali (2002) *The Clash of Fundamentalisms* (London: Verso); Ken Booth and Tim Dunne (eds.) (2002) *Worlds in Collision: Terror and the Future of Global Order* (New York: Palgrave).
40. Mark Juergensmeyer (2003) *Terror in the Mind of God* (Berkeley: University of California Press).
41. George Sefa-Dei (1997) *Anti-racism Education and Practice* (Halifax: Fernwood), Chap. 2.
42. Mark A. Burch (2000) *Stepping Lightly* (Gabriola Island: New Society).
43. Peter Knudtson and David Suzuki (eds.) (1992) *Wisdom of the Elders* (Toronto: Stoddart).
44. Alliance of Religions and Conservations (n.d.). "Faith & Ecology," www.arcworld.org/faiths.asp?pageID=75 (accessed January 3, 2008); Roger S. Gottlieb (ed.) (1996) *This Sacred Earth* (New York: Routledge); Rosemary Radford Ruether (1992) *Gaia and God* (San Francisco: Harper).
45. Dennis Edwards (2006) *Ecology at the Heart of Faith* (Maryknoll: Orbis Books).
46. Gary T. Gardner (2006) *Inspiring Progress: Religions Contributions to Sustainable Development* (New York: W. W. Norton).
47. Patricia M. Mische and Melissa Merkling (eds.) (2001) *Toward a Global Civilization? The Contribution of Religions* (New York: Peter Lang).
48. *Lao Tsu—Tao Te Ching* (1991) (London: Wildwood House) Translated by Gia-Fu Feng and Jane English.
49. Dietrich Bonhoeffer (1995) *The Cost of Discipleship* (New York, NY: Touchstone), 178.
50. David Tacey (2003) *The Spirituality Revolution* (Sydney: Harper Collins).
51. Charlene Spretnak (1991) *States of Grace* (New York: Harper Collins).
52. Nhat Hanh Thich (1991) *Peace is Every Step* (New York: Bantam); Christopher S. Queen (ed.) (2000) *Engaged Buddhism in the West* (Boston: Wisdom).
53. Hamza Yusuf (2004) *Purification of the Heart* (Illinois: Starlatch Press).

Part II

Locating Civilizational Dialogue in International Relations

Chapter 5

Civilizationism and the Political Debate on Globalization

Raffaele Marchetti

The focus of the debate on globalization is the inadequacy of the current institutional framework and its normative bases for a full development of the political sphere at the global level. Traditional political canons anchored in the nation-state and its domestic jurisdiction are increasingly perceived as insufficient, or indeed, self-defeating, in a world where socioeconomical interaction is, to a significant degree, interdependent and multilayered. Acknowledging the limits of this political tension, alternative projects of global politics have been developed in recent decades. What they have in common is their attempt to go beyond the centrality of the sovereign state toward new forms of political participation that allow new subjects to "get into transnational politics" from which they have been excluded. These new would-be or quasi-global political actors are part of the broad category of non-state actors, which includes international nongovernmental organizations (INGOs), transnational corporations (TNCs), networks and campaigns of civil society organizations and faith-based groups, transnational social movements (TSMs), transnational criminal networks, transnational political parties, regional public institutions,[1] international private bodies, and individuals. Despite minor institutional experiments, most of these actors share the characteristics of effectively being excluded from international decision-making mechanisms, and yet being more and more active on the global stage.[2] International exclusion constitutes the critical target of most of the alternative projects of global politics that occupy the centre of the public debate on globalization.

Among the principal competing visions of global politics that are currently advanced in the public discourse about globalization, this chapter specifically investigates that of civilizationism as an alternative model of transnational political inclusion.[3]

The first part of the chapter develops an analysis of ideal models as cultural resources that grounds the different readings of human bonds. The second part applies the notion of ideal models to the new scenario of globalization. Section three identifies and briefly sketches four alternative interpretations of the notion of global politics, namely, Neoliberalism, Cosmopolitanism, Alter-globalism, and Dialogue among Civilizations. The forth part focuses on the model of civilizationism and draws the principal characteristics of this notion in comparative terms, with the competing models of global politics.

Ideal Models as Cultural Resources

Underpinning the debate on the global political deficit are a number of ideological readings of globalization that can be considered as archetypes or ideal models of global politics. These ideal models can be considered as "meta-tanks" or cultural resources from which political actors draw their ideas and principles in order to formulate their political reference.[4] In being normatively substantiated, they form part of the shared understandings that shape actors' identity and interests:[5]

> Ideal-types are heuristic devices, which order a field of enquiry and identify the primary areas of consensus as well as contention. They assist in clarifying the primary lines of argument and, thus, in establishing the fundamental points of disagreement. They provide an accessible way into the mêlée of voices—rooted in the globalization literature but by definition corresponding to no single work [or] author.[6]

To better illustrate the notion of an ideal model, a parallel can be drawn between ideal political models and ideologies.[7] While both constitute fairly pervasive, integrated, and long-standing sets of beliefs and values, ideologies have a more wide-ranging scope, in contrast to the politically limited scope of ideal models, as intended here. Ideologies can be conceptualized as interpretations of modernity in its entirety. More modestly, ideal models concentrate on normative politics, on its principled and institutional dimensions.

Political actors actively deploy ideal political models and ideologies to construct their contentious political references in what has been named the interactive "politics of signification" or "collective action framing." Three elements can be distinguished in this process of political referencing: ideal models (composed by the condenzation and coherentization of different elements of the frames), frames (cognitive social processes producing a determined reading of political reality), and political projects (specific programmes for changing or preserving the political reality as interpreted according to the frame).[8] What distinguishes ideal models from political projects is their detachment from any specific political actor or action (content-orientation rather than action-orientation).[9] In opposition to the hybrid characteristics of political projects, an ideal model remains "uncontaminated," more static, and clearly distinguishable from other ideal models. Nonetheless, "intellectuals in a vacuum" do not create ideal models in the abstract. They are actually influenced in turn by social reflection, thereby including frames and political projects. Equally, while being rooted in ideologies and ideal models, frames are neither determined nor isomorphic with any single ideal model, and they are in continuous reciprocal relation with the social construction of politics. In the final analysis, however, the single actor creates its own political project by selecting and accentuating elements belonging to distinct ideal models and frames.

The formulation of the concrete political projects advanced by political actors passes through a complex process in which longstanding ideologies and ideal political models, midterm political visions and circumstances, and contingent factors are combined and filtered through master frames and specific group frames, and rendered politically active. Accordingly, it must be noted that an actor can hold more than one model for different reasons. A political actor, for instance, is often a collective body (either an institution or a forum), and so it is intrinsically plural and changes with time. Seen from a highly normative point of view, the "pick and choose" underpinning the construction of a political project by social actors produces a result that remains difficult to foresee and sometimes inconsistent. Yet, once a project is defined and adopted by political actors, it has a great impact in shaping the global public discourse by motivating actors toward political mobilization.

The academic discourse on ideal models of global politics is still underdeveloped. Few attempts have been made to map ideological background visions of global politics, and they either lack a number of important components or remain too shallow to grasp the most significant characteristics of each specific model. Moreover, the task of mapping a global political vision is also deficient to the extent that it fails to interconnect with political actors, interests, and actions. The links among ideas, actors, and actions are still fuzzy at the global level, requiring further investigation. In order to succeed, this kind of research needs to be interdisciplinary, for it requires the combination of a number of fields that are seldom integrated, including international political theory, international relations (especially the debate on norms), transnational political sociology, globalization studies, and international political economy.

In this chapter we will primarily concentrate on the model of global politics of civilizationism rather than on actors and actions. A relationship will be identified between this specific model and a set of actors and actions. However, as mentioned earlier, any actor shapes its own political project by choosing different components from various models, and this choice varies over time, therefore the kind of association between models and actors later suggested can only be considered contingent.

Global Politics and Its Ideal Models

Patterns of globalization have accentuated the diminishing exclusivity of states as actors in international affairs.[10] Following an almost conventional definition, interpreting global transformations as a,

> process (or set of processes) which embodies a transformation in the spatial organization of social relations and transactions—assessed in terms of their extensity, intensity, velocity and impact—generating transcontinental or inter-regional flows and networks of activity.[11]

Globalization links distant communities and de-territorializes power relations, whilst simultaneously extending their reach beyond traditional domestic borders. While diminishing the exclusivity of states as international actors, this globalizing process has opened up spaces for new social actors.[12] Among non-state actors, three categories can be identified: (a) public-interest-oriented nongovernmental actors; (b) profit-oriented corporate actors; and, (c) public intergovernmental organizations. Nowadays, these non-state actors play a significant role in international affairs by providing expertise and information (e.g., technical help provided by NGOs in development programmes), and also because they influence political discourse, agenda setting, and lawmaking (e.g., lobbying activities of advocacy or TNCs networks), as well as due to the part they play in the implementation of decisions (e.g., service provider organizations in humanitarian actions).[13] Yet, non-state actors are for the most part still formally excluded from institutional power.

A typical phenomenon of any democratization process at the international level is precisely the sense of instability generated by the emergence of un-institutionalized actors and new legitimacy claims (previously unheard) in the public domain. These actors try to upgrade their missing political and institutional power in order to align it to their existing social and economic power. Those excluded actors claim inclusion into the political system by deploying different strategies, from mild lobbying to harsh protest. Within this context of new political agency, an unprecedented global public domain gets consolidated, in which old, state-centered visions of international affairs mix with new non-state-centered visions of global politics, producing a complex map of ideological positions. This has been possible through the partial replacement of the Westphalian international system, in which authority and legitimacy was circumscribed, to reciprocally exclude territorial jurisdictions interacting exclusively at the intergovernmental level.[14] The new global public domain remains a central place where underestimated dimensions and innovative applications of global legitimacy are developed and advanced in contrast to mainstream interpretations. This does not necessarily entail reformist or, indeed, revolutionary reading of legitimate global politics that influence concrete political action, but the mere chance of starting a dynamic of norms change in international politics makes this global public arena and its ideal content extremely important for current global politics.[15] It is at this global public discourse and its components that we need to look in order to understand the future, long-term transformation of global politics.

In this under-explored arena of discussion and contestation over the legitimate global social purposes, a number of distinct political positions can be identified. Few scholars have attempted such a classification. These attempts encompass broadly both antiglobalization and pro-globalization positions. Patrick Bond identifies five principal positions: global justice movements, third world nationalism, post-Washington consensus, Washington consensus, and resurgent rightwing.[16] However, David Held and Anthony McGrew acknowledge six positions: radicalism, statism/protectionism, global transformation, institutional reformer, liberal internationalism, and neoliberalism.[17] Mario Pianta and Federico Silva distinguish three projects: neoliberal globalization, globalization of rights and responsibilities, and globalization from below.[18] Chrisophe Aguiton discerns three groups: radical internationalist (beyond state and capitalism), nationalist (south), and neo-reformist (global governance).[19] While these categorizations provide a useful orientation in the debate, they are not fully satisfying for at least three reasons: (a) they provide only a limited range of alternatives (i.e., Held and McGrew; Pianta; Aguiton); (b) they fail to clearly distinguish between conventional (i.e., state-based) and the new nonconventional models (i.e., Bond; Held and McGrew; Aguiton); and more importantly (c) they fail to provide a valid method to interpret politically these categories in the context of globalization.

Such taxonomy offers a new interpretation of the visions of global politics that avoids the deficiencies of the previous categorizations. First, the current proposal offers a wider spectrum of models of global politics that includes civilizations. Second, it recognizes those models that in disputing the centrality of the state in international affairs fully recognize the role of new political actors such as nongovernmental actors and individuals. Accordingly, the taxonomy focuses only on nonconventional models, excluding models still anchored in the Westphalian paradigm, such as nationalism, liberal multilateralism, neo-imperialism, and anarchical realism. Third, and most important, such taxonomy combines two key parameters of global politics: formation of political power (bottom-up and top-down) and the attitude toward globalization (positive and negative). Studying how political power engages with the issue of institutionalization (formation of political power), on one hand, and with the impact of globalization on the politics-society-economics nexus (attitude toward globalization), on the other, suggests the contrasting political essence of the different models of global politics under examination. These are the two key variables used to categorize the models of global politics, as shown in table 5.1.

Accordingly, four key interpretations of the notion of world polity can be identified as delimiting the range of nonconventional ideal alternatives available to the global political debate: (a) the vision of world capitalism as associated to a global free market and private economic actors; (b) the project for the democratization of international institutions, as formulated in the cosmopolitan model with reference to individuals and supranational institutions; (c) the radical

Table 5.1 Principal variables in mapping models of global politics

		Formation of Political Power	
		Bottom-up	Top-down
Attitude toward Globalization	*Positive*	Cosmopolitanism	Neo-liberalism
	Negative	Alter-Globalism	Dialogue Among Civilizations

Table 5.2 Main characteristics of non-state-based models of global politics

	Neo-liberalism	Cosmopolitanism	Alter-Globalism	Dialogue among Civilizations
Formation of political power	Top-down by economic actors	Bottom-up by individuals	Bottom-up by civic groups	Top-down by cultural elites
Attitude toward globalization	Supportive	Reformist	Radical alternative	conservative
Human bond	Economic	Political	Social	Cultural-religious
Agency	Individual/collective (firms and consumers)	Individual (citizens)	Collective (grassroots groups)	Collective (civilizations and cultural elites)
Pluralism	Universalism homogeneity	Universalism homogeneity	Pluralism heterogeneity	Pluralism heterogeneity
Political principles	Freedom Competition globalism	Globalism universalism Participation Procedural fairness	Place-basedness Participation Autonomy Diversity Solidarity	Diversity Respect Goodwill Non-violence
Institutional project	Self-regulation	Federation of individuals	Groups networks	Macro-regionalism

vision upheld by most social movements in terms of alter-globalism associated to civil society groups; and, finally (d) the discourse on the dialogue among civilizations, which refers to macro-regional actors often defined in religious terms. More specific differences among the models are provided later and summarized in table 5.2, which comparatively draws the remaining key political features of each model.

Mapping Models of Global Politics

The attitude toward globalization expresses the perspective entailed by each model. The alter-globalism model is firmly against globalization for its detrimental effects on social life. Though it prescribes a different form of transnational organization, it clearly rejects the current form of globalization. Similarly, the dialogue among civilizations model is also against the current form of globalization due to its negative and homogenizing impact on cultures and civilizations. In opposition to this, cosmopolitanism has a more positive attitude toward globalization in that global transformations are seen as epochal changes that can generate new and fairer political arrangements. Finally, the neoliberal model is definitely the ideological paradigm underpinning the recent globalization of economic exchanges. Their attitudes toward globalization offer a clear reference in ordering the four suggested models. However, a complete categorization cannot be provided without taking into consideration a second crucial parameter.

The vision of political power formation offers the second key parameter for the present proposal. A formation of political power refers to the modes in which political power becomes institutionalized, as well as to the crucial modes of interpreting and doing politics. Two alternative interpretations of this process need to be taken into consideration. One is a bottom-up interpretation, according to which political power is diffused and disaggregated at the bottom of society. From these numerous and fluid centers of potential power, nonpolitical resources can be canalized into institutions in order to produce a political impact. This is the case for alter-globalism, with its reference to grassroots groups or to cosmopolitanism with its ultimate reference to individuals. Second, a top-down interpretation, according to which political power is intense and concentrated at the top of society. From these few centers of actual power, nonpolitical resources can be canalized into institutions in order to produce a political impact. In agreement with such vision are both dialogue among civilizations, with its recognition of few cultural actors representing the whole civilizations, and neoliberalism, with its acknowledgement of the primacy of the powerful global economic actors, especially transnational corporations.

A further consideration concerning human bonds needs to be taken into account before delineating the details of each ideal model. According to social theory, human actions can be interpreted with reference to four general bonds among individuals: social, political, economic, and cultural-religious.[20] While we assume that each frame of action includes elements belonging to several bonds, it is possible to identify the prioritized bond in each of them. Any action that is part of a larger frame can be interpreted as making a primary reference to a specific bond, while at the same time it is making a secondary reference to other bonds.

The four models described above offer a reading of global politics that at times valorize one or the other of the four traditional human bonds. In this way, these models of global politics cover the entire spectrum of human interaction. Having clarified the principal parameters that allow for a demarcation of the four models, we now move to the specific characteristics of each model.

The Competing Models

Before outlining civilizationism, it is worth briefly introducing the other three models.[21] While they cannot be fully analyzed, their significance lies in their capacity to expose civilizationism—for it is argued that such a model emerged in contraposition to the other three.

As mentioned earlier, these four models together developed as alternative accounts of world politics that challenged the traditional state-centered readings. Though independent from each other, their social construction underwent an intense public and intellectual debate in which the comparative and dialogical dimension was the key. This is why it is important to have a sketch of the other three models. In fact, only by having a comprehensive perspective can the specific characteristics of the model of civilizationism be fully understood.

The ideal model of neoliberalism is centered on the primacy of the economic bond. While acknowledging the relevance of other traditional human bonds, neoliberalism recognizes the predominance of the economic aspects of human existence. The model makes primary reference to private economic actors (entrepreneurs, firms, business networks, and consumers) as key agents in the political system. Accordingly, political power is interpreted as being managed in a decentralized way by consumers and, especially, entrepreneurs grouped in transnational elite networks. Powerful firms are seen as key players in a universal political system that is intended as homogeneous and minimal—as a sort of global invisible hand. Public institutions are seen as universal tools allowing for a fair political life, beyond the limitations of a state-based system. Within the political and economic context of globalization, neoliberalism offers the clearest project in support of a libertarian globalization.

The ideal model of cosmopolitanism is centered on the primacy of the political bond. While acknowledging the relevance of the other traditional bonds between human beings, cosmopolitanism recognizes predominance of the political and civic aspect of human life. The model makes primary reference to individuals as key actors in the political system. Accordingly, political power is interpreted as originated by citizens and managed in a global, multilayered way. Public institutions are foreseen as universal tools to allow for a fair political life—beyond the limitations of a state-based system. Within the political and economic context of globalization, characterized by a high degree of political exclusion, cosmopolitanism offers a reformist project based on social-democratic and liberal values, which aims to democratize the system of globalization without altering its fundamentals.

The ideal model of alter-globalism is centered on the primacy of the social bond. While acknowledging the relevance of the other traditional human bonds (i.e., political, economic, and cultural), alter-globalism recognizes predominance of the social aspect. The model makes reference to grassroots organizations (e.g., civil society organizations, social movements, transnational social networks) as key actors in the political system. Accordingly, political power is interpreted as being managed through a rich network of local groups that preserves pluralism and heterogeneity. Within the political and economic context of globalization, characterized by a high degree of political and economic exclusion, alter-globalism offers the clearest radical alternative to the current global transformations.

While a more detailed presentation and a full comparison cannot be developed, these brief remarks suffice to map the terrain in which the model of civilizationism can be implanted.

Dialogue among Civilizations

While the civilizational paradigm slowly emerged as a significant model of global politics only in the past few decades, it nonetheless constitutes a further robust component in the discussion about globalization. The civilizational model is centered on the primacy of the cultural and religious bond. While acknowledging the relevance of other traditional bonds, such as economic and political, the discourse on civilizations recognizes the cultural and religious aspect of human life as predominant. The model makes primary reference to civilizations and cultural elites as key actors in the political system. Accordingly, political power is interpreted as being managed in a decentralized way by intellectual and religious leaders. Religions and macro-regional bodies are seen as key players in a political system that preserves pluralism and heterogeneity. Within the political and economic context of globalization, characterized by a high degree of political and economic exclusion, the perspective of civilizations offers grounds for a conservative rejection of current global transformations.

The model of the clash/encounter of civilizations is centered on the notion of civilization being intended as the ultimate cultural reference, beyond any other local and national element. Civilization is thus the highest cultural grouping of people and the broadest level of cultural identity. While the notion of identity is reinterpreted as multilayered, civilizational identity is acknowledged as the ultimate, most encompassing layer. Civilizations are accordingly interpreted as double-natured. While externally civilizations present themselves as monolithic, internally they allow for moderate pluralism. Civilizations are relatively stable social references, though they may overlap, include sub-civilizations, and transform over time. In fact, civilizations have risen and fallen throughout history. What is interesting within the clash/encounter of civilizations approach is that with the recognition of the West's loss of centrality comes also the recognition of other non-Western civilizations' full status as antagonists/dialogical companions.

According to the thesis of the clash of civilizations, the key mode of the relationship between civilizations is conflict and competition. While states remain important actors in global politics, conflicts will spring up between civilizations through fault lines, that is, those states that are on the border or even divided between two civilizations (torn countries). Civilizations need not necessarily collide, but history has proved that this is the most likely outcome. Remaining anchored to history, the thesis of the clash of civilizations claims to be purely descriptive. Accordingly, the reasons for conflict will thus be more related to cultural aspects than to ideological or economical factors. Key factors contributing to conflict principally relate to the aspect of irreducible cultural differences. Civilizational divergences are basic and irreconcilable. Since they are less mutable, they are also less prone to compromise. Globalization also contributes to civilizational tension for a number of reasons. On one hand, globalization increases the awareness of the other; this allows for the rediscovery of one's own identity but also generates opportunities for conflict. On the other hand, economic modernization is blending long-term local identities and, as the differences in these identities fade, larger, civilizational, and world religion identities supply a functional substitute.[22]

While sharing the ultimate assumptions on the nature of civilizations with the clash of civilizations, the model of the encounter of civilizations is more inclined to conceive normatively the possibility of dialogue among different cultures, and also the possibility of political cooperation. Within this perspective, there are four key principles. First, *diversity* maintains that cultural frameworks are irreducible to be compatible with one another, and thus it rejects universalism in the name of a reaffirmed pluralism.[23] Second, *respect* entails equal treatment among different civilizations and refuses the normative hierarchies used by the nineteenth-century discourse on civilizations versus barbarians.[24] Third, *goodwill* is seen as the crucial component for starting up a dialogue that leads to reciprocal understanding (based on the hermeneutic method) and a coming together of different civilizations.[25] Finally, *non-violence* prescribes peaceful ways of interacting.[26]

According to the civilizational model, in both its conflict and dialogical variants, politics focuses on the high institutional level of exchange among elites. In contrast to the homogenizing tendency of current global transformations, this position fosters a multipolar world, in which mutual coexistence allows for the competition, or alternatively for the flourishing, of different cultural and political traditions. A major ideological foe of the model of civilizations is neoliberal globalization, as its equalizing tendency neglects cultural differences. Politically speaking, this means that multilateral projects aiming at developing regional cooperation within and among different civilizational areas have to be supported.[27] A possible reform of the UN Security Council with civilizational representation would offer a valid institutional framework for this model.[28]

Incipient attempts to recognize the centrality of the notion of civilization in international affairs occurred in the late nineteenth century, with the establishment of the Parliament of the World's Religions (1893), and in the first half of the twentieth century, with the creation of the World Congress of Faiths (1936). However, it was only in the 1970s and 1980s that a clear recognition of the civilizational factor as a key component of international relations emerged. It was doubtless the publication of Huntington's famous article on the "Clash of Civilizations" in 1993 that turned what had originally been a predominantly religious discussion into a full-fledged political debate.[29] The events of September 11 only boosted the attention given to Huntington's thesis and initiated a campaign of division along civilizational lines that is profoundly marking today's global politics.

In reaction to Huntington's thesis, a number of political statements and theoretical formulations in terms of dialogue among civilizations have been developed not only in academia but also in public discourse and in institutional discussion. In academia, Dallmayr and others offered a robust foundation for the dialogue of civilizations in hermeneutic terms.[30] In the public political domain, the backing of the idea of a dialogue of civilizations by the centennial meeting of the Parliament of the World's Religions (1993),[31] and the World Public Forum–Dialogue of Civilizations,[32] offered a concrete space for interaction. A number of key emergent global players supported the idea, including former Russian President Vladimir Putin (together with the Patriarch of Moscow and of All-Russia Alexius II),[33] Chinese President Hu Jintao,[34] and especially former Iranian President Khatami.[35] Beyond Iran, in the Islamic world, the idea of civilizations was also favorably received.[36] The European Commission, with its President Romano Prodi, established a High-Level Advisory Group for the Euro-Mediterranean Dialogue.[37] And above all, the UN's institutional backing—with the designation of 2001 as the year of the Dialogue of Civilization,[38] and with the initiative on the Alliance of Civilizations (2004) cosponsored by the Spanish Prime Minister Jose Luis Rodriguez Zapatero and his Turkish counterpart Erdoğan, which generated a United Nations High-Level Group on this topic[39]—was the key to the consolidation of this discourse.

Today, civilization is firmly established as a key concept for an interpretation of global politics beyond a limited state-based perspective. Its value resides in both its strong accent on the cultural and religious components of international affairs and its robust criticism of neoliberal globalization. On one hand, the model of civilizationism expresses at its best the relevance of the cultural and identity-based factors of international relations[40] in a consistent way with the most recent developments of the theory of social constructivism. On the other, the model of civilizationism voices a strong dissent from the prophets of neoliberal globalization intended as a universalistic and consumerist project of (a-)political transformation. In fact, the model has been adopted by many counter-hegemonic international actors, from Russia and Iran to China and the European Union, who aim to dispute the current unipolar trend in favor of a multipolar world order. While it may well, at times, be used to mask power positions, especially with reference to subunits in the alleged unitary civilizational spaces, this model provides a highly relevant critical stance in world politics that cannot be easily avoided.

Conclusion

In this chapter, the debate about the future of global politics in the age of globalization has been presented with a specific reference to the model of civilizationism. These models of global politics constitute the ideal background to the current political project advanced by non-state actors in the global arena. While translating to the global domain a number of characteristics of domestic politics, these models also present an innovative conceptualization of the political discourse. Going beyond traditional state politics, as anchored in parties and national representations, these models envisage a new system from which new actors and new social claims can emerge. Ideal models of global politics denounce the current exclusionary system of international affairs, stressing instead the need for its reconstruction on a different basis. What is claimed is a political voice—a recognition in global affairs from which they are excluded. From the religious perspective to participatory democracy, from transnational citizenship to global market, new understandings of the polity that challenge traditional intergovernmental politics emerge within the framework of globalization. The future of global politics will perhaps emerge from here. Traditional state-centered approaches to international relations will inevitably have to engage with these new forms of political agency in the age of globalization. The end result cannot be foreseen.

However, it is reasonable to expect the partial inclusion of a number of tenets of these alternative models in the overall international institutional framework. If we take into consideration their increasing social and economic power, the voice that this kind of actors claim in global politics cannot be denied indefinitely without exposing the system to a certain degree of instability. The most likely result—signs of which are already evident in some instances of global governance—will be a combination of traditional intergovernmental mechanisms with new forms of governance structures in which these non-state actors will have an increasing significance and political power.

Notes

1. Throughout this chapter, public institutions and intergovernmental organizations are taken to be primarily an expression for the institution itself rather than of the single member states.
2. Jan Aart Schote (2004) *Democratizing the Global Economy: The Role of Civil Society* (Warwick: Centre for the Study of Globalisation and Regionalisation), 22; Raffaele Marchetti (2005) "Interaction-Dependent Justice and the Problem of International Exclusion," *Constellations* 12 (4), 487–501.
3. For an overview of the different models of global politics, see Raffaele Marchetti (2008) *Global Democracy: For and Against. Ethical Theory, Institutional Design, and Social Struggles* (London and New York: Routledge); and (2009) "Mapping Models of Global Politics," *International Studies Review* forthcoming in 11 (1).
4. David A. Snow and Robert D. Benford (2000) "Clarifying the Relationship between Framing and Ideology," *Mobilization* 5 (1), 55–60.
5. Alexander Wendt (1995) "Constructing International Politics," *International Security* 20 (1), 71–81.
6. David Held and Anthony McGrew (eds.) (2000) *The Global Transformations Reader: An Introduction to the Globalization Debate* (Cambridge: Polity), 2.
7. Ernesto Laclau (1996) "The Death and Resurrection of the Theory of Ideology," *Journal of Political Ideologies* (1), 201–220; John Gerring (1997) "Ideology: A Definitional Analysis," *Political Research Quarterly* 50 (4), 957–994.
8. Ervin Goffman (1974) *Frame Analysis: An Essay on the Organisation of the Experience* (New York: Harper Colophon); Enrique Laraña, Hank Johnston, and Joseph Gusfield (eds.) (1994) *New Social Movements: From Ideology to Identity* (Philadelphia, PA: Temple University Press); Doug McAdam, John D McCarthy, and Mayer N. Zald (1996) "Comparative Perspectives on Social Movements: Political Opportunities, Mobilizing Structures, and Cultural Framings" (Cambridge: Cambridge University Press); Kim Fisher (1997) "Locating Frames in the Discursive Universe," *Sociological Research Online* 2 (3); Robert D. Benford and David A. Snow (2000) "Framing Processes and Social Movements: An Overview and Assessment,"

Annual Review of Sociology (26), 611–639; Massimiliano Andretta (2005) "Il framing del movimento contro la globalizzazione neoliberista," *Rassegna italiana di sociologia* XLVI (2), 249–274.
9. Pamela Oliver and Hank Johnston (2000) "What A Good Idea! Ideology and Frames in Social Movement Research," *Mobilization* 5 (1); Snow and Benford "Clarifying the Relationship."
10. Ernst Otto Czempiel and James N. Rosenau (1992) *Governance without Government: Order and Change in World Politics* (Cambridge: Cambridge University Press); David Held, Anthony McGrew, D. Goldblatt, and J. Perraton (1999) *Global Transformations: Politics, Economics and Culture* (Cambridge: Polity); David Held and Anthony McGrew (eds.) (2002) *Governing Globalization: Power, Authority and Global Governance* (Cambridge: Polity); UNDP (ed.). (1999) *Human Development Report 1999—Globalization* (Oxford: Oxford University Press).
11. Held et al., *Global Transformations*, 16.
12. Robert Keohane and Joseph Nye (1972) *Transnational Relations and World Politics* (Cambridge, MA: Harvard University Press); Richard A Higgott, Geoffrey R. D. Underhill, and Andreas Bieler (eds.) (2000) *Non-State Actors and Authority in the Global System* (New York: Routledge); Virginia Haufler (2001) *A Public Role for the Private Sector: Industry Self-Regulation in a Global Economy* (Washington, DC: Carnegie Endowment for International Peace); Richard Price (2003) "Transnational Civil Society and Advocacy," *World Politics* 55 (4), 579–607.
13. Bas Arts, Math Noortmann, and Bob Reinalda (eds.) (2001) *Non-State Actors in International Relations* (Aldershot: Ashgate).
14. John G. Ruggie (2004) "Reconstituting the Global Public Domain—Issues, Actors, and Practices," *European Journal of International Relations* 10 (4), 499–531.
15. Martha Finnemore and Kathryn Sikkink (1998) "International Norms Dynamics and Political Change." *International Organization* 52 (4), 887–917; Ian Clark (2007) *International Legitimacy and World Society* (Oxford: Oxford University Press).
16. Patrick Bond (2004) *Talk Left, Walk Right: South Africa's Frustrated Global Reforms* (Scottsville: University of KwaZulu-Natal Press), 20–21; and (2007) "Reformist Reforms, Non-Reformist Reforms and Global Justice: Activist, NGO and Intellectual Challenges in the World Social Forum," *Societies Without Borders* 3, 4–19.
17. David Held and Anthony McGrew (2002) *Globalization/Anti-Globalization* (Cambridge: Polity), 99.
18. Mario Pianta and Federico Silva (2003) *Globalisers from Below. A Survey on Global Civil Society Organisations* (Roma: Globi Research Report), 235–238.
19. Christophe Aguiton (2001) *Le monde nous appartient* (Paris: Plon).

20. Peter Wagner (2006) "Social Theory and Political Philosophy," in Gerard Delanty (ed.) *Social Theory and Political Philosophy* (London: Routledge), 25–36; Nathalie Karagiannis and Peter Wagner (eds.) (2007) *Varieties of World-Making: Beyond Globalization* (Liverpool: Liverpool University Press).
21. Marchetti, "Mapping Models."
22. Samuel P. Huntington (1996) *The Clash of Civilizations and the Remaking of World Order* (New York: Simon and Shuster).
23. Fred Dallmayr (1996) *Beyond Orientalism: Essays on Cross-Cultural Encounter* (New York: State University of New York Press). Fabio Petito (2007) "The Global Political Discourse of the Dialogue among Civilizations: Mohammad Khatami and Vaclav Havel," *Global Change, Peace & Security* 19 (2), 103–126.
24. Abbas Manoochehri (2003) "Enrique Dussel and Ali Shari'ati on Cultural Imperialism," *Intercultural Studies* (1), http://www.intercultural-studies.org/ICS1/Manoocheri.html (accessed July 30, 2008).
25. Fred Dallmayr (2001) "Dialogue of Civilizations: A Gadamerian Perspective," *Global Dialogue* 3, 67–75.
26. Majid Tehranian and David W. Chappell (eds.) (2002) *Dialogue of Civilizations: A New Peace Agenda for a New Millennium* (London: I. B. Tauris).
27. Joseph A. Camilleri (2004) "Rights and Pluralism in a Globalising World: The Role of Civilizational Dialogue," paper presented at the Islamic-Western Dialogue on Governance Values: Rights and Religious Pluralism Workshop, Canberra; Joseph A. Camilleri, Kamal Malhotra, and Majid Tehranian (2000) *Reimagining the Future: Towards Democratic Governance* (Melbourne: La Trobe University); Franco Cassano and Danilo Zolo (eds.) (2007) *L'alternativa mediterranea* (Milano: Feltrinelli).
28. Simon Mundy (2006) "Thinking Beyond Nations: A New Approach to World Regions," paper presented at the World Public Forum—Dialogue Among Civilizations, Rhodes, Greece.
29. Samuel P. Huntington (1993) "Clash of Civilizations?," *Foreign Affairs* 72 (3), 22–49; (1996) *Samuel P. Huntington's The Clash of Civilizations? The Debate* (New York: Foreign Affairs/W. W. Norton); Huntington, *The Clash of Civilizations and the Remaking*.
30. Fred Dallmayr (2003) *Dialogue Among Civilizations: Some Exemplary Voices* (London: Palgrave).
31. Hans Küng and Karl-Josef Kuschel (eds.) (1995) *A Global Ethic: The Declaration of the Parliament of the World's Religions* (London: Continuum).
32. World Public Forum (2004) *Rhodes Declaration 2004* (Rhodes: World Public Forum—Dialogue of Civilizations).

33. Vladimir Putin (2005), Speech delivered at the High-Level Plenary Meeting of the 60th UN General Assembly, New York.
34. Hu Jintao (2006) Speech delivered at Yale University (New Haven, April 21); and, (2008) "Continuing Reform and Opening-up and Advancing Win-Win Cooperation," Speech delivered at the Opening Ceremony of The Boao Forum for Asia Annual Conference (Boao, Hainan, April 12).
35. Mohammad Khatami (1998) *Islam, Liberty, and Development* (Binghamton, NY: Binghamton University); (2000) *Islam, Dialogue, and Civil Society* (Canberra: The Center for Arabic and Islamic Studies, the Middle East and Central Asia-ANU); (2001) *Dialogue Among Civilizations [in Persian]* (Teheran: Tarh-e-No Publication); and, (2006) "Message to the Third Meeting of the High-Level Group for the Alliance of Civilizations" (Tehran).
36. ISESCO (2001) *White Book on Dialogue among Civilizations* (Rabat: Islamic Educational, Scientific and Cultural Organization-ISESCO); and, (2004) *Islamic Declaration on Cultural Diversity*, adopted by the 4th Islamic Conference of Culture Ministers (Algiers: Islamic Educational, Scientific and Cultural Organization-ISESCO).
37. European Commission (2004) *Dialogue between Peoples and Cultures in the Euro-Mediterranean Area*, Report by the High-Level Advisory Group established at the Initiative of the President of the European Commission (Brussels: European Commission).
38. Giandomenico Picco (ed.) (2001) *Crossing the Divide: Dialogue among Civilizations* (South Orange, NJ: Seton Hall University); United Nations (2001) *Global Agenda for Dialogue among Civilizations* (New York: UN General Assembly), (A/RES/56/6); United Nations (2001) "Report of the Secretary-General on the United Nations Year of Dialogue among Civilizations," New York: UN (A/56/523).
39. United Nations (2006) *Alliance of Civilizations: Report of the High-Level Group*, November 13; Manuel Manonelles (2007) "Building an Alliance of Civilizations" *Pace diritti umani* IV (1), 41–50.
40. Pavlos Hatzopoulos and Fabio Petito (eds.) (2003) *Religion in International Relations: The Return from Exile* (New York: Palgrave).

Chapter 6

Anti-Cosmopolitanism, the Cosmopolitan Harm Principle and Global Dialogue

Richard Shapcott

Introduction: Cosmopolitanism and Anti-Cosmopolitanism

Cosmopolitans, from the Stoics through to Kant, have argued in favor of a universal moral realm. Despite the division of humanity into separate historically constituted communities, it remains possible to identify oneself with, and have a moral concern for, humanity. To have such a concern requires that no one is *prima facie* excluded from the realm of moral duty. The most sophisticated formulation of this fundamental value occurs in Kant's "categorical imperative" requiring that we "treat others not merely as a means but always as an end in themselves."[1] The major tasks of cosmopolitan theory are to defend this universalism, to develop an account of an alternative political order based on it, and to explore what it might mean to follow Kant's imperative in a world divided into separate communities.

This chapter presents the case for a cosmopolitanism understood as stemming from an ethical predisposition of universal friendship, which means that obligations to fellow nationals are not exclusive of obligations to outsiders, and which can be reconciled with anti-cosmopolitan concerns for plurality and communal autonomy. The main premise is that cosmopolitanism is both consistent with, and sustaining of, moral pluralism and communal autonomy. The argument presented below is that such reconciliation can be achieved by incorporating a principle of dialogue into a cosmopolitan harm principle.

Until relatively recently, liberal cosmopolitan thinking has been dominated either by a certain form of Rawlsianism or by utilitarian theories of global justice, both of which focus on the distributive implications of justice as impartiality. Cosmopolitan liberal accounts of global distributive justice have provided a major cause of concern for "communitarians" and pluralists. This version of cosmopolitanism is associated with hostility to communal belonging stemming from the commonly made claim that national membership is "morally irrelevant."[2] For anti-cosmopolitan critics, cosmopolitanism is equated with the universalization of a particular, liberal, account of justice and is therefore problematic for a number of reasons. The anti-cosmopolitan tradition emphasizes the primacy of moral obligations to the nation-state, or some other, less than universal, human community. Anti-cosmopolitans come from a number of different perspectives and include Marxists, realists, postmoderns, liberals, and conservatives. What unites this otherwise diverse group is their skepticism toward substantive universalism and liberal global egalitarianism, rather than any particular ideology. From the Athenian generals of the Peloponnesian War to Georg Wilhelm Friedrich Hegel, and from twentieth-century realists to communitarians such as MacIntyre and Walzer, anti-cosmopolitans have sought to depict the moral realm as being fundamentally constrained. Some of these accounts have been based on notions of moral hierarchy (Aristotle), others by the "romance" of the nation-state and the idea of communal authenticity (Hegel), while still others have highlighted the circumstances of international anarchy and the ensuing tendencies of states to seek power and security rather than justice (Hans Morgenthau). Running through these various positions, and evident in the writings of today's authors, are several recurring themes and arguments that are used to defend significant, but not absolute, restrictions of human loyalties, and to give moral priority to less-than-universal communities.[3]

For the critics of cosmopolitanism, the presence of significant cultural diversity, and thus of significantly different accounts of the nature of justice, mean that in practice there is no consensus on the nature of justice that would permit a liberal solution. In addition to this practical limit, many anti-cosmopolitans argue that the liberal solution is morally undesirable because it amounts to the imposition of a culturally specific conception of justice upon others and contributes to the dissolution of a desirable plurality of forms of human life. Anti-cosmopolitans agree that "cosmopolitanism" is both unrealistic and inappropriate in a world characterized by radical moral pluralism.

At the core of this tradition is a set of claims that cosmopolitanism is both impossible (impractical) and undesirable. In particular, cosmopolitan universalism is depicted as requiring a universal state that is impossible and undesirable because of: (a) the international state of nature; (b) the existence of profound cultural and normative pluralism that entails the lack of a universal agreement about the "good" or the "right"; (c) the fact that any attempt to act in or realize universal values would be an unjustified imposition of one account of "the good society" upon others; and (d) the fact that a world state would be a source of violence and domination and tyranny. Any defense of cosmopolitan ethics therefore must address the issues arising from the attempt to enact a universal moral realm in a situation where universalism is either contested or simply lacking.

Contemporary anti-cosmopolitanism emerged in the context of the development of liberal, and especially (but not always) Rawlsian, accounts of cosmopolitan justice, beginning with the work of Charles Beitz and including those of Peter Singer, Brian Barry, Thomas Pogge, Charles Jones, Darrell Moellendorf, and Simon Caney.[4] Equally important, since Rawls, defining the nature of justice has been understood in terms of settling the basic institutions of society.[5] Therefore, it follows that the answer to questions of global distributive justice (GDJ) will almost necessarily require an account of a globally just society modelled on liberal, if not Rawlsian, principles. According to these authors there is nothing within the Rawlsian framework that suggests the need to restrict its account of justice to the domestic realm. The Rawlsian account is universalizable for two reasons: first, the account of the nature of the moral person is correct; and second, the extent of global economic interaction means that the world as a whole could be depicted as a system for mutual cooperation, that is, as a single global society. As a result, it is possible, they argue, to graft the Rawlsian account of justice onto the world as a whole (though differences arise as to how this might be done).

It is precisely this aspect that is most contested by anti-cosmopolitans, including Rawls himself, and not without good reason.[6] The Rawlsian theory of justice is based on an assumption about its compatibility with certain values, the reflective equilibrium of values common to liberal, and particularly American, society. As such, it is an account of justice for liberal societies. For the critics, any attempt to universalize liberal justice is bound to fail because the prerequisites of a shared political culture is absent from the international realm.

For these reasons, anti-cosmopolitans argue that national boundaries provide important ethical constraints. They are easily, but not always rightly, associated with the realist argument that moral duties stop "at the waters edge" and no "higher" duty exists than to one's own state or nation. In fact (at least) two different streams of anti-cosmopolitanism can be identified: realism and pluralism. Realism claims that the facts of international anarchy and sovereignty mean that the only viable ethics are those of self interest and survival. Pluralism argues that anarchy does not prevent states from agreeing to a minimal core of standards for coexistence. Both realism and pluralism begin from the "communitarian" premise that morality is "local" to particular cultures, times, and places.

This chapter argues that the liberal "do no harm" principle—or in Feinberg's phrase, "the harm principle"[7] indicates a significant potential for common ground between cosmopolitans and anti-cosmopolitans, and it can be used to correct the depiction of cosmopolitanism as hostile to "pluralism." Transboundary harms raise the issue of the nature of obligations to outsiders and present an arena in which cosmopolitan principles can be applied in the absence of a world state or a global cosmopolitan community. A cosmopolitan harm principle illustrates that the absence of a universal conception of justice should not prevent the recognition of an obligation on the part of states to limit transboundary harms.

Following from this observation, the chapter argues that the principle of communal autonomy and the preservation of plural conceptions of the good are both consistent with a Cosmopolitan Harm Principle (CHP), which recognizes that harm to well-being can occur in the realm of identity as well as in the realm of the physical. The final section of the chapter argues that the standard anti-cosmopolitan critique of liberal cosmopolitan accounts of GDJ does not apply to a CHP. It is argued that the question of "who is harming whom?" provides a better starting point for thinking about global poverty than the question of what is justice.

The Cosmopolitan Harm Principle

The risk accompanying the development of universal norms—of imposing a culturally specific conception of justice, or the good society, upon others—is a significant challenge for cosmopolitanism.

Nonetheless, it is possible to question and refute the accuracy of the anti-cosmopolitan depiction of cosmopolitanism. It is legitimate to ask whether cosmopolitanism necessarily requires, or rests upon, an ethical version of the domestic analogy[8] in which the international realm must be made to resemble the domestic realm of consensus and uniformity characteristic of a centralized state. It is possible to argue that the insights of the anti-cosmopolitan position have only limited purchase. In particular, the equating of cosmopolitanism with liberal schemes for global distributive justice diverts attention from more fundamental principles that may be more consistent with anti-cosmopolitan sensitivities.

The prospects for identifying and building common ground between cosmopolitans and their critics lie in defining cosmopolitan principles that predate a concern with global distributive justice. At its most simple, cosmopolitanism demands that "[i]f we really do believe that all human beings are created equal and endowed with certain inalienable rights, we are morally required to think about what that conception requires us to do with and for the rest of the world."[9] The liberal do no harm principle expresses the primary cosmopolitan commitment to equality and friendship for the world. If we wish to treat "outsiders" as equals, we must attempt to avoid harming them and recognize the possibility that in "the desire to do the best for our fellow citizens...we collude in imposing unacceptable costs on outsiders."[10] To impose harm upon someone is to treat them without moral respect and to exclude them from the realm of obligation. Therefore, the key to responding to the claims of anti-cosmopolitans is not to abandon the cosmopolitan project altogether, but rather to understand it in a more expansive context. Interpreted through a cosmopolitan lens, the principle "do no harm" can provide guidance for those who are convinced by cosmopolitan values and who wish to employ them in their treatment of "outsiders" and strangers in a way that is consistent with a world divided into nation-states.

The concept of harm is not without its ambiguities and confusions. Therefore, the first task in defending a harm principle is to construct a working definition and to clarify the concept as it is being used here. A cosmopolitan harm principle is primarily a negative duty of harm limitation and avoidance. As far as possible, our acts and practices should not knowingly or intentionally impose (or export) harms on outsiders.[11] According to Pogge, one definition of harm refers to avoidable negative changes in circumstances over time: "someone is harmed when she is rendered worse off than she was at some earlier time, or than she would have been had some earlier arrangements continued undisturbed."[12]

This definition sees harm in part as a relative measure (worse off in relation to prior circumstances), while at the same time providing a baseline (the undisturbed earlier arrangements) from which harms can be assessed. Beyond this, harm to someone must also be measured in relation to some substantive qualities. This is best understood as violations of core interests in physical and mental wellbeing. For Pogge, this is most conveniently expressed in terms of human rights.[13] According to Andrew Linklater, citing the Oxford English Dictionary definition: "harm is 'evil (physical or otherwise) as done to or suffered by some person or thing: hurt, injury, damage, mischief.' Its effects include 'grief, sorrow, pain, trouble, distress, affliction.'"[14]

Neither of these definitions provides any means for assessing which harms are worse than others or how responsibility can be determined. Nor do they provide an account of the difference between imposing a harm and causing a harm. For instance, do we harm a company by increasing taxation, which might reduce its profitability? For some companies this might mean no profit; for others it might mean only a reduced profit. Without further qualification, a mere reduction of profit may still conceivably qualify as harm. For this reason we need a more comprehensive definition that distinguishes between harms and costs and between imposition and causation.

In relation to the latter, David Miller draws a distinction between causative responsibility and moral responsibility; that is, between things we have caused for which we are responsible and things we have caused for which we are morally blameworthy.[15] The notion of imposition provides a means for determining the harms for which we are both causally and morally responsible. By the word impose, it is meant that harm is forcefully—without reasonable consent and with reasonable knowledge of the effects of the action—committed against another. Actions that cause harm to other communities and to individuals, but that are not knowingly imposed, also entail responsibility, but of a different kind. Unintended harmful actions can be penalized, but they cannot be proscribed as such, in the sense that accidents cannot be outlawed, but can be punished. Harms can be either intended or unintended, but they must be foreseeable or anticipated outcomes of actions in order to be proscribed.

According to Henry Shue, it is not wrong to inflict costs per se—we do it all the time—rather it is the costs of imposed harm that are morally serious. There are at least three criteria that can be employed to identify harm: "the first factor is that the damage done is physical... the second is that it is serious, possibly fatal, and the third that it is irreversible." To these three, Shue adds the further criteria of undetectability, unpredictability, avoidability, and high probability of fatality. These criteria are added to distinguish mere harms from prohibited harms. A harm is "prohibited because, chosen in ignorance maintained by others, it is inflicted by those others who obscure its nature and its likelihood as they introduce it."[16] Thus, what makes an act prohibited is not that it is in itself harmful, but that harm is knowingly or foreseeably inflicted or imposed rather than chosen.[17] The injustice of the harm is aggravated when it is imposed, rather than being freely chosen with full knowledge of the facts. Thus, a harm is worse than a cost incurred, and a harm that is imposed is worse than one that is freely accepted.

Shue's argument elucidates the double nature of the harm that is committed when "outsiders" are excluded from the realm of moral consideration, but it also indicates a means by which anti-cosmopolitan concerns can be overcome. Another consequence of the distinction between costs and harms is that the "essential contestability [of the concept] of harm" can then be circumvented,[18] because it becomes more possible to identify the harms that are likely to be considered important by everybody. According to Linklater, the universality of the harm principle extends from "two universal features of human existence: first, all human beings are susceptible to particular (though not identical) forms of mental and physical pain...; second, shared (though unequal) vulnerability to mental and bodily harm gives all human beings good reason to seek the protection of a harm principle."[19]

It also follows that the more serious or fundamental the nature of the harm, the more likely it is to be identified as such by people in diverse situations. Starvation is a clearly harmful condition that is close to being both objectively identifiable (the point at which life can no longer continue) and commanding of a near universal consensus as to its harmful status. Likewise, having one's identity, or community of belonging, removed or destroyed (harmed) is also something that might well command such a consensus. Genocide is perhaps one condition that states have agreed (in principle) overrides national sovereignty, thus recognizing it as a universal crime (or harm) against communities as well as individuals. The core of the Genocide Convention is not only the physical destruction of a community but the destruction of a group identity through a variety of means, including, but not restricted to, murder or mass killings.[20] Therefore, because all people experience these types of harm, it follows that there is a common interest, which is provisionally universal or universalizable, in protecting oneself and one's community from harm. It also follows that this is a reasonable thing to reciprocate.

Thus, even if one disagrees with the language of more substantive universalism, such as Rawlsian GDJ, it is still possible to employ the universal principle of harm avoidance in a way that can be reconciled with a great variety of ethical worldviews. Incorporating a "do no harm convention" into "our" relationship with outsiders does not necessarily require the existence of an already fully formed global community, instead, in the simplest form, it can apply "unilaterally" in a world of separate sovereign states. The core argument, which is consistent with anti-cosmopolitan and pluralist values, is that we ought not impose harms upon other communities (and individuals) without their consent, because imposing a potential harm upon another without this recognition constitutes another harm. Hence, in the discussion below, the focus is on recognizing and avoiding the transboundary harms that one community might knowingly export to, or impose on, others.

The harm principle can prospectively form the basis of a comprehensive cosmopolitanism that is consistent with respect for cultural difference, ethical pluralism, and communal autonomy while still addressing global poverty and inequality. Many cosmopolitans and pluralist "communitarians," or what Charles Beitz calls "social liberals," agree that membership in "thick" embedded communities is essential for human well-being, including moral development.[21] At the core of the pluralist position is a statist harm principle of nonintervention stating that political communities are not morally free to cause unjustifiable harm to outsiders. Therefore the concern to prevent harm to the communities that sustain individuals' well-being is consistent with limiting the harms that one community can export to another.

Harm and Dialogue

As Shue's analysis reveals, failing to engage in such dialogue or to seek consent can itself be considered harmful. Instead, the obligation to consult and achieve consent gives rise to a further positive duty to engage in dialogue concerning the harmful effects of transboundary activities. This can be considered the second component of a cosmopolitan harm principle.

A commitment on the part of states to "do no harm" invokes further obligations that go beyond a principle of mere tolerance or coexistence. A commitment to do no harm, because of the essentially contested nature of "harm," requires a commitment to dialogue and consultation in order to fully assess the scope and nature of harms between political communities and to accommodate different understandings of what it is to harm and be harmed. What constitutes harm differs according to time, context, culture, tradition, and worldview. There is not only disagreement about which harms are to be prohibited or condemned and which are to be condoned or at least accepted, but also fundamental differences about what actually constitutes a harm that may extend from different cultural starting points. This observation requires that any account of a harm needs to include the means for addressing divergent interpretations and for distinguishing between different levels of seriousness of harms.

Assessment of whether a particular act is harmful and whether it ought to be subject to sanction requires both consent and communication. In order to define any particular substantive concept of harm, a task of translation, dialogue, and engagement between the "harmer" and the "harmed" is necessary. Beyond deprivation of life and physical well-being, harms need to be assessed in a dialogical process whereby cross-cultural understandings can be achieved and consent to transborder practices can be sought. Dialogue is the principle means by which harms generated by misunderstandings and ignorance can be averted and by which differing conceptions of harm can be translated. Dialogue is also the principle means by which consent or agreement to actions can be achieved.[22] In many cases such consent is the only way of ascertaining whether a harm has occurred or is perceived.

While it is not without its own attendant controversies, the dialogic ethic is a primary means of avoiding the imposition of any single cultural standard upon others. The obligation to engage in dialogue is a cosmopolitan duty that does not immediately lead to the establishment of a unitary global state. At the same time, it is a moral advance toward an ethics of coexistence, because it involves a more complete recognition of the moral standing of outsiders.[23]

To date, anti-cosmopolitans have not paid sufficient attention to the necessity of intercultural dialogue in achieving their goal of cultural autonomy. Thinking about harm and dialogue in this way allows states and others to more completely recognize each other's claims to difference and autonomy while acting on cosmopolitan principles in their relationships with outsiders. The remainder of this chapter seeks to further consolidate this claim by examining the utility of a global harm principle in relation to GDJ.

Harm, Global Poverty, and Inequality

As noted above, discussions of world poverty and inequality have been dominated by the universalization of a particular, usually liberal, account of distributive justice. Arguably, the problem here extends from the assumption that liberalism of one version or another can be unproblematically universalized. The idea that liberalism represents a culturally neutral or impartial account of global distributive justice is rejected by anti-cosmopolitans, who conceive of liberal accounts of GDJ as harmful because they represent the universalization of a culturally specific conception of justice. However, an alternative way to address the issue of global poverty and inequality is to start by asking "who is harming who?" rather than "what is justice?"

The liberal or Rawlsian account of GDJ focuses theorizing on the ideal conditions of justice and pays scant attention to the causes of world poverty.[24] In particular, relatively little attention is directed toward the question of how particular state practices, and rules of the existing world order, harm some people more than others. Because they are not much concerned with the actual causes of poverty and inequality, it appears almost inevitable that liberal solutions appear impractical and idealistic. However, if global poverty and severe inequality are seen as the more immediate problem to which GDJ is an answer, then a cosmopolitan solution requires beginning with the causes of this harm. It begins with the question "who in the global economy is harming who and how?" and "what is a just response to that harm?" This focus transforms the traditional "inside out" approach of cosmopolitan liberalism where justice is exported to others with a focus on the harms or injustices that "we" might export or in which "we" are complicit. In this more problem-oriented approach, the solution to injustice begins with a negative duty to cease harming and, beyond that, to redress past harms that contribute to present inequalities.

The most convincing demonstration of this sort of cosmopolitanism has been provided by Pogge.[25] According to Pogge, the current international economic order and its governing principles constitute harm; that is, they are a cause of global hunger and poverty. As a result, there is a significant obligation upon those who have created this order to address the harms it perpetrates. Pogge argues that addressing the rules of the current international economic order (IEO), and reforming them in relatively minor ways, will go a long way to solving the problem of global poverty and starvation. Pogge's argument for a global obligation to those affected by the actions of others relies for its moral force on the recognition of a negative duty to cease harming rather than a positive duty to create global equality. In particular, and unlike Beitz and Moellendorf, Pogge demonstrates that the basis for an account of obligation lies not merely in the existence of economic relations between communities but in the characterization of those relations as unnecessarily harmful.

Therefore, given that an international economic order that causes harms exists *now*, there are good reasons to accept that certain universal rules ought to be devised to limit, redress, alleviate, or eradicate such harm and to prevent it in the future. This being the case, there is significant reason, as Pogge argues, for thinking that first-world states have a substantial duty to address those elements of global poverty stemming from historical and contemporary causes for which they are responsible. If Pogge is correct, then rich states should seek to reform their own practices and rewrite the rules of the international order to facilitate a substantial eradication of poverty and an increase in well-being for the worse-off members of the species (in this he is clearly Rawlsian). These rules would not require intervening in a foreign state's domestic affairs or overriding their system of justice.

However, the cosmopolitan harm principle is not necessarily a principle of thick global egalitarianism (in distributive terms); it is a recognition that treating others as ends in themselves requires not harming outsiders or making them suffer. At its simplest, it means that "our" economic well-being cannot come at the expense of the survival or suffering of outsiders. In other words, whatever the condition of our domestic social contract, we cannot consider it legitimate if it imposes unnecessary suffering or harm on those not party to it. Thus it is possible to develop a defense for limiting the harms done to other communities via international economic arrangements, which is consistent with a plurality of conceptions of justice and which would go a long way to meeting the challenge of serious global inequality.

In addition, the second part of the cosmopolitan harm principle incorporating a dialogic ethics requires that any solution to global poverty—including any rewriting of the rules of international order—must be agreeable to those affected by it. In that fashion, there is a responsibility on the part of the rich not only to cease the current harms but also to prevent future harms or problems that might arise in the redrafting of the rules of international economic life. Furthermore, they must not compound their harms by excluding the interests and arguments of the poor. Therefore, the solution must not be imposed without the consultation and agreement of the poorest people and their representatives. Nowhere in this solution is the prospect of imposing a particular account of the good upon others raised as an option. Instead, the opposite is true: the rich have an obligation to cease imposing an unjust institutional order on the poor.

It should also be noted that the dialogic component of harm avoidance helps to overcome the objections that not all harms trigger obligations, in particular, that some suffering is "self incurred" or purely a domestic responsibility (Miller), or that lines of causation are too diffuse or hard to determine. The cosmopolitan harm principle begins with the harms that states have imposed, that is, harms that have not been consented to by those who are harmed. Corresponding to the duty to not harm is a positive duty to consult outsiders about any issue that may have harmful effects upon them, in order to assess whether it does constitute a harm, whether it is acceptable or not, and where the responsibility lies. As Pogge's arguments about the role played by the global economic order in contributing to global poverty demonstrate, there are very few instances where responsibility is purely domestic, because all domestic policy is conducted within a global context as well. So, for instance, if a population in one country experiences hunger or severe poverty, it may be due to any number of factors, including domestic mismanagement (or worse), or it may be due largely to external factors attributable to a single or a diffuse range of sources. Under these circumstances there is a good case that, before responsibility for harm can be determined, all parties who may reasonably be thought to be contributing to the situation in some measure have a responsibility to consult each other to assess the lines of causation and the proportion of responsibility born by each. While this is a morally demanding implication of the harm principle, it is one that buttresses the rights of independent communities, even while limiting their absolute freedom of action.

On the other hand, a minimally just solution that solves the immediate problem of severe poverty might require only that states be responsible for the harms that they participate in or benefit from. This conception of the relationship between harm and global poverty may not be sufficient to address the problem of either global poverty or inequality. There is the possibility that harms that are "self incurred" can be identified as significant contributors to poverty and therefore provoke few international or global duties.[26] In this case, however, the humanitarian commitment to a base level of acceptable living standards comes into effect. This positive obligation applies regardless of causes and, therefore, if actually adhered to by states, would likely address this problem. States who can, but do not, adhere to this obligation should be considered to be morally compromised and to be committing a further harm by denying a basic good that would otherwise be available.

In conclusion, it is worth noting that it seems that the only way in which anti-cosmopolitans might object to such an argument is if they are willing to give moral priority to harm that might occur in the realm of identity or communal autonomy before the arguably more fundamental harms associated with poverty and starvation. In the case of the communitarian critique of global distributive justice, the preservation of communal identity appears to be valued at least as highly as material or distributive justice. The possibility of GDJ, it is implied, is more harmful than the status quo, which causes massive starvation and enduring poverty, because it risks harming those communities who do not share the values underpinning any given account. To make this defense requires an account of the moral priority of community over its individual members that most anti-cosmopolitans are unwilling to make, emphasizing as they do the necessity of communal belonging for individual well-being.[27]

Conclusion

This chapter has presented a case for an account of moral duties to humankind that can be reconciled with particularist duties to compatriots. It has demonstrated how a CHP provides a means for balancing competing claims to human loyalties. Such a principle refers to the *minimal* duties that communities and their citizens ought to owe each other and outsiders. It may also be possible to derive more demanding obligations, coming closer to the community envisioned by twentieth-century liberal cosmopolitans. However, the weight of argument here has been toward the "minimal" end of the spectrum. Although derived primarily from universalist arguments, the harm principle is compatible with a plurality of conceptions of the good. The basic cosmopolitan injunction to treat others as ends in themselves does not require the type of homogenous political community envisaged by the anti-cosmopolitans, and can be reconciled with a world formally divided into separate political communities. In this way, cosmopolitanism does not need to take the further step that liberal accounts of GDJ often do, developing a "thick" account of global justice extrapolated from contested culturally specific assumptions. The argument has been that all cosmopolitanism requires, as Linklater has noted,

> is friendship towards the rest of the human race, support for the Kantian notion of respect for persons or some equivalent notion of the equality of all human beings, and the conviction that there ought to be harm conventions.[28]

Cosmopolitanism means that no individual person or group of people is ruled out of moral consideration a priori or by virtue of their membership of different communities. Cosmopolitanism implies that obligations to friends and neighbors—our fellow countrymen—must be balanced with obligations to strangers and to humanity, and that at times humanity must be given first priority. It recognizes that humans are situated in both the community of their birth (or adoption) and the community of humankind, and that being so situated requires that neither realm is exclusive of the other nor exhausts our moral responsibilities.

The commitment to a principle of universal dialogue provides the means by which the abstract principle of harm avoidance can be negotiated in different cultural settings. This is not just a practical matter of translation but a moral/ethical component of treating others as ends in themselves. By conducting a dialogue regarding acceptable and unacceptable forms of harm, different communities recognize each other's needs and their cultural autonomy while agreeing to be ruled by shared values.

The ethical challenge that this chapter has addressed takes the form of the question: "how can everybody be treated as ends in themselves in a world that is not a 'kingdom of ends?'" In other words, how do those who wish to defend universalism act as cosmopolitans in a non-cosmopolitan world in which most people give moral priority to their local or national community and in so doing make themselves the enemy of humankind? The principle of harm avoidance provides at least a minimal account of what cosmopolitanism entails for those persuaded by the basic principle of human equality.

Notes

1. Andrew Linklater (1990) *Men and Citizens in the Theory of International Relations* (London: Macmillan), 100.
2. Martha Nussbaum (ed.) (1966) *For Love of Country: Debating the Limits of Patriotism* (Boston: Beacon Press), 133.
3. See, for e.g., Edward Hallett Carr (1939) *The Twenty Years Crisis, 1919–1939* (London: Macmillan); Hans Morgenthau (1960) *Politics Among Nations: The Struggle for Power and Peace* 3rd edn. (New York: Knopf); Michael Walzer (1994) *Thick and Thin: Moral Argument at Home and Abroad* (University of Notre Dame); Alasdair Macintyre (1999) "Is Patriotism a Virtue?," in M. Rosen and J. Wolff (eds.) *The Oxford Raeder in Political Thought* (Oxford: Oxford University Press); Robert Jackson (2000) *The Global Covenant* (Oxford: Oxford University Press).
4. Charles Beitz (1979) *Political Theory and International Relations* (Princeton University Press); Peter Singer (1972) "Famine, Affluence and Morality," *Philosophy ad Public Affairs* 1 (1), 229–243; Thomas Pogge (1989) *Realizing Rawls* (Ithaca, NY: Cornell University Press); Brian Barry (1989) *Theories of Justice: a Treatise on Social Justice* vol. 1 (Hemel Hempstead: Harvester-Wheatsheaf); Brian Barry (1999) "International Society from a Cosmopolitan Perspective," in D. Maple and T. Nardin (eds.) *International Society* (Princeton, NJ: Princeton University Press), 144–163; Brian Barry (1999) "Statism and Nationalism: a Cosmopolitan Critique," in I. Shapiro and L. Brilmaye (eds.) *Global Justice: NOMOS vol. XLI* (New York: New York University Press), 12–66; Charles Jones (1999) *Global Justice: Defending Cosmopolitanism* (Oxford: Oxford University Press); Darrel Moellendorf (2002) *Cosmopolitan Justice* (Boulder: Westview); Simon Caney (2005) *Justice Beyond Borders: A Global Political Theory* (Oxford: Oxford University Press).
5. John Rawls (1972) *A Theory of Justice* (Oxford: Oxford University Press).
6. John Rawls (1999) *The Law of Peoples* (Cambridge, MA: Harvard University Press).
7. J. Feinberg (1984) *Harm to Others: The Moral Limits of the Criminal Law* (Oxford: Oxford University Press).
8. See Hidemi Suganami (1989) *The Domestic Analogy and World Order Proposals* (Cambridge: Cambridge University Press).

9. Nussbaum *For Love of Country*, 13.
10. Andrew Linklater (2002) "Cosmopolitan Communities in International Relations," *International Relations*, 16 (1), 150.
11. However, not all forms of harm are unjustifiable, some crimes require punishment or harming and some harms are less harmful than others. The issue then is which harms are justifiable and which are not, and which are proscribed and which are not proscribed but punishable.
12. Pogge *World Poverty and Human Rights*, 4.
13. See for instance the discussion in *Ethics and International Affairs* (2005), 19 (1).
14. Andrew Linklater (2001) "Citizenship, Humanity and Cosmopolitan Harm," *International Political Science Review* 22 (3), 265.
15. David Miller (2004) "Holding Nations Responsible," *Ethics*, 114, 240–268.
16. Shue "Exporting Hazards," 121.
17. The costs and benefits of any given practice must be consented to under conditions of informed knowledge: "harms…may not be imposed without asking those who will suffer them. The potential victims of the harms might, once fully informed, accept them anyway as the least of the available evils." Shue "Exporting Hazards," 125. In the absence of that consent the prima facie argument is that we shouldn't harm them, until consent can be given, and not the other way around, that is, that we can harm them until they protest.
18. Andrew Linklater (2006) "The Harm Principle and Global Ethics," *Global Society*, 20 (3), 336.
19. Linklater "The Harm Principle," 20.
20. Donna Lee (2005) "The Dehumanisation of the Other: Genocide, Film and the Ethical," PhD thesis (Deakin University).
21. Charles Beitz (1999) "Social and Cosmopolitan Liberalism," *International Affairs*, 75 (3), 512–599. See for instance A. Buchanan (1989) "Assessing the Communitarian Critique of Liberalism," *Ethics*, 99 (4), 852–882.
22. The recognition that different cultures and people may interpret harm differently could be said to reinforce the opposition to cosmopolitan universalism. However, this would be so only if one accepts a radical incommensurability thesis regarding the impossibility of translation and interpretation. Such a reading would render the possibility of translating the concept of harm beyond our reach. It would make it impossible to identify any circumstances where our actions "harm" others, by their standards.
23. See Richard Shapcott (2001) *Justice, Community and Dialogue in International Relations* (Cambridge: Cambridge University Press).
24. This point has also recently by made by Thomas Nagel (2005) "The Problem of Global Justice," *Philosophy and Public Affairs*, 33 (2), 112–147.

25. Although working within a Rawlsian framework, Pogge's (2002) approach is substantively different from other Rawlsians precisely because he begins with the nature of the harms perpetrated by existing global institutional arrangements.
26. Globalization makes this harder to determine, which puts the emphasis back onto the global rules within which national decisions are made but which have not been consented to by particular states.
27. It is arguable that Walzer comes closest to this position in his defense of the "supreme emergency" doctrine that allows states to abandon the doctrine of noncombatant immunity. In this case the survival of one's own community overrides the harm to civilians in another. See Daniel Warner, "Searching for Responsibility/Community in International Relations," in D. Dampbell and M. Shapiro (eds.) (1999) *Moral Spaces: Rethinking Ethics and World Politics* (Minneapolis: University of Minnesota Press).
28. Andrew Linklater (2001) "Citizenship, Humanity and Cosmopolitan Harm Conventions," *International Political Science* 22 (3), 264.

CHAPTER 7

FINDING APPROPRIATE FORMS OF DIALOGUE FOR ENGAGING WITH THE POLITICS OF SECURITY

Phillip Darby

At the broadest level, there is unlikely to be much dissent from the aphorism often attributed to Winston Churchill, but that is said to go back to Bismarck: "To jaw jaw is always better than to war war."[1] (We could argue, of course, about how much either man actually lived by it.) Where the rub sets in is that dialogue has been hauled into the service of quite different objectives. It is therefore necessary to think along the lines of "horses for courses." That is to say, the form dialogue takes and the efficacy it might have, depend on the work we expect it to do. This chapter takes as its fundamental concern dialogue that might contribute to recasting the relationship between North and South. Yet, even this is too broad to tackle in a single essay, given the range of registers involved. I have therefore chosen to situate the chapter primarily in relation to a project about reimagining security from the everyday, which looks mainly at the experiences of South Asian people and Australia's indigenous communities.

Taking its cue from these remarks, the chapter begins by briefly sketching the assumptions upon which the project goes forward. These assumptions are put in broader relief by considering the perspectives on dialogue that emerge from the disciplinary literature and the practices of North-South relations as they have evolved since colonial times. We then turn to examine the nature of the dialogue envisaged as an integral part of the project, pointing to some of the difficulties and possibilities involved. A short conclusion reflects on the politics of different approaches to dialogue.

Reimagining Security from a Postcolonial Perspective

While still in its early days, our project goes forward under the aegis of the Institute of Postcolonial Studies in Melbourne.[2] Its approach is broadly postcolonial. By this I mean it looks back to the colonial experience to better understand the colonial mindset that remains with us today. It also attempts to recover non-European knowledges and practices that were suppressed or subordinated during the period of European rule, in the hope that they might offer alternative ways of proceeding with this subject. Three features of our approach have a bearing on the question of dialogue as addressed in this chapter. First, there is a hope to loosen the linkage between security and the state by giving prominence to practices of self-securing on the part of ordinary people. Yet, we accept that almost everywhere the state has deeply penetrated everyday life and that it has important tasks to perform. What is required is to break the hold of the traditional thought process that sees security as a "top-down" process and to encourage initiatives from the grassroots. Second, recognizing that security and insecurity are mutually constituted, we wish to foreground insecurity, arguing that it can create openings for recognition of the Other. Here we are interested in the potentialities of pain, suffering, and grief to help bring about greater understanding across difference and distance. Third, given the contemporary narrowing of the zone of the political and the parameters of acceptable dissent—think here of the globalization of neoliberalism, the impact of September 11 and the "war on terror," the increasing reliance on "experts"—there is a need to extend the archive of knowledge about security. Of particular significance for present purposes, we turn to the performative and creative arts as sources of alternative thinking. As Iain Chambers has observed: "To refuse to neatly cleave poetics from politics opens up a path into the question of economic and state power that provokes another way of inhabiting these conditions while questioning their grounds, language and logic."[3]

Thus understood, the paradox of security goes to the heart of the political as we now know it. Indeed, it can be argued that the paradigms of security derived from Westphalia 1648—or perhaps more accurately the myth of Westphalia—have a broader reach than even before. These paradigms have been extended globally, colonizing thought in the non-European world, often displacing or pushing to the sidelines other approaches that were rooted in local culture or drew on what Nandy has called recessive elements in Western culture, as was the case with Gandhi's nonviolence. And increasingly they have been insinuated within societies, threatening the democratic life anchored in the social sphere. Witness, for example, the rise of gated communities, private security industries, and an intolerance of difference.

Thanks to work in critical security studies, postcolonial studies, and the like, there are now constituencies in which it is recognized that all too often difference is seen as threatening and associated with danger. This awareness has been slow in coming. For many years, phrases such as "the comity of the civilized world" and "the expansion of international society" served to conceal how difference was dealt with. The others we cannot know—the "barbarian at the gate," the "stranger among us"—have long informed the popular imagination about security. Despite the enormous changes that have occurred in Western thinking over the past century, we appear to be stuck in a time warp when it comes to the Other and security. As we all know, in the wake of September 11 and in the succession of crises about refugees and asylum seekers, the mainstream Western response has been of the same ilk: hunt them down, keep them out, make those at home conform. Yet the real threat to security lies not in the existence of difference but in its denial and the attempt to make the Other just like the Self.

Dialogue has a crucial role to play as an alternative approach. Bringing other voices into the conversation and encouraging relatively open communication hold the prospects of arriving at an acceptance of alterity. The hope is that an interchange of this nature will break the hold of distorted representations of the Other and lead to a self-reflexive approach to the culture and politics of home. Clearly, on this reading, dialogue between the parties would need to be replicated within the respective selves—the "inner-personal," as it has been called. Seen in this light, dialogue merges with conflict resolution and processes of reconciliation and represents a way of changing the workings of international politics.

But, of course, very often in the past it was not seen in this light, and it is by no means clear how widely it is so seen today. The multiple understandings of dialogue in themselves represent a problem that needs to be confronted. What I am suggesting is that dialogue is too open to co-option and that all too easily it can be pulled into the service of upholding the existing world order. It is worth fleshing this out a little by taking a few fragments from the historical experiences of dialogue and then writing about it. They suggest that the track record so far, as far as the Third World is concerned, is hardly very encouraging.

Some Cautionary Remarks on Dialogue

We might begin by observing that, in the European tradition, security always involved dialogue. International relations could be regarded as a conversation between princes, in which security lay at the nub. This can be seen most clearly in the Concert of Europe, where ground rules were observed about channels of communication and diplomatic contrivances, such as alliances and buffer states. The costs of this system to those outside it were high, and this was most apparent in the second expansion of Europe from about 1870 through to the First World War. Stability in Europe was secured by horse trading in the tropics for colonial possessions and credits. (After France's defeat in the Franco-Prussian War in 1871, Germany encouraged France to find provinces in Africa for those lost in Europe. As Bismarck so graphically put it to the French Ambassador in 1879, "the Tunisian pear is ripe and...the time has come for you to pluck it!"[4]). A caveat should be added that at times non-European voices were also heard—maharajahs, emirs, sultans, and even tribal chiefs. This brought short-term benefits to some, but long-term costs to most non-European peoples, particularly bearing in mind that the mixture of direct and indirect rule contributed to the violence of decolonization and thereafter.

The position was not so different in the era of the Cold War—though this is not how we in the West like to tell the story. We like to think, along with John Gaddis, that the diplomacy of security, anchored in the strategy of containment, played a key role in making the post-Second World War period one of the more orderly and stable periods of modern times.[5] Perhaps this is so if one's gaze is restricted to the level of central balance. But the paradigms of security developed for what was seen as the crucial arena were extended outward to cover the world. And following the precedent of imperial times, stability in Europe was achieved at the expense of instability and violence in the colonial world, both former colonies and current ones.[6] More than this, we should take into account the Third World precursors to dialogue, or perhaps I should say earlier attempts at dialogue that went under different names. Nonalignment is the most important, because it was understood by many in the Third World as a system of communication that presented an alternative model of international relations grounded in cooperation rather than power—an approach particularly associated with Jayantanuja Bandyopadhyaya, an internationalist scholar based in Calcutta. Think also of agitational diplomacy, for instance, with respect to the New International Economic Order in the 1970s, initiatives with respect to mediation and peace areas, and the challenge to the body of international law by jurists such as Christopher G. Weeramantry. Overwhelmingly, such attempts at dialogue were dismissed by the First World as so much "puff and wind." Initially this was largely because of the influence of stratagems of geopolitics; later it was more the result of the conviction in the West that the Third World had little to contribute to the management of the international economic system—or at least that what was said was mostly politics, not economics at all.

One might ask about the knowledge gained of the Other and the personal connections made during the long encounter between Europe and the world outside. On the first point, Tzvetan Todorov in his remarkable book *The Conquest of America* offers a sobering commentary: "What Cortés wants from the first is not to capture but to comprehend."[7] We should not be surprised, Todorov observes, that in the encounter of the Indians with the Spaniards, "that the specialists in human communication should triumph in it."[8] So it is that Todorov, who begins his study with the claim that the discovery of America is "certainly the most astonishing encounter of our history," ends with "the astonishing fact that the other remains to be discovered." Had we the space, the story could be carried forward through "the native informant," the politics of early anthropology, and the development of area studies, till the present times.

Except in its earliest phase, modern colonialism took great care to minimize personal relations between ruler and ruled. A few, of course, were brave enough to break ranks, but mostly they were already situated at the margins of the culture of the colonies for reasons of some perceived difference, such as their sexuality.[9] The power relations, the herd instinct, and the geography of empire ensured that such broader crossings were rare. You will recall the final scene in E. M. Foster's *A Passage to India* when Fielding asks Aziz: "Why can't we be friends now?" The novel closes with the passage about the horses, the earth, the sky, and so on not wanting it—Foster mostly avoided the hard politics when he could; Rudyard Kipling is more telling in this regard. Today, in many, though by no means all, respects, the climate has changed. But not the facts of dominance.

In an era of globalization, the very currency of dialogue as a way out of our present impasse should make us wary. All too easily it can be pulled into the service of the existing world order. Knowledge about the global has its own colonizing practices that help shape the thinking of even those who oppose it. It has been said, for instance, that the World Social Forum, in the course of challenging economic globalization, has shown a strong tendency to globalize socioeconomic and political problems, which were formerly considered matters of local provenance.[10] In an essay published in 1998, Nandy observes that although the modern West may have well-honed tools for conversing with other civilizations, culturally, it has an exceedingly poor capacity to live with strangers. He goes on to assert that the West's "centrality in all intercultural dialogues of our times has been ensured by its dominance of the cultural language in which...dialogue takes place."[11] At the very least, therefore, we must attempt to put "speed bumps" in place, which might facilitate the emergence of non-European perspectives and experiences. Indeed, on occasions, there will be so little room for dialogue that it might need to be held in abeyance or be accompanied by defiance. Such might be the case in Australia with respect to the government's approach to the recognition of the claims of Aboriginal people over the past decade, or the contemporary Latin American response to the United States' economic agenda for the region. In other words, in such circumstances confrontation may be regarded as a necessary condition if there is to be any dialogue at all. Then there are the difficulties associated with positing dialogue, as between cultures, religions, and civilizations. The search for commonalities and connections between such constructs works to discount the heterogeneity of human experience. Huntington has much to answer for in the way he pursued the idea of dividing the world into discrete chunks. Not least that in his scheme Africa is given a doubtful status. And where might indigenous people fit in? Or for that matter the diasporas? Pitching dialogue at the global level may also work to entrench the privileged position of the state—as for instance in the cause of good governance.

Questions should also be raised about the role of institutions promoting dialogue. Without casting doubt on their good intentions, organizations have interests and insecurities of their own, which may impede the dialogical process or push it in a direction that may not be very productive. I am thinking, for instance of UN agencies, international nongovernmental organizations, and similar actors that often share a community of thought with the states and act in a similar top-down manner. Then there is the case of universities and disciplinary formations that are perhaps more likely to sponsor dialogue of the kind we are addressing in this chapter. Yet, clearly, there are potential difficulties that may impinge on their role as brokers and facilitators of dialogue when it comes to relating to the everyday events. As a consequence of economic shortfalls, universities have increasingly accommodated themselves to the neoliberal order.[12] In short, the influence of neoliberalism has been twofold. Instrumental knowledge is coming to be privileged over knowledge that is critical and reflective. Knowledge transfer, not knowledge exchange, appears to be the ruling paradigm. Both developments compound the problem, for long apparent but seldom addressed, of the screening out of noninstitutionally accredited knowledges, mostly in non-European societies. There is often an Otherness associated with such knowledges, embedded as they are in lived experience, which means that they are understood as custom, culture, belief, or superstition. In the view of Marcia Langton: "There is an epistemological and an ontological gap between the academy and the actual lives of indigenous people."[13]

Dialogue in the Context of Everyday Life: Two Workshops

The above thoughts direct attention to the practice of dialogue, to issues such as who participates and how the process is guided, which are raised in the introduction to this book and in Dallmayr's reflections in chapter 2 on the linkage between the institutional setting and change at the international level. We now turn to consider what dialogue might mean in the context of our rethinking on the security project. At the nub of the project we plan to have two mobile workshops. The first will be held in Darwin, northern Australia, and will be concerned with episodes in Aboriginal pasts about encounters with strangers. The second, to be held in Delhi, will be about how pain and suffering might be a means of relating to the Other. These workshops will be the fora for testing the hypotheses set out at the beginning of the chapter. For instance, we will be looking for feedback concerning the dilemmas of working with the everyday.

It would hardly be appropriate here to go into details about the mechanics of the workshops or how they might function.

Nonetheless, the workshops raise issues that reflect on arguments advanced earlier in the chapter that need to be drawn out. In addition, they direct our attention to some of the problems encountered in other attempts to develop alternative political perspectives. It is, therefore, instructive to address some of the potential difficulties that could impede or even derail the dialogical process.[14]

Given the backgrounds of the likely participants, there is reason to think that once the workshops are underway the main thrust of dialogue would occur across a restricted range of topics without any special pleading. However, that may not be so. In any case the issue of steering the deliberations needs to be addressed. Our aim would be to so structure the workshops as to encourage open discussion. But clearly there are limits if dialogue is to be productive. In this regard, it is worth considering the experience of the World Social Forum in Bombay in 2004—which in the view of Immanuel Wallerstein and some others showed that decision-making resided at the top.[15]

Account should also be taken of Arturo Escobar's argument that it is important to nourish self-organizing behavior because many environments suppress it. He therefore argues that "[s]elf organisation needs to be steered in specific ways."[16] On the other hand, steering is obviously a very delicate business and it can easily go askew. Here I have in mind the workshops put in place by Yale University psychologist Leonard W. Doob to develop cross-cultural communication, with the hope of reaching some creative consensus on how to begin to resolve conflicts between states. One such workshop held in the Tyrol in Italy was directed at border disputes in the Horn of Africa. The eighteen participants were drawn in equal number from Somalia, Ethiopia, and Kenya and were mostly academics, with a sprinkling of civil servants. Contrary to expectations, Doob and his colleagues found that nationality became more salient as the workshops proceeded.[17] Another of Doob's workshops addressed the bitter sectarian divide between Protestants and Catholics in Northern Ireland. Of the fifty-six participants, about a quarter came from middle-class backgrounds, with the remainder coming from the working class.[18] According to one account, based on interviews with participants, the peace-promoting techniques backfired and "Doob created more conflict than he resolved."[19]

Returning to our own workshops, a little more need to be said about their content to give purchase to the contentions that follow. Basically the Darwin workshop will be concerned with precolonial approaches to the Other. Our plan is to begin by examining the relationship that developed between Aboriginal, especially Yolngu, people in northeast Arnhem Land and Macassan seafarers who came from Sulawesi in what is now Indonesia to harvest trepang and to trade in tobacco, cloth, and metals. Despite a number of violent clashes, an intimate connection was established between the Yolngu and the Macassans, which is fondly remembered today. We wish to discuss how it survives in language, identity, song cycles, and performance traditions, and how it informs ideas about "membership and remembership," reconciliation, and proposals for management of the sea.[20] The workshop will then open out to consider other banks of knowledge in the South, mostly local in nature and drawing on traditional thought and practice that might enrich our approach to security and insecurity. Many such knowledges are mediated through ceremony or oral conventions and address what today we would call conflict resolution or accord-building.

Recovering and working with the knowledge of others raise questions of access (positionality) and ethics (whose knowledge and for what purposes?). Over thirty years ago, Doris Lessing observed the following of black society in Rhodesia (as it then was): "if you are a white writer, it is a story that you are told by others."[21] John von Sturmer, who has a rich knowledge of Aboriginal cultures and who is a collaborator in our project, spoke at the Institute of Postcolonial Studies in August 2006, and in an endeavor to negotiate a way through some of the problems to which I have drawn attention, he wrote a script for a performance involving members of the audience, instead of giving an address from the lectern. The script included these lines:

> The right to know. Where did that come from?
> Who said you should know?...
> Who said you could just bowl in and please yourself?[22]

Von Sturmer has also expressed concern about the practices of the academy, which lend support to my earlier argument that disciplinary ways of proceeding might hinder enquiry during the workshops. It is his view that often the language of academic analysis forestalls thought and works to produce closure. For our purposes, a particular problem is created by the translation of Otherness into the pre-given categories and frames of academic thought. One aspect is the false claims of "reason" for what is but the application of familiar, existing forms of reason, which foster intervention rather than warn against it. Von Sturmer continues:

> The "deadness" of academic talk is not merely an attribute; it is an "active" product. This equates security with deadness. There is little or no attempt to activate or to enliven. My own concern—or at least one of them—is the relationship between event and enlivening.[23]

The aim of the Delhi workshop will be to extend the body of thinking about pain and suffering and to bring it into the fold of reconceptualizing security. The first item on the agenda is how to recognize the suffering of the Other—which is not as obvious as it might appear. Victims may not wish or may not be able to speak or write of their experiences, as was the case for many years with the survivors of the violence that accompanied the partition of India in 1947. There are the problems of language, representation, and narration, so well brought out by Veena Das, Michael Taussig, Allen Feldman, and others. It has also been said that sometimes pain finds its outlet not in words but in art and music, as was the experience of the Jaffna Tamils in Sri Lanka.[24] Then there are overtly political acts such as hunger strikes or the sewing of lips, which may be read as a form of communication, a desperate attempt to trigger dialogue with the Other. These related difficulties must be confronted, and they may indeed prove very productive themselves in that they can challenge the privileging of the state, the rational, and the normal that is characteristic of so much disciplinary discourse.

From Theory to Practice: Social Suffering and Performativity

Once it is accepted that suffering is a social experience, we can begin to think about how it might serve to connect different peoples. There are several suggestive leads in the literature that need to be taken up. Judith Butler has reflected on how the experience of vulnerability and loss might contribute to an awareness of dependence upon anonymous others, and therefore provides a basis for imagining different forms of political community.[25] Despite her pessimism about the prospects, Das writes compellingly about the possibilities of a tolerable peace, given acknowledgement of "the vulnerability and fallibility to which we are all subject."[26] Both these lines of thinking could connect with Julia Kristeva's proposal to engage with what she has called "the foreignness within ourselves."[27] But how might we move from theory to practice? What steps could be taken to channel private cross-border understanding, through suffering and grief, into the public sphere? Might material from the first workshop on ceremonial exchange or other traditions of communities more vulnerable to the environment be relevant here? It is questions of this nature that will be the primary concern of the workshop. In many ways the work we will undertake in this sphere is also relevant to dialogue. Although concerned with speech more than emotions, the case for dialogue runs along parallel tracks.

"Social suffering," three pioneering scholars in the field declare, "results from what political, economic and institutional power does to people."[28] It is a recurrent theme in the literature that in attempting to alleviate suffering, these forms of power very often appropriate the suffering of victims, thus intensifying their problems. Das goes a step further: "the conceptual structures of our disciplines...leads to professional transformation of suffering which robs the victim of her voice and distances us from the immediacy of her experience."[29] These contentions mesh with the presuppositions of our project and will inform the Delhi workshop. It may be that new insights will emerge in the workshop that can be taken up in the final stage of the project.

There is one other aspect of the workshops that needs to be mentioned here, and that is their performative nature and the importance we attach to it. Dialogue at the workshops goes beyond what is said, to how it is said (different speech patterns), how it is received (which, in part, will not be expressed in words in public), to whom points are addressed, and how they are taken up. We are interested in gestures, looks, and other forms of body language that change the dynamics of exchange and the context of discussion.[30] As we all intuitively know, this broadened understanding of communication informs everyday life, yet seldom is it recorded in the written transcripts of academic proceedings. Extending our understanding of dialogue in this way will be of particular significance in developing our ideas about insecurity, for example, in relation to the ways in which insecurity of address is a means of securing the attention of others. It may also be of importance in bringing to the surface what is not said but privately accepted. One illustration that comes to mind in the field of development is the reluctance of aid organizations to publicly acknowledge that the provision of overseas aid is deeply political.[31]

Our interest in performance is not restricted to the workshops: it extends to many other parts of the project as well. It may be thought that the phrase "the performance of everyday life" is but a rhetorical flourish, but this would be quite mistaken. As I have intimated, performance is embedded in the protocols that regulate day-to-day exchange, the ceremonies and song and dance of traditional societies as well as modern ones, in the role of meeting places that help shape the conventions of social and political life (and hence it has a direct relevance to the design of public space). Rustom Bharucha has written of the performativity of suffering, which can be both a means of recovering subjectivity and also an expression of the difficulty of so doing.[32] He has also brought his knowledge of performance to bear on environmental matters, for instance, the part played by musical instruments and folk songs in relation to water resources and their management in rural Rajasthan.[33] Then there is the role of performance in the theatre, film, and other art forms, which is increasingly recognized as a key source of critique, as politics in traditional fora has come to be characterized by closure.[34] At times the politics of performativity are "in one's face." At others, one is uncertain of what is happening, which can lead to a rethinking about what was previously taken for granted—such as the security imaginary. As Johannes Birringer has put it, we are then so placed as "to be able to imagine different realities, under and above our normal ways of seeing."[35]

To round off, a few remarks about how dialogue at the workshops might stand in relation to dialogue between contending knowledge formations. Dialogue in the latter register is, of course, fundamental to the project. It will take the form of a dialogue between geopolitical understandings of security and security conceived in terms of conflicting identity practices, reaching back to socialization and trust, the role of the state, and so on. No less important, there will also be a dialogue between critical security studies and human security. Intersecting with these debates will be another debate seeking some accommodation between approaches to differences anchored in perception and communication and sharply contrasting approaches proceeding on the basis of the primacy of hard interests. One of the lessons I draw from the literature on conflict resolution is the importance of addressing the question of interests quite early so that dialogue can proceed on a fruitful basis.[36] One might therefore expect the nature of dialogue to change over the course of the project, broadening out and probably encountering more resistance in reaching accommodation at those points when different knowledge formations are brought into engagement with each other.

Taking Stock

In this chapter my argument has been that dialogue needs to be approached differently in different contexts; that an understanding along the lines of "one size fits all" has major shortcomings. Taking the case of security and examining it in relation to the North-South divide, I contend that the historical record has established that non-European attempts at dialogue with the First World have mostly been rejected out of hand or have worked to the advantage of the dominant. Moreover, in an era of globalization, when the First World determines the currency of exchange, there is little to suggest that the prospects have become more favorable. At the root of the problem is a deeply engrained resistance to the acceptance of alterity. Thus, if dialogue is to proceed in a productive manner, it may not only, at times, need to be accompanied by defiance, but also should go forward along substantially different lines from most of the contemporary rhetoric.

This thinking has led us to critically engage with the practice of dialogue. At least so far as security is concerned, there is much to support the contention that dialogue conducted between representatives of states is unlikely to produce significant changes because states share a community of interest and predominantly act in a top-down manner—as do international agencies and most nongovernmental organizations. Instead, we argue, dialogue should attempt to capture something of everyday life, focusing particularly on practices of self-securing and the experience of pain and suffering. One potentially fruitful source of insight is the experience of stateless societies in earlier times. Another is the role of performance. By enlarging the archive in this way, the hope is to break down the self-referential nature of Western knowledge systems and the disciplinary conventions that inhibit more open conversation. Thus refurbished, dialogue would be able to draw on an extended repertoire of procedures and techniques to enable people to better relate to each other.

Notes

I gratefully acknowledge many stimulating conversations with Paul Carter, Marcia Langton, Ashis Nandy, and John von Sturmer. I also extend my warm thanks to Edgar Ng and Greg Lavender for their help in getting this chapter together.

1. Churchill is said to have so remarked at a private luncheon at the White House on June 26, 1954, *New York Times* (June 27, 1954), 1.

2. The principal researchers are Paul Carter, Marcia Langton, Ashis Nandy, John von Sturmer, Edgar Ng, and myself.
3. Iain Chambers (2001) *Culture After Humanism: History, Culture, Subjectivity* (London: Routledge), 42.
4. Quoted in Nicholas Mansergh (1949) *The Coming of the First World War: A Study in the European Balance 1878–1914* (London: Longmans, Green and Coy), 44.
5. John Lewis Gaddis (1987) *The Long Peace: Inquiries Into the History of the Cold War* (New York and Oxford: Oxford University Press), 245.
6. On this see Ranabir Samadder (2000) "State in the Revision of Space and History Today," in Ranabir Samadder (ed.) *Space, Territory and the State: New Readings in International Politics* (Hyderabad: Orient Longman), 166–183.
7. Tzvetan Todorov (1984) *The Conquest of America: The Question of Other* (New York: Harper and Row, translated from the French by Richard Howard, first published 1982), 99.
8. Todorov, 97.
9. On this, see Leela Gandhi (2006) *Affective Communities: Anticolonial Thought, Fin-de-Siècle Radicalism and the Politics of Friendship* (Durham and London: Duke University Press).
10. R. R. Ariyaratne (2004) "Global Defiance of Globalisation? The World Social Forum at Mumbai, January 16–21, 2004," *Regional Centre for Strategic Studies Newsletter* (Colombo) 10 (2), 6.
11. Ashis Nandy (1998) "Defining a New Cosmopolitanism: Towards a Dialogue of Asian Civilisation," in Kuen-Hsing Chen (ed.) *Trajectories: Inter-Asia Cultural Studies* (London: Routledge), 142–149.
12. I have argued this more fully in Phillip Darby (2003) "Reconfiguring 'the International': Knowledge Machines, Boundaries and Exclusions," *Alternatives* 28, 141–166.
13. Marcia Langton in conversation with Phillip Darby (2006) "The Changing Complexions of Race," in Phillip Darby (ed.) (2006) *Postcolonizing the International: Working to Change the Way We Are* (Honolulu: University of Hawai'i Press), 228.
14. In addition to the research team, about twelve invited participants will be involved in each workshop, chosen on the basis of their knowledge of, or personal experience with, the issues to be discussed. As the aims of the workshops will be clearly set out in advance, it is reasonable to expect broad agreement about the privileging of the local and the everyday. The thoughts that follow in the body of the text may not reflect the view of my collaborators, as we have not yet addressed some of the issues relating to the practice of dialogue.
15. On this, see Heikki Patomäki and Teivo Teivainen (2004) "The World Social Forum: An Open Space or a Movement of Movements?," *Theory, Culture and Society* 21 (6), 145–154.

16. Arturo Escobar (2004) "Other Worlds Are (Already) Possible: Self-organisation, Complexity and Post-Capitalist Cultures," in Jai Sen, Anita Anad, Arturo Escobar, and Peter Waterman (eds.) *The World Social Forum: Challenging Empires* (New Delhi: Viveka Foundation), 354.
17. Leonard W. Doob (ed.) (1970) *Resolving Conflict in Africa: The Fermeda Workshop* (New Haven and London: Yale University Press), 105–107.
18. Leonard W. Doob and William J. Foltz (1973), "The Belfast Workshop: An Application of Group Techniques to a Destructive Conflict," *The Journal of Conflict Resolution* 17 (3), 489–512.
19. Michael Chinoy (1975) "How Not to Resolve a Conflict," *New Society* (September 4), 516.
20. Ian S. McIntosh (2000) *Aboriginal Reconciliation and the Dreaming: Warromiri Yolngu and the Quest for Equality* (Needham Heights, MA: Allyn and Bacon for Cultural Survival). See especially 82–89 and 104–105.
21. Preface to the 1973 edition of Doris Lessing, *This was the Old Chief's Country* (London: Michael Joseph).
22. John von Sturmer (2006) *"Gunbanjng, sorry to say these words…" An occasional performance piece for many voices* (Melbourne: Institute of Postcolonial Studies), August 19, 4. www.ipcs.org.au (accessed January 15, 2007).
23. Communication with the author (December 23, 2006).
24. E. Valentine Daniel (1996) *Charred Lullabies: Chapters in an Anthropograbhry of Violence* (Princeton University Press), 145.
25. Judith Butler (2003) *Precarious Life: the Powers of Mourning and Violence* (London and New York: Verso).
26. Veena Das (2002) "Violence and Translation," *Sarai Reader 02: The Cities of Everyday Life* (Delhi: Centre for the Study of Developing Societies), 209.
27. Julia Kristeva (1991) *Strangers to Ourselves*, trans. Leon S. Roudiez (New York: Columbia University Press).
28. Arthur Kleinman, Veena Das, and Margaret Lock (eds.) (1998) *Social Suffering* (Delhi: Oxford University Press), ix.
29. Veena Das (1995) *Critical Events: An Anthropological Perspective on Contemporary India* (Delhi: Oxford University Press), 175.
30. It would be revealing to have an account of the role of performance at the conference that gave birth to this book. It might well be that the performative elements involved in the cut and thrust of the informal exchange would tell a different story from that of the prepared papers. I was especially struck by the way the performance of a few of the participants, at times somewhat extravagant, changed the nature of the dialogue. Performativity was also significant in changing the relationship between invited speakers and others, which had been spatially structured with the speakers seated around

tables and others in rows behind—the inner and outer circles, as one participant put it.
31. On this, see Brian Smith (1990) *More than Altruism: The Politics of Private Foreign Aid* (Princeton University Press), 280–281.
32. Rustom Bharucha (2000) *The Politics of Cultural Practice: Thinking Through Theatre in the Age of Globalisation* (London: Athlone Press), 113–117.
33. Rustom Bharucha (2003) *Rajasthan: An Oral History—Converstaions with Komal Kathari* (Delhi: Penguin Books).
34. On this, in 2006 and 2007 the Institute of Postcolonial Studies ran a three-semester seminar series entitled "Performance and Politics," featuring performances by leading Australian artists and writers and commentaries by Rustom Bharucha and John von Sturmer. See newsletters 21, 22, and 23 of the Institute, www.ipcs.org.au.
35. Johannes Birringer (1991) *Theatre, Theory, Postmodernism* (Bloomington and Indianapolis: Indiana University Press), 100.
36. There is a cautionary tale to be told about the difficulties of dialogue between John W. Burton and his critics over Burton's techniques of controlled communication to resolve international conflicts. The method was developed at the Center for the Analysis of Conflict at University College, London, in the 1960s, and it passed lightly over the salience of interests. See John W. Burton (1969) *Conflict and Communication: The Use of Controlled Communication in International Relations* (London: Macmillan), and for instance, Ronald J. Yalem (1971) "Controlled Communication and Conflict Resolution," *Journal of Peace Research* 8 (3–4), 263–272.

Part III

Civilizational Dialogue between Empire and Resistance in the Post-September 11 Context

Chapter 8

Monologue of Empire versus Global Dialogue of Cultures: The Branding of "American Values"

Manfred B. Steger

In recent years, the number of publications focusing on "Empire" has been skyrocketing. Since the arrival of the "unipolar moment" following the fall of the "Evil Empire" in 1991, the term has been usually associated with the United States and its expanding sphere of influence. One notable exception, of course, is Michael Hardt's and Antonio Negri's much publicized perspective on Empire as a radically new paradigm of authority and control that cannot be reduced to American power—a "new global order" composed of a series of national and supranational organisms that supersede old, nation-state-centered forms of sovereignty.[1] But the enormity of the Al-Qaeda attacks and the ensuing belligerent response that the Bush administration was bent on waging, what former Central Command's General John Abizaid calls, the "long war on global terror," brought the public discourse on Empire back to the role of America in the world—sparking the process over whether the world's irate "hyper-power" had embarked on a "new imperialism."[2] Soon, the post-September 11 cacophony over American Empire merged with long-standing high-profile debates on "globalization" to form narratives that explored the meanings and normative implications of what I have referred to elsewhere as "imperial globalism."[3]

To take but two recent examples, Chalmers Johnson and Jan Nederveen Pieterse have argued that rapid growth of the American military-corporate complex has been a powerful impetus for the rise of imperial globalism after September 11. Similarly critical of the role of American Empire, these prominent social scientists nonetheless disagree on one fundamental point. Johnson thinks that September 11 spelled the beginning of the end of globalization by encouraging the Bush administration to shift from neoliberal "economic imperialism" to neoconservative "military imperialism." Conversely, Pieterse holds that globalization constitutes a dynamic of far greater significance and historical duration than American Empire. In his view, the current "imperial moment" represents the most recent yet passing phase in globalization's glacier-like evolution over centuries, if not over millennia.[4] Hence, we ought to consider whether globalization and empire are clashing dynamics or perfectly capable of integration in hybrid constellations that contain features of both market globalism and militaristic Empire.

Though conceding the *possibility* of Empire, overwhelming market globalism, my response leans toward Pieterse's perspective. Indeed, this chapter analyzes the ongoing American public diplomacy strategy of winning hearts and minds around the world—especially in the Middle East—as one concrete face of "imperial globalism" embedded in the evolving dynamics of globalization. I argue that post-September 11 American public diplomacy has been based on a unilateral and unidirectional model of communication to which I refer in this chapter as "monologue of Empire." This singular communicative process has been designed to win the hot war on terror by "branding" so-called "American values," such as liberty, opportunity, and democracy, as premium commodities for global consumption. Thus, this ideological discourse merges traditional war propaganda with cutting-edge marketing techniques developed by the corporate advertising industry in its drive to "go global." Ignoring even the most basic dialogical principles, American public diplomacy fails to engage in genuine cultural exchanges that take seriously the values of pluralism and human dignity. In my view, the monologue of Empire is a perfect example for the hybrid nature of American empire—a constellation Pieterse calls "neoliberal empire." As he notes,

> Neoliberal empire twins practices of empire with those of neoliberalism. The core of empire is the national security state and the military-industrial complex; neoliberalism is about business, financial operations, and marketing (including the marketing of neoliberalism itself).[5]

Unfolding *within* the discursive parameters of market globalism, the monologue of Empire does not spell a sudden death for neoliberal globalization, as Johnson suspects. But this strained marriage of convenience between the two dominant currents of globalism raises a number of troubling questions—not only with regard to public diplomacy's pragmatic prospects for "success," however defined, but also in relation to its failure to encourage sustainable cross-cultural dialogue on the basis of equality, sincerity, reciprocity, and mutual respect.

America's Sagging Global Image after September 11

Six years after Al-Qaeda's devastating attacks on the most recognized symbols of American power, it is easy to forget the worldwide outpouring of sympathy that followed at the heels of the strikes. Granted, some individuals may have revelled in the callous notion that the United States had finally received what it deserved, but most people around the globe appeared to be genuinely upset by the massive loss of life in New York City and Washington, DC. Even the most inveterate critics of American foreign policy paused in amazement as the headline of a major French newspaper proclaimed that "we are all Americans now," and thousands of Iranian youths staged touching solidarity vigils in downtown Tehran.[6] Unable to rally the Muslim world behind its violent vision, Al-Qaeda actually presented the United States with a unique opportunity of enhancing its global leadership by assembling a transnational coalition of equal partners committed to punishing those responsible for the atrocities of September 11.

Failing to take advantage of this auspicious moment, the Bush administration rushed instead into a global war on terror, thereby not only elevating the political status of a private network to that of a war-making entity, but also casting an exceedingly wide semantic net around the notion of "terrorists." Unwilling to involve itself in genuine multilateral efforts to combat global terrorism, the US government acted as though it had all the right answers, demanding from its allies nothing less than unquestioning loyalty. Claiming that his country's responsibility to history was to "rid the world of evil," President George W. Bush famously put the world on notice that whoever was not with the United States was against it.[7] Bush's persistent Manichean portrayal of his country as the force of good battling the barbaric hordes of evil—combined with his administration's obvious disdain for the United Nations—fuelled public perceptions around the world that America was an arrogant bully indifferent to the rest of world. Within months of the attacks, the prospect of a caring America leading a collective struggle for a better world had turned into a vengeful "hyper-power" unleashing its awesome military arsenal without much international consultation.

A series of global opinion polls tracked the rising tide of anti-Americanism, particularly in the Muslim world. For example, a 2002 Pew Charitable Trust Poll found that 69 percent of Egyptians, 75 percent of Jordanians, 59 percent of Lebanese, 69 percent of Pakistanis, and 55 percent of Turks had unfavorable views of the United States.[8] Surprised by the sharp increase of negative perceptions, the US government remained nonetheless wedded to its militant unilateralism, doggedly pursuing its imperial vision for a "new American century."[9] Wrapped in its flag and donning the rhetorical cloak of waging a "just war on terror," the United States escalated its military operations in the Middle East, whilst simultaneously seeking to convince skeptical audiences around the world that its real aim was to bring noble "American values" such as "freedom" "opportunity," "prosperity," and "democracy" to the oppressed people of the region.

This double-pronged strategy was rooted in the influential view that the global war on terror involved both military and ideological confrontations with radical Islamism. As many US foreign policy experts emphasized, winning the "battle for the hearts and minds" in the Muslim world was impossible without simultaneously launching a major public relations effort.[10] Touted as "twenty-first-century public diplomacy," the US State Department devised a massive campaign to enhance America's global image as a force for good in the world. Substituting neoliberal advertising for a genuine cross-cultural dialogue committed to addressing serious problems such as the global redistribution of wealth and technology, the Bush administration, supported by pundits of all kinds, formulated "imperial globalism."[11] However, in the months following the launch of the State Department's monologue of Empire, there were clear signs that anti-American sentiments around the world were intensifying rather than subsiding. Since then, ongoing efforts to showcase a new and improved "Brand USA" have sputtered along without achieving their stated goals. As the sun sets on the Bush era in 2008, no real progress has been made—a fact reiterated by Democratic Presidential nominee Barack Obama on his quest for the White House.

US Public Diplomacy before September 11

Coined in the mid-1960s by Dean Edmund Guillon at Tufts University, "public diplomacy" (PD) referred to government-sponsored programs and initiatives designed to inform and shape public opinion in other countries with the objective of promoting US national interests.[12] While complementing and supporting traditional diplomacy, PD did not engage other governments but sought to influence diverse nongovernmental segments of foreign societies. Moreover, as Peter van Ham notes, it focused on *values* as opposed to diplomacy's traditional concerns over *issues*.[13] Created specifically for media consumption and carried out by a variety of public and private agents, PD has been an amorphous enterprise operating primarily at the level of rhetoric. As former US ambassador Richard Holbrooke put it, "[c]all it public diplomacy, or public affairs, or psychological warfare, or—if you really want to be blunt—propaganda."[14] Indeed, as Carnes Lord notes, other terms that have been associated in the last fifty years with various aspects and dimensions of PD include "psychological operations," "public information," "strategic communication," "strategic influence," and "global communication."[15]

Given Americans' long-standing suspicions of government propaganda, US public diplomacy never enjoyed the high status it was afforded in other countries. Early efforts by Benjamin Franklin and Thomas Jefferson to cultivate a "decent respect for the opinions of mankind" represented a rather instrumental strategy by a young republic eager to establish itself as a full-fledged member of the international community. Indeed, it was not until US entry in the First World War that public diplomacy turned into a substantive enterprise. The Wilson administration created the Committee on Public Information, which, at its peak, employed some 150,000 people. The objective was not only to strengthen the "war will" among an ethnically diverse home population, but also to convince foreign publics that a reliable and invincible United States would defeat the German war machine and "make the world safe for democracy."[16]

After the Second World War, public diplomacy added a new dimension with US Senator J. William Fulbright's immensely successful scholarly and cultural exchange programs designed to "tell the American story" in academic settings. In 1953, the Eisenhower administration inaugurated the era of modern public diplomacy by creating the gigantic US Information Agency (USIA). Still wary of government-sponsored propaganda, Congress made sure to expressly prohibit the domestic distribution of its periodicals, newspapers, magazines, articles, broadcasts, and films.[17] Operating on a billion-dollar budget and employing some 12,000 people at its peak in the mid-1960s, USIA oversaw such well-known broadcast programs as Voice of America, Radio Free Europe/Radio Liberty, Radio Free Asia, and Worldnet TV, which reached millions in dozens of countries. Born out of the dynamics of the Cold War, USIA developed a surprisingly decentralized and semiautonomous organizational structure, led by public affairs officers with a keen eye for cultural and linguistic diversity existing in the vast world outside of the United States. The heads of the Agency's posts in each country were given some leeway to design their own programs and to decide how much or how little of Washington-produced media material they wanted to include in their initiatives.[18]

At the same time, however, US public diplomacy during the Cold War operated in a foreign policy climate characterized by America's acquired tendency to treat the whole world as a proper sphere for its political influence. Thus, imperial globalism was born out of Pearl Harbor and represented an ideology dedicated to the spread of "American values"—freedom, democracy, opportunity, rule of law, and so on—ostensibly for the benefit of humankind.[19] Indeed, at the core of imperial globalism one finds the unshakable conviction that the universality and superiority of American values justify and even necessitate the *global* projection of US power.

Imperial globalism, in turn, cannot be understood apart from a broader cultural matrix that developed around the religious idea of American exceptionalism. Siobhan McEvoy-Levy identifies two major strands of this doctrine. One calls for the wholesale remodeling of the world according to American ideals, the other promotes American superiority within the limits of the established international order.[20] But even the proponents of the second, more moderate variant of American exceptionalism regard liberty, democracy, individualism, diversity, and free markets as values that are fundamentally "American" in character. Their assumed universal applicability implies that anyone opposed to those values can only be "irrational," "ungrateful," or outright "evil." In fact, the vehement rejection of imperial globalism, for example, during the long years of the Vietnam War or the 1980 Iran hostage crisis, tended to generate in many Americans sentiments of anger and humiliation as they struggled to understand why anybody would want to reject their country's precious gifts to the world. Anger was usually followed by one of two extreme reactions: temporary retreat (fuelling, in turn, the flames of isolationism, nativism, and protectionism) or aggression, manifested in blunt attempts to impose American values and social arrangements on dissenting nations.

During the 1980s, US President Ronald Reagan's preference for the second approach resulted in the creation of an Office of Public Diplomacy dedicated to "managing" foreign media. Moreover, it was created also to encourage popular support at home and abroad for America's arms race with the Soviet Union and its aggressive military interventions in Central America.[21] Assuming the presidency after the collapse of the "Evil Empire" and President George H. W. Bush's successful prosecution of the 1991 Gulf War, President Bill Clinton developed his approach to public diplomacy in the shadow of Fukuyama's influential idea that American liberalism had defeated all of its ideological competitors, thus leaving the world no alternative to Anglo-American democracy and free markets. As van Ham notes, the main conclusion following from this ideological framework was that the newly liberated East European nations would spontaneously opt for the market-oriented "American model."[22] The staying power of this idea is obvious in similar assumptions made by the Pentagon planners of the 2003 invasion of Iraq. Neoliberal reliance on the "free market" as the "natural" agent for the global spread of American values meant that the state had to leave public diplomacy to a phalanx of corporate forces that made the case for a new world order based on "turbo-capitalism." Arguing that the "new economy" of the information society required radical economic deregulation and trade liberalization, market globalists in the Clinton era primarily opted for "soft power" to secure US hegemony: the use of cultural and ideological appeals to shape favorable outcomes without commanding allegiance.[23] As Julia Sweig notes, the Clinton administration embraced democratization and economic globalization as the organizing mission of US foreign policy. Indeed, it operated on the assumption that, "if the United States could extend its model to the globe, then conflict, the stuff of history, would finally be no more."[24]

The widespread worship of free-market fundamentalism during the 1990s spawned a fiercely deterministic doctrine centered on the ideological claim that globalization—understood as the liberalization of and global integration of markets *as well as* the worldwide spread of American values—was inevitable and irreversible.[25] This faith in economic providence translated not only in a significant drop in US military spending, but also in a decrease of government funds earmarked for public diplomacy. Between 1989 and 1999, USIA's annual budget shrank by $150 million, or 10 percent. The resources for its mission in Indonesia, the world's largest Muslim nation, were cut in half.[26] By the end of the decade, USIA had ceased to exist as an independent agency as it was decided to "integrate" it into the State Department as the Office of International Information Programs and the Bureau of Educational and Cultural Affairs under the jurisdiction of a new Undersecretary of State for Diplomacy and Public Affairs.[27] As William Kiehl notes, the once formidable public affairs agency was "reduced to a shadow on the periphery of foreign policy."[28]

US Public Diplomacy after September 11

September 11 marked the reversal of the Clintonian laissez-faire approach to public diplomacy, as it became clear that the magnitude of the terrorist challenge required the development of an effective war propaganda by the US government. Neoconservatives in the Pentagon vied with neoliberals in the State Department for control over US public diplomacy. The cohorts of Defense Secretary Donald Rumsfeld eventually self-destructed when their ill-conceived attempt to set up an Office for Strategic Influence (OSI) was derided in the national media as the creation of an "Office for Disinformation" designed to spread false "news stories" to the foreign press. Secretary of State Colin Powell emerged as the clear winner in this contest, but his sole control over the public diplomacy agenda ended abruptly in January 2003 when President Bush established the White House Office of Global Communications, an agency charged with "improving America's image abroad by better conveying U.S. policies."[29] In the aftermath of September 11, however, the main responsibility for dealing with the rising tide of anti-Americanism still rested with the State Department in the person of Charlotte Beers, the newly appointed Under Secretary of State for Public Diplomacy and Public Affairs.

Powell's choice of Beers reflected the emerging partnership between government, reinvigorated by the new security agenda, and a corporate sector struggling to maintain its globalist project of expanding markets and trade in a time of global insecurity. Prior to her appointment, Beers had served as chief executive of J. Walter Thompson and Ogilvy & Mather (two of the world's top

Monologue of Empire vs. Global Dialogue ≋ 155

ten advertising corporations), handling the multimillion advertising accounts of such powerful clients as IBM. Thus, she brought to her new government job a thorough understanding of cutting-edge commercial marketing and public relations techniques developed specifically to meet the new challenges of the global information society. Hence, it is hardly surprising that she approached the task of improving America's image in the world in terms of "branding," that is, an attempt to establish a positive relationship between the commercial "product"—American values—and its "users" or "buyers" abroad.[30]

Convinced that four decades in the advertising industry had been the perfect preparation for her new position, Beers saw herself as the salesperson-in-chief hawking America's "intangible assets—things like our belief system and our values"—to her "target audience" in the Muslim world. Thus, a hybrid monologue of Empire mixing imperialist and consumerist images and metaphors was born. As Pieterse reminds us,

> Neoliberal empire is a marriage of convenience with neoliberalism, indicated by inconsistent use of neoliberal policies, and an attempt to merge America whose business is business with the America whose business is war, at a time when business is not doing great.[31]

Indeed, for Beers, public diplomacy and commercial advertising abided by the same market logic:

> You'll find that in any great brand, the leverageable asset is the emotional underpinning of the brand—or what people believe, what they think, what they feel when they use it. I am much more comfortable with that dimension of the assignment, because I have dealt with it before.[32]

Agreeing wholeheartedly with Beers's Madison Avenue approach to public diplomacy, Secretary Powell countered public criticisms of appointing a politically inexperienced advertising executive to such an important post by saying: "There is nothing wrong with getting somebody who knows how to sell something." "After all," he added, "we are selling a product. We need someone who can rebrand foreign policy, rebrand diplomacy. And besides, Charlotte Beers got me to buy Uncle Ben's rice."[33]

As first order of business, Undersecretary Beers met with the Ad Council—an umbrella organization of the advertisement industry specializing in so-called "public service announcements"—to develop a series of television commercials that would capture the "essence" of "American freedom and democracy." The most striking of these advertisements shows a typical American suburban street with the caption "9-11 has changed the USA forever," followed by a depiction of the same street with flags flying from every house while a confident voice praises the patriotism exhibited by US citizens. Carried by national television networks, such messages violated the traditional prohibition against the domestic dissemination of government propaganda. As van Ham observes, Beers countered this charge by arguing that the advertisements were part of "a broader exercise to reposition and recharge the 'American brand.'"[34]

Upon launching her public relations campaign in early 2002, Undersecretary Beers identified three main strategic goals for a new and improved "Brand USA": (1) countering anti-American sentiments by effectively conveying genuine American values and beliefs to the rest of the world, especially in the Middle East, and by applying the most up-to-date communication techniques and methods; (2) demonstrating the global opportunities that result from democratization, good governance, and open markets; and, (3) supporting an appropriate education of the younger generation in crisis regions. At the same time, however, she consistently emphasized that her task was not to participate in policymaking, but to inform "many publics of the content of US policy—accurately, clearly and swiftly."[35] To those ends, the under secretary hastened to sign off on a number of new initiatives.

Perhaps her most substantive project was the creation of the Middle East radio network "Sawa" (Arabic for "together") and a twenty-four-hour Middle East television network. The latter was meant to compete with al-Jazeera and other regional Arabic broadcast networks. Specifically targeting listeners under thirty years, Radio Sawa's programming was music-driven, with periodic newscasts that presented the US government's view. In addition, Beers oversaw the creation of a brochure on September 11 titled "The Network of Terrorism." More than a million copies were distributed in the Muslim world. She also collaborated with California-based Globe TV to fund an exchange of Arab and US journalists, including Shereen el Wakeel, the anchorwoman of the popular Egyptian television show "Good Morning Egypt." Moreover, her office embarked on the systematic search for thousands of foreign professionals, students, and artists who previously participated in US government-sponsored exchange programs, hoping to convince them to serve as "mini-ambassadors" for the United States. Finally, she advocated English teaching to foreigners in their own schools as "an effective way of exposing them to American values and preparing them for productive lives in a modern world."[36]

When Beers resigned unexpectedly in March 2003—ostensibly for health reasons—commentators were united in their negative assessment of her campaign. After all, world opinion polls actually pointed to the intensification of anti-American sentiments. The war in Iraq and the difficult occupation of the country by coalition forces made matters only worse. Even in the United Kingdom, America's closest and most sympathetic partner, positive attitudes toward the United States dropped from 75 percent in July 2002 to 58 percent in March 2004.[37] Congress was so dismayed at the results of Beers' efforts that it appointed a special commission to recommend new and better public diplomacy strategies for the Muslim world. Indeed, none of the ensuing reports and studies over the past several years by a variety of official and independent bodies across the political spectrum disputed the poor condition of American public diplomacy. Criticisms of Beers' performance included lack of strategic directions; failure to take into consideration the fundamental cultural differences between Americans and Arabs; absence of scientific measures on the impact of her public relation efforts on her target audience; and her unwillingness to spend enough time in the Middle East. Indeed, a few days before her resignation, the frustrated Under Secretary conceded that "the gap between who we [Americans] are and how we wish to be seen and how we are in fact seen, is frighteningly wide."[38]

Tellingly, however, the main culprit of her failure—the arrogant monologue of Empire—was not identified as such in any of these reports. In fact, Beers' successors Margaret Tutwiler and Karen Hughes continued to run American public diplomacy in the same mode of imperial globalism. Let me offer four reasons for why I believe this to be both counterproductive and dangerous. First, the central metaphor of the imperial monologue—"American values"—is historically incorrect, culturally insensitive, and politically foolish. Given that broad ideals like freedom, democracy, opportunity, and diversity can be found in almost all cultures at various times, the exclusivist claim of any single country to these values runs the risk of generating intense sentiments of resentment and inferiority in non-Americans. For example, the widespread American conviction that "democracy" was "invented" in Greece 2,500 years ago and culminated in the American republic overlooks a number of important qualifications: (1) ancient Greece was culturally much closer to the Mediterranean societies of West Asia and North Africa than to those of Northern Europe; (2) Greek democracy was never "democratic" in the modern sense; (3) the evolution of democracy did not lead smoothly from point A (Greece) to point Z (United States), but is characterized by long interruptions, dramatic reversals, and vital contributions from many cultures; (4) existing forms of democracy are far too varied and complex to be reduced to one ideal type; (5) American democracy consistently fails to live up to its advertised standards. This last point has been most clearly demonstrated in the draconian policies of the Bush administration regarding citizens' surveillance, the status of "unlawful combatants," the abusive treatment of suspects at Abu Ghraib prison in Baghdad, and the existence of the US prison camp at Guantanamo Bay, to name but a few examples.

The constant representation of freedom and democracy as "American" values reveals the unabated strength of exceptionalist thinking in US politics—the cultural impulse behind the rise of imperial globalism and its mission to remake the entire world in its image. In fact, the semiotic prominence of American values in the Bush administration's communicative strategy reveals its cultural embeddedness in powerful diffusionist and orientalist models that portray modernization and globalization as civilizing processes originating in the West. Imagined as the permanent navel of the world, the West is inscribed with a superior cultural essence to be proliferated to the inferior, "backward" periphery. The West represented the active masculine principle, whereas the East appeared as a passive feminine vessel waiting to be filled with accidental knowledge. Historian James Blaut has referred to this hegemonic conceptual regime as "the colonizer's model of the world"—a worldview constructed by Europeans and their American descendents to explain, justify, and assist their colonial expansion. It is not grounded in facts of history and geography, but in imperialist and colonialist ideology.[39]

An instructive example of the contemporary pervasiveness of such pejorative and historically flawed strains of diffusionism pervading imperial globalism can be found in the writings of influential foreign policy experts such as Michael Mandelbaum, who boldly asserts that "the ideas that conquered the world" (peace, democracy, and free markets) were "invented" in Britain and France in the seventeenth and eighteenth centuries. Claiming that "it was natural for Britain and France to lead the world into the modern age," Mandelbaum never acknowledges that these countries owe much of their "meteoric rise" to the previous scientific and cultural contributions made by non-European civilizations.[40]

Cultural insensitivity and the failure to recognize the achievement of others are crystallized in the notion of "American values." It explains, at least in part, why the monologue of Empire of Beers and her successors has faced such opposition in the Muslim world. After all, it operates on a symbolic level that is easily recognizable by the inhabitants as yet another form of Euro-American imperialism. Hence, the cultural assumptions underlying American public diplomacy makes such efforts counterproductive because they are actually *more likely* to generate anti-Americanism. They are also dangerous because, by suggesting that Middle Eastern values need to be "Americanized," they make people in the region feel that they lack valuable cultural resources of their own, thus fanning long-standing sentiments of humiliation and resentment.

In addition, the State Department's attempt to "rebrand USA" treats values such as freedom and democracy as marketable commodities not unlike, say, a can of Pepsi or a Big Mac. Obviously, the intrinsic, noninstrumental value of liberty evaporates as soon as it is turned into a product to be bought and sold on the market. By commodifying people's deepest civic aspirations, the campaign waged by Beers and her successors unwittingly lends credence to Osama bin Laden's accusation that America is a soulless, materialist wasteland devoid of any genuine spirituality. In other words, the very means chosen to convey such a message devalue "Brand USA" in the eyes of many in the Muslim world.

Furthermore, as Naomi Klein has pointed out, another serious obstacle facing the rebranding of America concerns the very nature of the marketing process itself. Successful branding requires a carefully crafted message delivered with discipline and consistency. Anything that threatens the homogeneity of the message dilutes a corporation's overall strength. But freedom, democracy, and diversity are values that are inherently incompatible with "discipline" and "homogeneity." Hence, Klein makes a convincing point when she argues that powerful marketing techniques driving businesses could be fatal when applied to politics: "When companies try to implement global image consistency, they look like generic franchises. When governments do the same, they can look distinctly authoritarian."[41] In short, celebrating difference by employing sameness turns out to be a counterproductive endeavor that undercuts the very values it tries to "sell."

Finally, and perhaps most importantly, no marketing technique can compensate for a flawed product. This is not to say that freedom and democracy are not noble and worthwhile values—quite the opposite. However, by failing to incorporate these norms on a consistent basis, US foreign policy has generated much anger and frustration around the world. This is especially true in the Middle East, where the US employment of "double standards" has been painfully visible for decades. As is well known, the vast majority of the September 11 hijackers came from authoritarian Saudi Arabia. Saudi money has financed scores of radical Wahabbi organizations around the globe. Yet, Saudi Arabia has been treated by the Bush administration as a "staunch ally" in the global war on terror. Much of the same is true for Pakistan, a country still ruled by small military and political elites that stockpile weapons of mass destruction, including nuclear arms. The United States waged war in 1991 on the tyrannical regime of Saddam Hussein in the name of "liberating" an equally undemocratic regime in Kuwait. The list goes on, and also includes the rather biased American approach to the Israel-Palestine conflict. Easily discernable by people in the region, the instrumental mode by which the United States selects friends and foes and pursues its interests around the world often contradicts its professed ethical commitment to "American values." Shaping a foreign policy merely by devising policies based on strategic decisions made upstairs, Beers and her successors never bothered to address the central problem of "double standards."

Conclusion: From Monologue of Empire to Dialogue of Cultures?

Even in the age of globalization, the US government is entitled, indeed obligated, to articulate a detailed and substantive version of what values America subscribes to and what its proper role should be in the twenty-first century. But a monologue of Empire anchored in Madison Avenue marketing principles is unlikely to either improve America's image or weaken the ideological appeal of jihadist globalism around the world. In fact, even in the current flawed status of public diplomacy, such diplomacy has been given low priority in the State Department. In order to keep pace with the budgetary priorities currently in place in comparable countries, the US government would have to sign off on a tenfold increase, from the current $1.2 billion to at least $12 billion. This figure may sound exorbitantly high, but in comparative terms it amounts to only 3 percent of the total US military budget.[42]

So, what is to be done? In my view, for both pragmatic and ethical reasons, the new administration, of President Obama, needs to replace the current American public diplomacy model with a new paradigm based on three broad imperatives: (1) facilitate genuine intercultural dialogue in place of the current ideological monologue of Empire; (2) pursue legitimate American security interests within a multilateral public diplomacy framework that seeks to counter global threats such as terrorism by addressing its local roots; (3) eliminate as much as possible the existing "double standards" in US foreign policy. Senator Obama's repeated intentions to seek "dialogue" even with Iran stand in stark contrast to Senator McCains more belligerent pronouncements. Hence, an Obama administration appears to be more likely to carry out some or all of these imperatives.

The implementation of the first imperative relies on the US government's genuine willingness to take into account views and opinions expressed outside its borders. Virtually all reviews into the failed Beers campaign found that the United States made a serious mistake by adopting a one-way advertising strategy rather than opting for a two-way "engagement approach" that involves building of dialogue and relationship as well as increasing the amount and effectiveness of public opinion research.[43] As Joseph Nye succinctly puts it, "to communicative effectively, Americans must first learn to listen."[44] There are many proven ways of facilitating multicultural encounters conducted globally in the inclusive spirit of mutual learning, including the creation of new dialogic institutions and networks connecting governmental and non-governmental sectors of the international community, the dramatic expansion of academic and cultural exchange programs, the organization of high-profile conferences on intercultural understanding, and so on. However, the success of these programs critically depends on the willingness of Americans to turn away from exceptionalism and recognize that freedom and democracy are not "American values" but are common norms to be polished through cross-cultural dialogue.

The second imperative constitutes an extension of the first into the arena of national security. It is anchored in the recognition that public diplomacy programs centered on global dialogue and cultural exchange have the potential to provide better security for the American people than Apache helicopters, laser-guided missiles, or unmanned surveillance drones. For example, the creation of a sizeable US public diplomacy corps operating in local settings and committed to solving concrete problems such as poor sanitation, inadequate education, and crumbling infrastructure might change the image of America in "crisis regions" more dramatically than superficial television commercials that showcase American Muslim celebrities such as Muhammad Ali. In general, US public diplomacy has not paid sufficient attention to the opportunities emerging from what James Rosenau describes as the "interactively reinforcing processes of globalization and localization" in the turbulent early twenty-first century world.[45]

Finally, the third imperative makes public diplomacy the voice of conscience that holds US foreign policy accountable to its espoused values. To be sure, in the harsh world of power politics, there always remains a gap between policy and ideals. However, to let this unavoidable discrepancy manifest into a systematic practice of double standards fatally undermines American credibility in the world. The Bush administration's disdainful rejection of the World Court's ruling that Israel's so-called "security fence" violated the human rights of Palestinians is but an example of such double-standard policies that generate intense anti-American sentiments in the Muslim world. If the new US government made a concerted effort to build its public diplomacy around these three imperatives, its claim to world leadership would find a more receptive global audience.

But how likely is it that such a fundamental transformation of American public diplomacy will occur in the foreseeable future? As I noted above, it really depends on who will be elected president. As Lord points out, both the State Department and the White House are centers of political power capable of making decisive changes to American public diplomacy.[46] After all, there has been at least one relatively recent occupant of the Oval Office who promulgated a new mission for US public diplomacy that comes much closer to the ideal of cross-cultural dialogue among equal partners. In 1978, President Jimmy Carter openly called into question the monologic, "propagandistic" character of American self-representation to the rest of the world. Affirming the importance of letting other nations and cultures "know where this great country stands and why," he also claimed that "it is in our interest—and in the interest of other nations—that Americans have the opportunity to understand the histories, cultures, and problems of others, so that we can come to understand their hopes, perceptions, and aspirations."[47] Without such a "regime change" in the United States, Johnson's fears of a second, global coming of the Roman Empire might well be realized sooner than we think.

Notes

1. Michael Hardt and Antonio Negri (2000) *Empire* (Cambridge, MA: Harvard University Press).
2. See, for example, the special issues on "American Empire" in *New Political Science* 26 (3) (2004) and *Ethics and International Affairs* 17 (2) (2003).
3. Manfred B. Steger (2005) "Ideologies of Globalization" *Journal of Political Ideologies* 10 (1), 11–30; (2005) *Globalism: Market Ideology Meets Terrorism*, Second Edition (Lanham, MD: Rowman and Littlefield); and (2008) *The Rise of the Global Imaginary: Political Ideologies from the French Revolution to the Global War on Terror* (Oxford and New York: Oxford University Press).
4. Chalmers Johnson (2004) *The Sorrows of Empire: Militarism, Secrecy, and the End of the Republic* (New York: Metropolitan Books); and Jan Nederveen Pieterse (2004) *Globalization or Empire?* (New York: Routledge).
5. Ibid., 45.
6. *Le Monde* (September 12, 2001).
7. George W. Bush, "Address to Joint Session of Congress and Americans," September 20, 2001, in J. W. Edwards and Louis de Rose (2002) *United We Stand* (Ann Arbor, MI: Mundus), 7–11; and "Remarks in the National Cathedral," Washington, DC, September 14, 2001, www.whitehouse.gov/news/releases/2001/09.html (accessed May 21, 2007).
8. See Erik C. Nisbet, Matthew C. Nisbet, Dietram A. Scheufele, and James E. Shanahan (2004) "Public Diplomacy, Television News, and Muslim Opinion," *Harvard International Journal of Press/Politics* 9 (2), 11–37. The article also includes a comprehensive world opinion poll conducted between November 2003 and February 2004 in nineteen countries. It found that 55 percent of respondents believed that the United States exerted a negative influence in the world. See World Public Opinion Poll published by the Program on International Policy Attitudes (PIPA), June 4, 2004, www.pipa.org/OnlineReports/Global_Issues/globescan_press_06_04.pdf (accessed March 30, 2007).
9. For an enlightening discussion of the neoconservative "Project for a New American Century," see Tom Barry and Jim Lobe (2003) "The

People," in John Feffer (ed.) *Power Trip: U. S. Unilateralism and Global Strategy after September 11* (New York: Seven Story Press), 39–49; and Claes G. Ryn (2003) "The Ideology of American Empire," *Orbis* 47 (2) 383–397.
10. See, for example, Peter G. Peterson (2002) "Public Diplomacy and the War on Terrorism," *Foreign Affairs* 81 (5), 77; Christopher Ross (2002) "Public Diplomacy Comes of Age," *The Washington Quarterly* 25 (2), 75–83; and Antony J. Blinken (2002) "Winning the War of Ideas," *The Washington Quarterly* 25 (2), 101–114.
11. I prefer the term "market globalism" to "neoliberalism," defined as an ideology endowing the buzzword "globalization" with norms and meanings that not only legitimate and advance corporate interests, but also seek to cultivate consumerist cultural identities in billions of people around the world. Since power elites concentrated in the United States constitute the main proponents of this ideology, globalism has a decidedly "American" cultural flavor. In my most recent studies on the subject, I use the term "imperial globalism" to refer to the post-September 11 militarized version of market globalism. See Steger (2008) *Rise of the Global Imaginary*; (2005) *Globalism*; and (2003) *Globalization: A Very Short Introduction* (Oxford: Oxford University Press).
12. For various definitions of "public diplomacy," see Jarol B. Manheim (1994) *Strategic Public Diplomacy and American Foreign Policy: The Evolution of Influence* (New York: Oxford University Press).
13. Peter van Ham (2003) "War, Lies, and Videotape: Public Diplomacy and the USA's War on Terrorism," *Security Dialogue* 34 (4), 429.
14. Richard Holbrooke, "Get the Message Out," *Washington Post* (October 28, 2001). For an excellent study of public diplomacy as rhetoric, see Siobhan McEvoy-Levy (2001) *American Exceptionalism and US Foreign Policy: Public Diplomacy at the End of the Cold War* (New York: Palgrave).
15. Carnes Lord (2006) *Losing Hearts and Minds? Public Diplomacy and Strategic Influence in the Age of Terror* (Westport: Praeger), 7–9.
16. John Brown (2003) "The Anti-Propaganda Tradition in the United States," *Bulletin Board for Peace* (June 29). Full text available at www.publicdiplomacy.org/19.htm (accessed July 22, 2007).
17. A. A. Bardos (2001) "'Public Diplomacy': An Old Art, a New Profession," *The Virginia Quarterly Review* 77 (3), 424.
18. Ibid., 433.
19. John Fousek (2000) *To Lead the Free World: American Nationalism & the Cultural Roots of the Cold War* (Chapel Hill, NC: University of North Carolina Press), 7.

20. McEvoy-Levy, *American Exceptionalism and US Foreign Policy*, 24. For a comprehensive exploration of "American exceptionalism," see Seymour Martin Lipset (1997) *American Exceptionalism: A Double Edged Sword* (New York: Norton).
21. Van Ham, "War, Lies, and Videotape," 430.
22. Ibid.
23. Their preference for "soft power" methods does not mean that American globalists disavowed the imposition of their "Washington Consensus" through economic pressure exerted by US dominated, international lending institutions such as the IMF and World Bank. While the terms "hard power" and "soft power" have been coined by Joseph S. Nye, the power dynamics in question have been described and analyzed in different words by generations of political thinkers influenced by the writings of Antonio Gramsci. For the latest elaboration of Nye's perspective on power, see his (2004) *Soft Power: The Means to Success in World Politics* (New York: Public Affairs).
24. Julia E. Sweig (2006) *Friendly Fire: Losing Friends and Making Enemies in the Anti-American Century* (New York: Public Affairs), 42–43.
25. For a detailed discussion of globalism's core claims, see Steger, *Globalism*, 2nd ed., Chapter 3.
26. Joseph S. Nye (2004) "The Decline of America's Soft Power: Why Washington Should Worry," *Foreign Affairs* 83 (3), 17.
27. For an informative overview of the organizational structure of US public diplomacy, see Rosaleen Smyth (2001) "Mapping US Public Diplomacy in the 21st Century," *Australian Journal of International Affairs* 55 (3), 421–444.
28. William P. Kiehl (2003), "Can Humpty Dumpty be Saved?" (November 13), www.publicdiplomacy.org (accessed November 17, 2006).
29. Associated Press, "New Office Aims to Bolster U.S. Image," *New York Times* (January 21, 2003).
30. Charlotte Beers interviewed by Alexandra Starr, in "Building Brand America," *BusinessWeek online* (December 10, 2001), www.businessweek.com/bwdaily/dnflash/dec2001/nf20011210_2325.htm (accessed September 4, 2005).
31. Pieterse, *Globalization Or Empire?*, 45.
32. Beers interview, "Building Brand America," *BusinessWeek online* (December 10, 2001).
33. Colin Powell cited in Naomi Klein (2002) "Failure of Brand USA," *InnerSelf Magazine* (September), www.innerself.com/Essays/brand_usa.htm (accessed September 23, 2002).
34. Van Ham, "War, Lies, and Videotape," 434.

166   Manfred B. Steger

35. Charlotte Beers (2002) "U.S. Public Diplomacy in the Arab and Muslim Worlds," remarks at the Washington Institute for Near East Policy, Washington, DC, May 7, www.state.gove/r/us/10424.htm (accessed May 10, 2002). See also Charlotte Beers cited in Robert Satloff (2002) "Battling for the Hearts and Minds in the Middle East: A Critique of U.S. Public Diplomacy Post-September 11," *Policywatch* 657, www.washingtoninstitute.org/watch/Policywatch/policywatch2002/657.htm (accessed September 17, 2002); and Charlotte Beers cited in Barry Zorthian (2004) "Public Diplomacy Is Not the Answer," www.publicdiplomacy.org/29.htm (accessed June 12, 2004).
36. Charlotte Beers (2002) "Funding for Public Diplomacy," Statement before the Subcommittee on Commerce, Justice, and State of the House Appropriations Committee, April 24, www.state.gov/r/us/9778.htm (accessed April 15, 2005).
37. Pew Research Center for the People and the Press Poll (March 16, 2004), www.preople-press.org/reports (accessed May 7, 2006).
38. Charlotte Beers cited in Associated Press (2003) "Senators Urge Bush to Work on U.S. Image," *New York Times* (February 27).
39. James M. Blaut (1993) *The Colonizer's Model of the World: Geographic Diffusionism and Eurocentric History* (New York: Guilford Press). See also Edward Said (1978) *Orientalism* (New York: Vintage).
40. Michael Mandelbaum (2002) *The Ideas that Conquered the World: Peace, Democracy and Free Markets in the Twenty-First Century* (Washington, DC: Public Affairs), 79.
41. Klein, "Failure of Brand USA."
42. Nye, *Soft Power*, 123. As Nye points out, France and the UK each spent approximately 3 percent of their total military budget on public diplomacy (124).
43. See, for example, the reports submitted by Peter G. Petersen, Chair of the Independent Task Force on Public Diplomacy sponsored by the Council on Foreign Relations (2002) "Public Diplomacy and the War on Terrorism," *Foreign Affairs* 81 (5), 74–94; and Ambassador Edward Djerejian (2004) Chair of the Congressional Advisory Group on Public Diplomacy, "Statement to House Committee on Appropriations" (February 4) www.appropriations.house.gov (accessed February 7, 2004).
44. Nye, "The Decline of America's Soft Power," 20.
45. James Rosenau (2003) *Distant Proximities: Dynamics Beyond Globalization* (Princeton: Princeton University Press).
46. Lord, *Losing Hearts and Minds?* Chapters 7 and 10.
47. Jimmy Carter cited in ibid., 67.

CHAPTER 9

TERROR, COUNTERTERROR, AND SELF DESTRUCTION: LIVING WITH REGIMES OF NARCISSISM AND DESPAIR[1]

Ashis Nandy

> That we have dreamed of this event, that everybody without exception has dreamt of it, because everybody must dream of the destruction of any power hegemonic to that degree—this is unacceptable for Western moral conscience. And yet, it is a fact. [...]
>
> It is almost they who did it, but we who wanted it. If one does not take that into account, the event loses all symbolic dimensions to become a pure accident, a purely arbitrary act, the murderous fantasy of a few fanatics, who need then to just be suppressed. But we know very well that this is not the way it is. Thus, all those delirious, counter-phobic exorcisms: because evil is there, everywhere as an obscure object of desire. Without this deep complicity, the event would not have had such repercussions.
>
> This goes much further than hatred for the dominant global power from the disinherited and the exploited, those who fell on the wrong side of the world order. That malignant desire is in the very heart of those who share (this order's) benefits.
>
> —Jean Baudrillard (Le Monde, November 2, 2001)[2]

Interpretations of September 11, and the political and intellectual responses to them, have oscillated between a concern with the wrath of the disinherited and exploited and the elements of self-destruction built into a hegemonic system. Keeping in mind Baudrillard's warning, I shall focus on the rage of those who feel they have been deceived by the present global system and have no future within it. This feeling has acquired an ominous edge in recent times and developed close links with the self-destructiveness inherent in any global system. The rage often does not have a specific target, though it is always looking for one; and regimes and movements that latch on to that free-floating rage can go far. Indeed, once in a while, their targets too have the same need to search for and find enemies—to reaffirm their raw power and to recapture the evaporating sense of mission in the managerial ethics of a global system. The two sides then establish a dyadic bond that binds them in lethal mutual hatred.[3]

Terror in Culture, Culture in Terror

Seven years after September 11, there has been a narrowing of cognitive and emotional range all around the world. The global culture of common sense has concluded that it is no longer a matter of realpolitik and hard-eyed, calculative interest-based use of terror of the kind favored by the mainstream culture of international relations and diplomacy—as for instance, the repeated attempts the US Central Intelligence Agency (CIA) has made over the last six decades to assassinate recalcitrant rulers presumed hostile to the United States—but a terror that defies rationality and abrogates self-interest, a terror that is deeply and identifiably cultural. Global common sense also seems to insist, to judge by the responses to September 11, that there are only two ways of looking at the link between terror and culture. One way is to emphasize cultural stereotypes and the way they hamper intercultural and interreligious amity. This way presumes that the West with its freedoms—political and sexual—and its lifestyle, identified in popular imagination with consumerism and individualism, has come to look like a form of Satanism to many millennial movements, particularly those flourishing in Islamic cultures. Multiculturalism and intercultural dialogue are seen as natural, if long-term, antidotes to such deadly stereotypes. So, in the short run, the emphasis shifts to "firm" international policing.

The other way is to locate the problem in the worldview and theology of specific cultures. What appear at first instance as stereotyping, prejudices, or scapegoating are really expressions of the "natural" political self of some cultures. At the moment, Islam looks like the prime carrier of a political self that is inclined to use terror to achieve political ends, though some other cultures are not far behind. The American senator, who ridiculed those who wore diapers on their heads, did not have in mind only the Muslims; nor did the American motorist who, when caught while trying to run over a woman clad in sari, declared that he was only doing his patriotic duty after September 11.

The first way—that of multiculturalism and intercultural dialogue—is of course seen as a soft option, the second, as harsh but effective. Hence, in the short term, the second option appears a more viable basis for public policy and decisive action. This preference for political "realism" is, however, not new. Terror has been an instrument of statecraft, diplomacy, and political advocacy for centuries. To see it as a new entrant in the global marketplace of politics is to shut one's eyes to the human propensity to hitch terror to organized, ideology-led, political praxis. Maximilien Robespierre said—on behalf of all revolutionaries, one presumes—that without terror, virtue was helpless.[4] Terror, he went on to claim, was virtue itself. When it comes to the serious business of international relations, such propensity enjoys a certain intrinsic legitimacy in many cultures of public life that today feign shock and dismay when facing terrorism. Despite recent pretensions, in international politics, violence does not have to be justified, but nonviolence has to be. The mainstream global culture of statecraft insists that the true antidote to terror can only be counterterror.

In this respect, the killers who struck at New York on September 11, 2001 and the regimes that claim absolute moral superiority over them share some common traits. Both believe that when it comes to Satanic others, all terror is justified as long as it is counterterror or retributive justice. Both believe that they are chosen and, hence, qualified to deliver life and death in the name of righteous causes. And both are posthumous children of the twentieth century—a century that installed the rights to hone technologies of terror and the capacity to inflict unlimited collateral damage at the centre of public life and public policy. Guernica, Hamburg, Dresden, Nanking, Tokyo, Hiroshima, and Nagasaki are all formidable names in the contemporary imagination of permissible political and strategic weapons. So are the attempts to hitch terror to virtue and efficient governance in a wide range of situations—from Jalianwallabagh to Lidice, from Sharpeville to Mi lai, and from Palestine to Kashmir. The culpable states include the autocratic and the democratic. Liberal democracy has not often been a good antidote for state terror. Few are now surprised that some of the iconic defenders of democracy, such as Churchill, were as committed to terror as Robespierre was. Not only was Churchill a codiscoverer of the concept of area bombing, as opposed to strategic bombing, he and the armies of the two most powerful democracies in the world did not intercede when supplied with evidence, including aerial photographs, of Nazi death camps.[5] Terror and counterterror are normal statecraft, but saying so is not.

Hence, there is also a widespread tendency to dismiss all ideas of fighting terror without using counterterror as romantic drivel. It is a basic tenet of the mainstream global culture of politics that only counterterror deters terrorists. Hence, there is also a tacit admiration for garrison states, such as Israel, in "softer" states such as Sri Lanka and India, and the attempts of such admirers to use Israeli "expertise," forgetting that Israel has been fighting terror with terror for decades without noteworthy success. All that Israel can really take credit for is that, in a classic instance of identifying with its past oppressors, it has succeeded in turning terrorism into a chronic ailment within its own boundaries, whilst in the process brutalizing its own politics and turning many of its citizens into fanatics and racists.

Terrorism as Self Destruction

Into this atmosphere, a new genre of terrorists has emerged during the past few years in Sri Lanka, Palestine, India, Pakistan, and, now, the United States and Iraq. The suicide bombers or suicide squads have made their presence felt in roughly twenty countries. They come prepared to die and, therefore, are automatically immune to the fear of counterterrorism. They usually view counterterrorism—and the reactions to it—as a useful means of mobilizing and polarizing communities.[6]

This is one form of political activism that the hedonic, self-interest-based, individualistic culture of the globalized middle class just cannot handle. It looks like an unwanted war declared by the death-defying on the death-denying. The former thrives on a theology and martyrdom, the latter on a psychology of hard, this-worldly individualism, which cannot but wonder what kind of a person one is if one does not want to keep any option open for even glimpsing the future one is fighting for, or to care about what might happen to one's family, neighborhood, or community in the backlash? Living in a hedonic, secularized world, unable to fathom why its secular hedonism seems evil to others, the cultural sensitivities of the globalized middle class, which was never high, has further narrowed in recent times. To the modern citizen, such suicidal activism looks like the negation of civilization, apart from being utterly irrational and perhaps even psychotic.

In the nervous, heated discussions that used to take place on the *kamikaje* sixty years ago, the doomed pilots usually appeared like strange, robotic killers and carriers of collective pathologies, driven by feudal loyalties, unable to distinguish life from death or good from evil. There have been attempts in recent years to view the self-sacrifice as an "irrationality" imposed by ruthless, scheming officials of the Japanese Army. To that extent, the *kamikaje* pilots now look less like perpetrators and more like victims. However, while there was ruthlessness and the Japanese Army did knowingly push more than 3000 young men to death, one cannot ignore the atmosphere of desperation and despair that allowed such a scheme to be acceptable to a sizeable section of the Japanese public.

Recent discussions of the suicide bombers of Hamas, Tamil Tigers of Sri Lanka, Al-Qaeda, and sundry terrorist groups in Pakistan and Kashmir are linked to similar imageries and fantasies in the mainstream, global awareness. Hence, probably the abortive attempts to rename suicide bombings as homicide bombings. The modern world always seems to be at a loss to figure out how to deter someone who is already determined to die. For most of us, such passions have no place in normal life; it can be only grudgingly accommodated in text books of forensic psychiatry as a combination of criminality and insanity. The expression "homicide bombing," used as a substitute for "suicide bombing," is an attempt to endorse this reading. The former sounds more decisively evil, stripped of the touch of the ambiguous, insane heroism of the latter. Outside the modern world too, few call it self-sacrifice. For, unlike the freedom fighters of India and Ireland who fasted themselves to death during the colonial period as an act of protest and defiance of their rulers, the self-sacrifice of the suicide bombers also involves sacrificing unwilling, innocent others, what we have now learnt to euphemistically call "collateral damage."

Yet, the key cultural-psychological feature of today's suicide bombers and suicide squads, despair, is not unknown to the moderns. Indeed, the idea of despair has become central to our understanding of contemporary subjectivities, and we also admit that it has shaped some of the greatest creative endeavors in arts and some of the most ambitious forays in social thought in our times. Van Gogh, Franz Kafka, or Albert Camus cannot be understood without invoking the idea of despair, nor can be Friedrich Nietzsche or Fyodor Dostoevsky. So powerful has been the explanatory power of the idea of despair that recently Harsha Dehejia, an art historian, has tried to introduce the concept in Indian classical art theory, by extending Bharata's theory of *rasa*s itself. Dehejia feels that without deploying this construct as a part of Indian theories of art, we just cannot explore contemporary Indian art using Indian categories.[7] One suspects that the desperation one sees in the self-destruction of the new breed of terrorists is the obverse of the same sense of despair that underpins so much of contemporary creativity. This despair expresses itself in strange and alien ways because it comes from defeated cultures that have remained mostly invisible and inaudible.[8]

Of the eighteen persons mentioned as members of the suicide squad that struck on September 11, fifteen were identified as Saudis. They came from a prosperous society where dissent was taboo, where political conformity and silence were extracted through state terror. Arguably, by underwriting the Saudi regime, which presided over Islam's holiest sites and had acquired undeserved reputation in some circles as an exemplary Islamic state, the United States had identified itself as the major source of the sense of desperation in the killers. The violence of September 11, Johan Galtung and Dietrich Fischer argue, presumes "a very high level of dehumanization of the victims in the minds of aggressors."[9] That dehumanization did not come in a day, nor can it be explained away as unprovoked. Pervez Hoodbhoy identifies another kind of dehumanization that turns the suicide bombers into drones that are only killing machines—you turn yourself into a weapon for a cause and for the sake of a leader who himself never sacrifices his own or his family's lives, though he routinely sends young recruits to death.[10] This total commitment and blind allegiance not merely become passports to instant salvation, but also the meaning of life. While it is tempting to agree with Hoodbhoy, imputing to hundreds of "crazed demagogues" such immense persuasive powers and ability to seize control of the minds of worshippers also flies in the face of all psychological knowledge.

Thanks to global news media, we are all too aware of the denominational loyalties of the terrorists who attacked the World Trade Centre. They were Wahhabis, given to an aggressively puritanical form of Islamic revivalism. But all Wahhabis do not turn into suicide bombers. Who are the ones that do?

Part of the answer lies not in the ethnic, religious, or class connections of terrorism, but in the fear of cultures that forces us to deny the desperation that has begun to crystallize outside the peripheries of our known world as a new bonding between terror and culture. This desperation may not be preceded by theocide, of the kind Nietzsche talks about, but it may be prompted by a feeling that God may not be dead but has surely gone deaf and blind. Situations such as that of the Palestinians are only one part of the story. The present global political economy has begun to reward all cultivated ignorance of how the unprecedented prosperity and technological optimism in many countries have as their underside utter penury and collapse of life support systems, often brought about by ecological devastations, threats to cosmologies, and no specific hopelessness.[11]

Nothing I have come across reveals the nature of this nihilistic, suicidal despair in some parts of the globe better than the following extract from a journalist's story, which I request the reader to read through despite its length:

> Late last year...I paid the last of many visits to...Brigadier Amanullah, known to his friends as Aman. Aman, in his early fifties and now retired, is lithe and gentle-natured and seemed to me slightly depressed....[A]s the secretary to Benazir Bhutto....[he] also keeps in close touch with old colleagues, who include many powerful people in Pakistan. Aman was once the chief of Pakistan's military intelligence in Sind Province, which borders India....That put Aman squarely in the middle of things....
>
> Aman noticed me looking at the painting and followed my gaze....He told me that one day when [Bhutto] was still Prime Minister, an unknown man, an ordinary Pakistani citizen, had come to the gate of Zardari House with the picture...Aman said that he was immediately transfixed by the painting....
>
> We both looked up at the painting in silence. "A rocket ship heading to the moon?" I asked.
>
> ..."No" he said. "A nuclear warhead heading to India."
>
> I thought he was making a joke....I told Aman that I was disturbed by the ease with which Pakistanis talk of nuclear war with India.
>
> Aman shook his head. "No," he said matter-of-factly. "This should happen. We should use the bomb."
>
> "For what purpose?" He didn't seem to understand my question. "In retaliation?" I asked.
>
> "Why not?"
>
> "Or first strike?"

"Why not?"

I looked for a sign of irony. None was visible....

"We should fire at them and take out a few of their cities—Delhi, Bombay, Calcutta," he said. "They should fire back and take Karachi and Lahore. Kill off a hundred or two hundred million people.... and it would all be over. They have acted so badly toward us; they have been so mean. We should teach them a lesson. It would teach all of us a lesson. There is no future here, and we need to start over. So many people think this. Have you been to the villages of Pakistan, the interior? There is nothing but dire poverty and pain. The children have no education; there is nothing to look forward to. Go into the villages, see the poverty. There is no drinking water. Small children without shoes walk miles for a drink of water. I go to the villages and I want to cry. My children have no future. None of the children of Pakistan have a future. We are surrounded by nothing but war and suffering...."

...He told me he was willing to see his children be killed. He repeated that they didn't have any future—his children or any other children.

I asked him if he thought he was alone in his thoughts, and Aman made it clear to me that he was not.[12]

Fear of Incommensurability

Clash of cultures and civilizations become possible not because some cultures suffer from psychological stigmata, but when, for whatever reason, sizeable sections in a society develop a heightened fear of "strange" cultures living with other moral universes. This is not a prerogative of the backwaters of the civilized world. This applies equally to societies that resonate to slogans, such as "multiculturalism," often as a means of cultural tolerance that is compatible with the dominant pattern of global common sense—cultures that can be safely consumed in the form of ethnic food, arts, museumized artifacts, ethnographies, or, as is happening in the case of Buddhism and Hinduism, packaged theories of salvation severed from the ways of life associated with these faiths. That is why the tacit solipsism of Islamic terrorism and its ability to hijack some of Islam's most sacred symbols is matched today by the narcissism of the policy elite in some countries wedded to the idea of their manifest destiny.

The confrontation becomes more serious when, for a large majority of the world, all rights to diverse visions of the future—all utopian thinking and indigenous visions of a good society—are subverted by the globally dominant knowledge systems and an accessible media as instances of maudlin nostalgia, otherworldly delusions, or brazen revivalism. The Southern world's future now, by definition, is nothing other than an edited version of contemporary North. What Europe and North America are today, the folklore of the globalized middle class claims, the rest of the world will become tomorrow. Once the visions of the future are defined so narrowly, the resulting vacuum is sometimes filled by pathological forms of millennialism, the primary concern of which is to negate, challenge, or subvert the seemingly unbreakable global consensus on values.[13] Some of these pathological forms are perfectly compatible with the various editions of fundamentalism floating around in the global marketplace of ideas today. In the luminal world of the marginalized and the silenced, desperation embraces millennialism at some corner to redefine violence as a necessary means of exorcizing one's inner ghosts and rediscovering an insane version of one's stolen future.

Terrorism's Religious Connotations

September 11, Gandhian activist-scholar Rajiv Vora and the Swarajpeeth initiative have reminded us, was the day Satyagraha was born in Johannesburg in 1906.[14] Satyagraha—militant nonviolence, to use psychoanalyst Erik Erikson's translation, and not passive resistance, as the global media usually calls it—was born in South Africa when it was a proudly authoritarian, racist, police state, not at all like British India, presided over by a reportedly benign, liberal colonial regime that, votaries of political realism assure us, ensured the success of Gandhi's nonviolence. Though the principle and the strategy of militant nonviolence, Satyagraha, was worked out by Gandhi, the first person to proclaim the principle from a public forum at Johannesburg was Abdul Gani, a Muslim merchant, and their closest associate was Haji Habib, another Muslim.[15] Does this coincidence of dates and the Islamic connection have something to tell us?

Recently, there has been animated debate on Robert Pape's proposal, based on empirical data, that suicide bombing is primarily a secular, not religious, enterprise.[16] Some have disputed Pape's formulation. However, there are at least two other ways of looking at the religious links of suicide terrorism, bypassing the debate but perhaps deepening it. One way is to compare the despair-driven, suicidal forms of terror with the suicidal defiance and subversion of authority through fasting to death, as in the cases of some Irish and Indian freedom fighters, to spot the points of contact between two cultures where violence turns outward and the points where it turns inward.

Such a comparison might reveal the religious meaning of some of the most secular acts of suicide "terror" and a secular meaning of some avowedly secular forms of self-destruction. Perhaps the most obvious of the difference between the two is the willingness to couple one's self-sacrifice with the willingness to sacrifice noncombatants.

The other way is to look at the two types of self-sacrificial intervention as tendencies or traits within every person or community. As an example, I draw the attention of the reader to the openly religious, militant nonviolence of an Islamic community known all over the world today for its alleged weakness for religion-based terror in Afghanistan and Pakistan. Pathans, the major ethnic community in Afghanistan and in so-called lawless northwest Pakistan, are known for their martial valor and were officially declared a martial race by British India in the nineteenth century, and they are today the ultimate symbols of mindless violence in the world. For many, there is continuity between the view of the Pathans as a traditionally violence-prone, martial community and the view of the Pathan as naturally predisposed toward fundamentalist violence.

Yet, in India at least, till quite recently, the Pathans were also a symbol of militant nonviolence of the "truly" courageous and martial. According to Gandhi himself, they were the finest exponents of militant nonviolence, which was directed against the British imperial regime in the 1930s.[17] The Pathans who participated in the Gandhian struggle—at the height of the movement, there were at least 100,000 of them who called themselves Khudai Khidmatgars (God's servants)—were the products of the same culture that has produced the Taliban and played host to Osama bin Laden and his entourage.

Can this inconsistency be explained away as only an effect of dedicated fundamentalist clerics, the brutalization in the wake of the anti-Soviet struggle in Afghanistan, or the skill and efficiency of the Pakistan's notorious Inter-Services Intelligence (ISI)? Or does the contradiction exist in human personality and the Pashtun culture itself?[18] The second possibility cannot be dismissed offhand. The behavior of the ordinary Afghans after the fall of the Taliban regime suggests that the Taliban enjoyed some support from the people they ruled. However, most Afghans also seemed genuinely happy to get rid of the harsh, puritanical reign of the Taliban.

Conclusion: In Search of the Real Pathan

Who is the real Pathan? The one sympathetic or obedient to the Taliban or the one celebrating the Taliban's fall? The one known for his martial values or the one who, in the 1930s, turned out to be a death-defying, nonviolent resister, facing ruthless baton charges and firing by the colonial police, never retaliating and never flinching? The Pathans evidently brought to their nonviolence the same fervor that the Afghan terrorists are said to have brought to their militancy. Are the Pathans as ruthless with themselves now as they were when resisting the colonial regime?

I shall avoid answering these questions directly and instead venture a tentative, open-ended comment in the end. Most cultures enjoin nonviolence, or at least seek to reduce the area of violence. These efforts often go hand in hand with cultural theories of unavoidable violence. Only a few, such as Sparta and the Third Reich glorified, prioritized and celebrated violence more or less unconditionally as the prime mover in human affairs or as the preferred mode of changing the world. In cultures that fall in the first category, violence and nonviolence both exist in the same person as human potentialities. By studying the life experiences of terrorists, we are only unlocking one of the potentialities in understanding the phenomenon—the other pertains to grasping the context surrounding terrorism.

I have told my story and, like Aesop, also appended a moral to it. However, an endnote is perhaps in order. A key factor that has in our times contributed to the growth of massive violence can often—though not always—be traced to the partial collapse of the communities and the normative systems they sustained. In many cases, the powerful and the rich have welcomed this collapse as a pathway to a freer, more individualistic, transparent, predictable world, which is more congruent with the dominant theories of progress. But flawed norms, one must remember, are norms nonetheless. The social flux and moral anomie that we see around us have condemned large sections of the humankind to live with a vague sense of loss, anxiety, and anger. They live with a sense of abandonment and a feeling that the vocations, cultural life, and ethics they have known are all being slowly invalidated. Many of them do not clearly perceive the hand of any agency in these changes; they try to bind anxiety and contain anger through consumerism and immersion in the world of total entertainment. That is called normality. But some others do identify an agency, rightly or wrongly. They end up with free-floating rage perpetually looking for targets or embrace ideologies that promise to supply them with ready-made targets of violence. Many forms of terror, particularly among non-state actors, originate from among them.

Only by engaging with these experiences and its associated suffering will it be possible to battle the worldviews or ideologies that organize vague experiences of injustice, abandonment, and uprooting into a work plan for terror. If one is unwilling to negotiate these life experiences or empathize with the pain and the suffering, if one consistently denies their existence and legitimacy and the normal human tendency to configure such experiences into something culturally meaningful, one contributes to and aggravates the sense of desperation and abandonment in many. One well-known Palestinian psychiatrist has claimed that in West Asia "it is no longer a question of determining who amongst the Palestinian youth are inclined towards suicide bombing. The question is who does not want to be a suicide bomber."[19] When you de-recognize these experiences or live as if they were only a psychiatrist's concern, you push the desperate and the abandoned toward a small, closed world of like-minded people who constitute a "pseudo-community" where nonspecific rage is perpetually seeking expression in desperate self-destructiveness, masquerading as self-transcending martyrdom. The self-transcendence may be questionable but the desperation is not.

Notes

1. This paper draws upon a keynote address at the International Symposium on Cultural Diversity and Information Network, Tokyo, on March 7, 2001, organized by Tamotsu Aoki and Masako Okamoto for the National Graduate Institute for Policy Studies; presentation made at a symposium on "Edward Said: Speaking Truth to Power," organized by the Institute for Research and Development in Humanities, Tarbiyat Modaress University, Tehran University, and the Center for Dialogue of Civilizations, Tehran, December 2–13, 2004. This version owes much to my long discussions with Nur Yalmin.
2. Jean Baudrillard (2001) "The Spirit of Terrorism," *Le Monde* (November 2), trans. Rachel Bloul.
3. Vamik D. Volkan (1988) *The Need to Have Enemies and Allies* (New York: Jason Aronson).
4. Quoted in Carl L. Becker (1958), *Modern History* (Morristown, NJ: Silver Burdett), 249–251.
5. See Stuart G. Erdheim (1997), "Could the Allies Have Bombed Auschwitz-Birkenau?," *Holocaust Genocide Studies*, 11 (2), 129–170.
6. This is recognized in Michael S. Doran (2002) "Somebody Else's Civil War," *Foreign Affairs* 81 (1), 22–42.

7. Harsha Dehejia, Prem Shankar Jha and Ranjit Hoskote (2000) *Despair and Modernity: Reflections from Modern Indian Paintings* (Delhi: Motilal Banarsidass).
8. One suspects that, appearances notwithstanding, some instances of suicide bombings are a response to American hegemony; directed not so much at the US Army per se as toward its near-absolute control of the global media.
9. Johan Galtung and Dietrich Fischer (2001), "The United States, the West and the Rest of the World" (September 20) *G21 World Forum*, http://www.jca.apc.org/g21/forumpage3.htm#johan2 (accessed June 27, 2008).
10. Pervez Hoodbhoy (2008), "They Only Know How to Kill: Pakistan's Suicide Bombers are Human Drones," *The Times of India* (March 12), 22.
11. That is why one of the most thoughtful intellectual responses to September 11 remains Wendell Berry (2002) "In the Presence of Fear," *Resurgence* 210 (Jan–Feb), 6–8; see also Jonathan Power (2001) "For the Arrogance of Power America Now Pays a Terrible Price," TFF Press Info 127, Transnational Foundation (September 13).
12. Peter Landesman (2002) "The Agenda: A Modest Proposal From the Brigadier, What One Prominent Pakistani Thinks His Country Should do with its Atomic Weapons," *The Atlantic Monthly* (March).
13. On this subject, see especially the writings of Ziauddin Sardar, for example, Sohail Inayatullah and Gail Boxwell (eds.) (2004) *Islam, Postmodernism and Other Futures: A. Ziauddin Sardar Reader* (London: Pluto Press).
14. Rajiv Vora, "11 September: Kaun si aur Kiyun," Unpublished Hindi paper circulated by Swarajpeeth and Nonviolent Peaceforce, New Delhi 2005; and Arshad Qureshi, "11 September 1906: Ek Nazar," Unpublished paper circulated by Swarajpeeth and Nonviolent Peaceforce, New Delhi, 2005.
15. Robert Payne (1969) *The Life and Death of Mahatma Gandhi* (London: Bodley Head), 163. Recent criticism of Gandhi's religion-tinged language of politics as an important cause of divisive politics in South Asia has not considered the possibility that the secular language of politics may have even less cross-religious and cross-cultural reach in some parts of the world. That, however, is another story. For readers who are curious, see Ashis Nandy (2003) "The Twilight on Certitudes: Secularism, Hindu Nationalism and Other Masks of Deculturation," *The Romance of the State and the Fate of Dissent in the Tropics* (New Delhi: Oxford University Press), 61–82; and Ashis Nandy, Shikha Trivedi, Achyut Yagnik, and Shail Mayaram (1995) *Creating a Nationality: The Ramjanmabhumi Movement and Fear of the Self* (New Delhi: Oxford University Press).
16. Robert A. Pape (2005) *Dying To Win: The Strategic Logic of Suicide Terrorism* (New York: Random House).

17. An ethnographic monograph that nevertheless captures the other self of the Pathan is Mukulika Banerjee (2000) *The Pathan Unarmed: Opposition and Memory in the North West Frontier* (Oxford: James Currey). For a hint that this is not merely dead history but a living memory for many, see Ayesha Khan (2005) "Mid-Way to Dandi, Meet Red Shirts," *Indian Express* (March 22). Also, the very well-researched documentary film, Terri McLuhan, *The Frontier Gandhi: Badshah Khan, A Torch of Peace* (2007).
18. See an insightful, sensitive discussion in the way that the same cultural resources can be used to legitimize and resist terrorism in Bhikhu Parekh (1989) "Dialogue with the Terrorists," *Colonialism, Tradition and Reform: An Analysis of Gandhi's Political Discourse* (New Delhi: Sage), 139–171.
19. Eyyead Sarraj, quoted in Chandra Muzaffar (2002) "Suicide Bombing: Is Another Form of Struggle Possible?," *Just Commentary* 2 (6) (June), 1–2.

Chapter 10

Quo Vadis, the Dialogue of Civilizations? September 11 and Muslim-West Relations

Chandra Muzaffar

In 1998, in a speech at the 53rd Session of the UN General Assembly, the President of the Islamic Republic of Iran, Mohammad Khatami, called "for a dialogue among civilizations and cultures instead of a clash between them."[1]

Khatami's clarion was motivated by a number of factors that can be culled from the UN address itself and from some of his previous pronouncements. First—and this is obvious—it was an explicit rejection of Huntington's infamous "clash of civilizations" thesis propounded in 1993.[2] Khatami has always subscribed to a more optimistic view of the evolution of human civilization. In his 1998 speech he asserted,

> From this rostrum and the pulpit of the United Nations, I announce that humanity despite all calamities and hardship, is heading towards emancipation and liberty. This is the unalterable Divine providence and human destiny. And the malice and depravity of no individual can ever violate Divine providence and the course of history.[3]

Second, by urging humanity to enter into a dialogue, which recognized the equality of all peoples and cultures, the Iranian president was also criticizing the notion of a unipolar world where a single nation dominated global affairs. In his own words,

> The fantasy of a unipolar world ruled by a single superpower is but an illusion, indicating the failure of its holders to keep pace with history. And, I am confident, that powerful nations, such as the American

people, will not accept that their good name, potentials and national prestige be exploited for the advancement of the dream of a unipolar world by the politicians, motivated by the short-sighted material and factional interests of a few. The evolution of public opinion in the West in support of peaceful relations on the basis of mutual respect testifies to this assertion.[4]

Third, in his advocacy for dialogue, Khatami accords primacy to the Divine as the pivot of history that will bring together the human family and guide it to its destiny. He had said in 1998, "[s]ince 'God created man with His Own Hand,' and in 'His Own Image' and since He breathed into him of 'His Own Spirit,' humanity is but a single entity, and so is human history."[5] He further added, "[n]ot only do all human beings originate from the one and the same origin and share a continuous and integrated history, but also one may further postulate a single end or telos: the telos of history is none other than spiritual culture and its requisite of genuine human liberty."[6]

It was largely because of Khatami's perseverance and commitment to dialogue that the UN sponsored a conference on "Dialogue Among Civilizations" in New York on September 5, 2000. At this conference, he adumbrated upon the purpose of the dialogue, connecting it to international relations. He emphasized that in proposing a dialogue of civilizations, his country was in fact presenting

> an alternative paradigm for international relations…we ought to learn from the world's past experience, especially from the tremendous human catastrophes that took place in the 20th century. We ought to critically examine the prevalent, and the glorification of might. From an ethical perspective, the paradigm of dialogue among civilizations requires that we abandon the will-to-power and instead pursue compassion, understanding, and love. The ultimate goal of dialogue among civilizations is not dialogue in, and of itself, but attaining empathy and compassion.[7]

Support for Khatami's idea of a dialogue of civilizations grew and the United Nations declared 2001 as the "Year of the Dialogue of Civilizations"—what Khatami had actually suggested in his 1998 address. In the first eight months of 2001, a number of conferences and seminars were held exploring the multifarious dimensions of the dialogue of civilizations. The UN and its agencies and affiliates, especially UNESCO and the United Nations University (UNU) were actively involved.[8] So also were other universities, think tanks, and some NGOs.

September 11 and Its Aftermath: Dialogue and Preoccupation with the "Muslim"

The dastardly assault upon the World Trade Centre in New York and the Pentagon in Washington, DC, on September 11, 2001, by a group of terrorists from Al-Qaeda under the direction of its leader, Osama bin Laden, which killed instantly almost 3000 men and women, was a huge setback for dialogue especially between the West and the Muslim world. In the immediate aftermath of the colossal catastrophe, Muslim individuals and groups living in the United States and in other countries were targeted. Muslims and their religion were vilified and stigmatized by sections of the media. Some American Church leaders and politicians joined the bandwagon. Islamophobia—the fear of, and antagonism toward, Islam and its followers—was on the rise.[9]

To make matters worse, other terrorist attacks, also initiated by Muslim groups, occurred in other parts of the world. There was the Bali bombing of 2002, the Madrid bombing of 2004, and the London bombing of 2005, among other similar episodes. Each episode—and the manner in which it was presented in mainstream media—further smeared and shamed the Muslim community.

As a result, public discourse had undergone a transformation. The cynosure of attention was the Muslim and often his/her religion. A number of dialogues, especially those pioneered by certain Western governments, universities, think tanks, and NGOs, seek to "understand" the Muslim and his/her alleged tendency to indulge in acts of terror. Though distinctions are sometimes made between those Muslims who resort to violence and those who do not, the public as a whole, in the West as well as in the East, perceives the Muslim as a problem.[10] The Muslim, to put it in graphic terms, is now on the psychiatric couch, subjected to countless examinations and reexaminations.

This trend in post-September 11 dialogue—a preoccupation with the "Muslim"—is by no means confined to politicians, journalists, academics, or activists from the West. A number of their Muslim counterparts also participate in these seminars and conferences, which sometimes degenerate into elaborate rituals of self-flagellation, with some or the other Muslim academic providing a pseudo religious or cultural explanation for the parlous state of the Muslim community or *ummah*.[11] Their concerns about Muslims and Islam appear to revolve around three themes, the most significant of which, of course, relates to terrorism and violence. There is also the issue of democracy and of women.

Terrorism, Violence, and the Forgotten Resistance to Hegemony

While it is true that a tiny fraction of the *ummah* is guilty of the type of carnage associated with September 11 and other similar episodes, the overwhelming majority of Muslims condemn the slaughter of civilians. There is no need to emphasize that the killing of noncombatants is prohibited in Islam. In war, children, women, the elderly, and the infirm are to be accorded full protection. Besides, the Qur'an denounces aggression. However, it allows Muslims to defend themselves from aggression and oppression.[12]

In this connection, if Osama is a hero of sorts in the eyes of a segment of the Muslim community, it is not because of his massacre of innocent people! He is seen, rightly or wrongly, as someone resisting US hegemony and US-Israeli occupation of Muslim lands.

Those who resist colonial and postcolonial hegemony have always been adored and applauded in the Muslim world. Thus, the secular Prime Minister of Iran, Mohamed Mossadegh, was showered with accolades in his time just as the religious Imam Khomeini occupies a sacrosanct status in contemporary Iran. Similarly, the nationalist Gamal Nasser was the darling of the Arab masses, because he resisted the British and the French in the Suez War of 1956, just as the cleric Hassan Nasrallah was loved by Muslims everywhere for his ability to stave off Israeli aggression against Lebanon in 2006. As an aside, it is important to remember that Muslims are not the only ones who lionize the resister. Look at the affection of the Vietnamese for Ho Chi Minh or of the Cubans for Fidel Castro.

And, it is true that, more often than not, the violence of the resister is a response to hegemony and occupation. After all, Al-Qaeda, which collaborated closely with US intelligence in resisting the Soviet occupation of Afghanistan, turned against the United States only when the latter decided to station its military personnel at the Dharan air base in Saudi Arabia.[13] It was seen by Osama as American military occupation of the land of the two holy mosques. There are other examples. In Palestine, it was the establishment of Zionist settlements in the 1920s and 1930s under the aegis of British colonialism and later the creation of the state of Israel through the occupation of

Palestinian land and the expulsion and subjugation of the Palestinian people that ignited armed resistance.[14] It is worth noting that non-violent resistance has also been an integral part of the Palestinian struggle for liberation, though it is seldom highlighted in the mainstream media. The violence in Iraq is a direct consequence of the Anglo-American invasion and occupation of that country. Even the Sunni-Shiite sectarian strife and a lot of the banditry are inextricably intertwined with the occupation.[15] In the case of Lebanon, the Hizbullah emerged as a resistance movement committed to armed struggle because of the Israeli invasion of the country in 1982.[16] Afghanistan is another country where the presence of NATO forces, viewed as occupiers, has spurred the revival of the Taliban, an ultra conservative religious-nationalist movement that ruled Afghanistan from 1996 to 2001.

All this shows that a great deal of contemporary Muslim violence—including acts of terror—is due directly or indirectly to hegemony and occupation, which in turn is linked largely to the United States and its close allies. In dialogues between the West and the Muslim world conducted by the centers of power in the West or groups allied to them, this irrefutable truth is seldom acknowledged. Strenuous efforts are often made to avoid any reference to this truth. At best, hegemony and occupation are treated as some inconsequential factor, which has very little bearing on current Muslim violence. By emphasizing hegemony and occupation, one is not suggesting for one moment that there are no other causes of violence. There are. They emanate from within the community and will be discussed later.

Democracy in the Muslim World and Its Distorted Western Representation

It is of course true that there are dictatorships and authoritarian governments in the Muslim world, just as there are such regimes outside the Muslim world. In fact, the most dictatorial regimes in the world today are in North Korea and Myanmar, both non-Muslim. What is even more significant is that the majority of authoritarian Muslim governments are not only allies of the United States but are also preserved and protected by that superpower. Most of them are feudal in structure with power concentrated in the hands of the royal family. Their lack of democratic credentials—from Brunei in Southeast Asia to Kuwait in West Asia—does not worry the US elite.

All that matters to the US elite and their partners is whether these monarchies will continue to allow them to control their oil.[17] It is no coincidence that almost every one of these monarchies is an important oil exporter.

This is the lesson one can draw from the relationship of feudal Muslim monarchies to the United States. As long as one is subservient to US interests and acquiesces with its dominance, no questions will be asked about one's autocratic power. On the other hand, if one refuses to yield to US hegemony, every institution will be scrutinized for its degree of adherence to democratic norms. This explains why Saudi Arabia, which has never had an elected parliament and where public dissent is severely curbed, has been treated with extra care by the Western media and Western leaders, while Iran, which has held open, competitive elections at various levels of society without fail since the Revolution of 1979, is often pilloried in the Western media for allowing a Council of Guardians to vet certain parliamentary legislation. It is because hegemony, not democracy, is the United States's real goal that it is so stark in its bias.[18]

Because their drive for hegemonic power overrides everything else, the United States and its allies have been utterly hypocritical in their attitude toward the actual workings of democracy in West Asia. When Hamas, an Islamic movement that refuses to recognize Israel because of its occupation of Palestine, won the parliamentary election in Gaza and the West Bank in January 2006, Israel, the United States, and other Western governments sought to prevent Hamas from functioning as the Palestinian Authority (PA). Israel withheld revenue that belonged to the PA while the United States and the European Union cut off much needed economic assistance with the aim of bringing Hamas to its knees. Though the Hamas victory was secured through an election that was certified as "free and fair" by the European Union and by independent monitoring groups from the United States, the verdict was not acceptable to the US and EU elites. For these illustrious champions of democracy, elections should produce outcomes that conduce toward their interests. Moreover, what are their interests in West Asia? It is the protection and perpetuation of US hegemony and the dominant power of Israel. In their reckoning, a movement such as Hamas, which is determined to resist hegemony, should not be allowed to succeed.[19]

The Hamas episode is not the first time that the champions of democracy have hobbled a democratically elected group in West

Asia from exercising effective power, or sanctioned the denial of the right of a popularly chosen movement to assume political authority in the Arab world. In 1953, British and American intelligence colluded to oust the democratically elected Prime Minister of Iran, Mossadegh, after he nationalized Iranian oil. They helped to restore the autocratic Shah, Reza Pahlavi, to his peacock throne. In 1992, the Algerian armed forces prevented the Islamic Salvation Front, which had won a convincing victory in the first round of the first ever general election held in Algeria, from assuming power. The French government, the mainstream French media, and the majority of French intellectuals endorsed the blatantly undemocratic move of the Algerian military junta. The US government acquiesced through its silence.[20]

When Muslim societies succeed in embracing democratic forms of governance, sometimes after decades of authoritarian rule, it is more often than not because of their own courageous efforts. For instance, democracy grew and developed in Turkey in an environment in which the military reigned supreme, largely because of the Turkish people's commitment to freedom. An even more outstanding example of a people's struggle for democracy is Indonesia, the world's largest Muslim nation. The people threw off the yoke of thirty-two years of authoritarian military rule through peaceful agitation and protest, which reached a crescendo in the aftermath of the 1997–1998 financial crises that undermined Suharto's iron grip. Suharto, it will be recalled, was supported for most of his tenure by the US government.

It is these realities about democracy in the Muslim world that are seldom highlighted in some of the post-September 11 intercivilizational dialogues. By downplaying the intimate nexus between the United States and some of the most retrogressive forces in the Muslim world holding back the quest for democracy, and by concealing the role played by the US ruling elite and its allies in thwarting the growth of democracy in certain parts of the Muslim world, some individuals and groups associated with the centers of power in the West have created the erroneous impression that it is the Muslims themselves who are averse to democratic values and principles. This distorted representation of Muslims is a barrier to dialogue between the two civilizations. It only serves the narrow interests of those groups who do not want people in the West to realize that it is the perpetuation of hegemony, not the dissemination of democracy, that is at the crux of much of US foreign policy.[21]

The Issue of Women—the Positive Side of Contemporary Muslim Female Seldom Heard

The third issue that keeps cropping up in dialogues between the West and the Muslim world is the status and role of women in the *ummah*. It is undeniably true that there is discrimination against, even subjugation of, women in some parts of the Muslim world. But it would be wrong to generalize. It would be wrong to suggest that there is no respect at all for the dignity of women in the entire global Muslim community.

Here again, it is significant that it is in some of the Muslim countries that enjoy the closest of ties with the United States that women are most marginalized. Saudi Arabia is a case in point. Women have no role in the nation's political or public life. It is only in recent years that Saudi women have begun to enrol in universities in sizeable numbers. Even certain rudimentary civil rights, which a lot of women elsewhere take for granted, are denied to the Saudi woman. She cannot drive a car or interact with males who are not her kin. She cannot travel abroad alone. Many professions are closed to her. She is, essentially, a second-class citizen.

Contrast the Saudi woman with her counterpart in Syria—a nation that is on the United States's list of rogue states. Syrian women are among the most advanced in the Arab world. They occupy high political office and are active in public life. Women constitute almost half of the total student population in institutions of higher learning.[22] In Lebanon, Egypt, Jordan, Tunisia, and Morocco, among other Arab countries, women are much better positioned than in Saudi Arabia.

There are other non-Arab Muslim societies where women, overall, can hold their heads high, compared to many other countries, both Muslim and non-Muslim. Malaysia, Indonesia, and Turkey are among them. In Malaysia, for instance, Muslim women are in some of the most important decision-making roles in the financial and economic sectors.[23] Many of them serve in the upper echelons of the public bureaucracy. They are also present in parliament, state assemblies, and the federal cabinet. Female students outnumber males in Malaysian universities and colleges.

In dialogues between the West and Islam, these concrete examples of the progress made by Muslim women in various countries are not given the prominence they deserve. The positive aspect of the contemporary Muslim female is seldom heard.[24] What attracts the attention of the dialoguers and the media are peripheral instances of female circumcision and honor killing, both of which have no basis in the Qur'an. Stereotyped images about Muslim women and their "perennial oppression" are then constructed and popularized through the media.

New Impediments for Western-Muslim Understanding

The negative stereotyping of Muslims and even of Islam within a significant segment of Western society, which, needless to say, is one of the most formidable obstacles to harmonious relations between the two civilizations, has a long history. Even before the crusades of the eleventh to the thirteenth centuries, pejorative, prejudiced caricatures of the religion and its Prophet had begun to appear in church circles in Europe. Of course, the bloody, brutal crusades exacerbated relations, which deteriorated further because of the long centuries of Western colonial dominance over Muslim lands.[25]

In the postcolonial period, a host of new factors have emerged that hamper and hinder Western-Muslim understanding. The American drive to control—and not just access—oil in order to exercise hegemony has led to a situation where US elites are determined, regardless of the consequences, in bringing oil exporting Muslim states under their aegis.[26] Moreover, it so happens that most of the oil that is exported flows beneath the feet of Muslims, especially those living in West Asia and North Africa. To justify control and dominance over this vital natural resource—the lifeblood of contemporary civilization—and the society that owns it, one has to find an explanation that will convince one's own constituency and the world at large of the need for some sort of action against the state in question. Thus, the British and American leaderships concocted horrendous lies about President Saddam Hussein's nonexistent weapons of mass destruction in order to justify their immoral invasion and occupation of Iraq in 2003.[27]

It is not just the desire on the part of the US elite and its allies to control oil, and what this implies, that divides the centers of power in the West from the Muslim masses. There is also the equally critical issue of Israel. Western leaders and the vast majority of Western citizens do not realize what a deep and painful wound the establishment of Israel is for the *ummah*. It is a wound that refuses to heal, partly because Palestinian land continues to be annexed, Palestinian children continue to be massacred, and Palestinian women continue to be humiliated on a daily basis. Since the US government offers unquestioning support to Israeli arrogance and intransigence, often with the endorsement of European governments, Muslims everywhere feel alienated from Western governments, which are perceived as protectors and defenders of an unjust and oppressive Israeli regime.[28] It is very apparent that Israel, and all that it conjures, has become a huge wall that separates much of the Muslim world from much of the West.

If this wall has become even more insurmountable over the years, it is because of the mainstream Western media that has a pronounced bias toward Israel in its coverage of the Israeli-Palestinian/Arab conflict.[29] Since the media omits or downplays Palestinian and Arab suffering while magnifying Israeli suffering, it commands very little credibility with Muslims. For a lot of Muslims, the media's bias is a reflection of the West's lack of fairness and even-handedness when it comes to issues of importance to the global Muslim community.

There is yet another emergent force that is driving a wedge between the Muslim world and the West. Right-wing evangelical Christians in the United States and their kindred spirits in various parts of the world have pushed the US government under George Bush into an even more hostile and antagonistic stance toward Muslim states in West Asia. The Christian Right, a significant segment of which identifies itself as Christian Zionists, believes that it is only when Israel triumphs and dominates West Asia that the Messiah will return to earth and Christianity will reign supreme throughout the world.[30] It goes without saying that the defeat of the Palestinians, the Arabs, and the Muslims as a whole is a prerequisite for this apocalyptic event to occur. Since the Christian Right has a massive following in the United States and had strong links to President Bush, its pronouncements, however outlandish, carried considerable weight. It is one of the reasons why Muslims feel more estranged than ever from Washington.

There is also a demographic factor that impacts upon the West-Muslim encounter. In the course of the past twenty or thirty years, the Muslim component in Europe has grown tremendously. There are about 27 million Muslims in the whole of the continent while the Muslim population in the United States is about seven million. For some right-wing European politicians and media outlets, the expanding Muslim community is a threat to Europe's identity.[31] Fear of the "Muslim Other" whose norms and values may sometimes be different has become yet another barrier to harmony between the two communities. It is partly because of this fear that a sizeable section of the European community is so reluctant to accept Turkey with its 70 million population into the European Union. In the United States, prior to September 11, there was hardly any fear of the steadily increasing Muslim population. Today, the Muslim demographic pattern is discussed in some conservative circles, but for the American populace at large the root cause of their apprehension about Muslims remains the politics of violence and terror.

Indeed, the violence and terror of a fringe within the Muslim community, which has been analyzed in some depth in this and other chapters, is one of the other obstacles impeding the emergence of a more positive relationship between people of the West and the Muslim world. When that violence is directed at civilians—for example, when a Palestinian "suicide bomber" blows to smithereens Israeli schoolchildren in a bus—the already tarnished image of the Muslim in the United States or Europe plunges even further. Viewed against the backdrop of other negative perceptions of Muslims in relation to democracy, women, and other such issues, it should not surprise anyone that the chasm that separates the two civilizations has been getting wider and wider.

American Hegemony versus Inter-civilizational Empathy

If we reflect upon the current impediments to a better understanding between the Muslim world and the West, it will become obvious that the single most important factor is Washington's hegemony, often aided and abetted by its allies. Hitherto we have examined how hegemony expressing itself through specific conflict situations, such as Palestine or Iraq or through control over oil or through manipulation of the media, affects inter-civilizational ties. What we should now look at is how hegemony as a phenomenon erodes and jeopardizes a whole gamut of values and attitudes, which, individually and collectively, are crucial for just and equitable relations between civilizations and cultures. For instance, the United States' military hegemony, which is the fulcrum of its global empire, creates fear among the nations and peoples of the world.[32] When a culture or civilization fears another, their relationship becomes inherently flawed. The victim of fear can never be equal to the party that generates fear. At the same time, since the hegemon is feared, it will not be able to elicit either respect or affection from the hegemonized. Likewise, hegemonic global politics that concentrates power and influence in the hands of the elite of the world's only superpower is antithetical to democratic participation and decision-making. If nations and peoples cannot participate in decisions that impact their lives, their sense of self-worth and self-respect will evaporate. Turning to the global economy, the hegemony of neoliberal capitalism results in the concentration of wealth in the hands of a few. The gap between the superrich, on one hand, and those who are struggling to eke out a living, on the other, becomes starker. If, at the same time, the bulk of the superrich are associated with a particular civilization, while the bulk of the poor are found in other civilizations, there can be no inter-civilizational bond between them. By the same token, if there is cultural hegemony, those cultures that are marginalized will feel alienated. Alienation can spawn feelings of bitterness and anger against the dominant culture, thus negating any attempt to narrow the gulf that separates one culture or civilization from another.[33]

Finally, it is the intellectual hegemony of a dominant center of power that endows ideas associated with that centre—about governance, democracy, human rights, and women's rights—with a sacrosanct glow. Ideas from other sources, however worthwhile, are invariably measured against the hegemon's standards and criteria. This often leads to the marginalization of ideas from civilizations other than the dominant one. When other ideas and other worldviews are sidelined by the dominant intellectual discourse, one cannot expect inter-civilizational amity to flourish. In a nutshell, hegemony—more than any other phenomenon—repudiates inter-civilizational empathy.

The good news is that the US-led hegemony that we have been exposed to for a couple of decades now is coming to an end. The economic ascendancy of China; the military and political reassertion of Russia; the revolt of a number of Latin American states against the Washington Consensus; the defiance of Iran; the resistance of Hizbullah and Hamas; and most of all, the utter failure of the Bush Administration to conquer West Asia through control of Iraq, all suggest that there is concerted opposition to hegemony. Besides, a sizeable segment of global civil society continues to stand up to Washington's attempt to dominate and control the rest of the world.[34] Indeed, more and more Americans themselves have become critical of what their leaders are doing not only to the human family but also to the environment.

Their critical attitude assumes some significance in light of the economic and social woes facing the United States. Partly because of its military adventures in Afghanistan and Iraq, the American debt crisis has become more serious than ever. The United States is the world's biggest debtor nation—burdened with both a budget deficit and a trade deficit. It is also a deeply divided society, which is not only over Iraq. On issues such as homosexual rights and their impact upon marriage and family, Americans are badly split. How long can a nation in the throes of such a profound economic and social malaise continue to try to dominate and control the world?

After the End of Hegemony

As US hegemonic power declines, it is quite conceivable that introspection and reflection within American society on how it should relate to the rest of the world will become more intense. There may be a greater realization of the importance of modifying US foreign policy especially in West Asia, aimed at ensuring that Israel's short-term self-interest does not supplant United States' long-term need for friends and partners in that part of the world. Even as it is, more and more Americans are listening attentively to American voices that are critical of overwhelming Israeli influence over US policy in West Asia.[35] Indeed, the audience for those who are arguing against the United States' present hegemonic role and are pleading for a different path, which accords with the values of the American Constitution and its Declaration of Independence, has expanded significantly in recent years. If the United States has a future, they argue, it is as a republic, not as an empire.[36]

A less aggressive, less belligerent, gentler, and a humbler American republic would be in a much better position to indulge in dialogue with other nations and cultures. It would have the psychological disposition to admit its mistakes, to correct its wrongdoings, and to listen and learn from others. Other civilizations and societies will also be more inclined to engage with the United States, to appreciate its great strengths, and to emulate the virtues of its people.

To be more specific, when power and the drive toward power cease to be the defining attributes of the American nation, the world at large will develop much more empathy for those stupendous accomplishments of the United States in the sciences and humanities, which have brought so much happiness to the human race over the last few decades. When the United States is no longer a hegemon bullying and bludgeoning other nations, the innovative spirit of the American people and their creative energies will be celebrated as the hallmark of a dynamic civilization that serves humankind. And yes, the American nation will have friends—not foes[37]—in every nook and cranny of the earth.

A non-hegemonic American republic relating to others with humility and civility will have a profound impact upon the Muslim world. Hopefully, it will pave the way for a just resolution of the Israeli-Palestinian conflict that will witness the establishment of a sovereign, independent Palestinian state and the return of Palestinian refugees to their homeland. United States and other foreign troops would have withdrawn from Iraq and Afghanistan, providing both countries with the opportunity to form their own stable, viable, representative governments. With the end of US-helmed hegemony—which will also spell the decline of Israeli power—other countries such as Lebanon, Syria, and Iran will no longer feel threatened.

When hegemony ceases to be part of the equation, Muslim governments and societies will be better positioned to isolate and even eliminate the terror and violence of Muslim fringe groups. Indeed, Muslims will have no choice but to confront senseless, mindless violence within their community, which is sometimes also directed at individuals and groups outside the community. The ideological motivations for some of this violence—such as the Sunni-Shiite conflict—in Pakistan and parts of West Asia will have to be rooted out.

There could be other positive changes too. Without the support of hegemonic United States and Western power, many of the feudal Sheikhdoms in the Muslim world may disappear. Authoritarian regimes that are dependent upon the same hegemonic infrastructure for their survival may also be in serious trouble.

What this implies is that with the end of hegemony, there may be tremendous scope for reform within the Muslim world. There should be a concerted, determined endeavor to improve the standards of governance. Corruption in particular, which is the bane of many a Muslim society, should be curbed and, if possible, eradicated altogether. Poverty, which is the number one challenge in a host of Muslim countries in sub-Saharan Africa, should be made history. Issues pertaining to women's rights should also be addressed with honesty and sincerity.[38]

It is important to clarify at this point that it is not because of US-led hegemony alone that problems such as poverty, corruption, and mediocre governance are rampant in some parts of the Muslim world. Irresponsible national elites with distorted priorities are also a major cause. Nonetheless, because hegemony, as we have seen, has a significant direct or indirect impact upon societies everywhere, its disappearance will have a salutary effect on a whole spectrum of challenges confronting the contemporary nation-states.

Indeed, in a non-hegemonic world it should be possible for different nations and cultures to work together at the regional or international level to solve the problem of poverty or corruption without being afraid that some powerful state may exploit the issue to dragoon a weaker, smaller state into submitting to its foreign policy dictates. This of course has been a legitimate concern of a number of Muslim and non-Muslim countries alike for some years now, particularly when issues pertaining, for example, to human rights or the environment are raised in international fora by the United States and some of its allies.

The end of hegemony could have yet another positive consequence. It should encourage Muslim societies in general to become more inclusive and universal in outlook. It is partly because of the fear that hegemonic power would erode their religious identity and integrity that some Muslims have become more exclusive and parochial. In a non-hegemonic environment, Muslims should not hesitate to embrace the Qur'anic spirit of respecting religious and cultural diversity—a spirit that was embodied in the Prophet Muhammad's Charter of Medina and was carried to its zenith in Andalusia from the eighth to the thirteenth centuries. It is this universalism that found expression in the inclusive vision of humanity that permeated the Sufism of illustrious souls such as Jallaludin Rumi and Ibn Arabi. Today, more than ever before, in an increasingly globalized world that is yearning for understanding and empathy between different civilizations, that universal dimension of Islam is vital.[39]

In all religions and civilizations, it is the inclusive, universal dimension that should be emphasized in order to promote dialogue and interaction. It was this dimension that Khatami highlighted in his call for a dialogue of civilizations. If it has not emerged as the defining characteristic of any religion or civilization, it is partly because of the overwhelming power of hegemony. This is why, in the ultimate analysis, the perpetuation of hegemony is the antithesis of the quest for our common humanity—which is the goal of the dialogue of civilizations.

Notes

1. See Statement by H.E. Mohammad Khatami (1998), President of the Islamic Republic of Iran, before the 53rd Session of the United Nations General Assembly (New York, September 21).

2. Samuel P. Huntington, the Eaton Professor of the Science of Government at Harvard University had argued that in the future civilizations would clash. Specifically, Islamic and Confucian civilizations will challenge the West. See his (1993) "The Clash of Civilizations?," *Foreign Affairs* 72 (3) and his (1996) *The Clash of Civilizations and the Remaking of World Order* (New York: Touchstone). My critique of the Huntington thesis can be found in (1994) "A Clash of Civilisations or Camouflaging Dominance?," *JUST Viewpoints* (Penang, Malaysia: Just World Trust) and in (2005) "A Clash of Civilisations?," in my *Global Ethic or Global Hegemony?* (London: ASEAN Academic Press).
3. Khatami (1998) Statement.
4. Ibid.
5. Ibid.
6. Ibid.
7. See a report on his speech on that occasion entitled "Empathy and Compassion," *The Iranian* (September 8, 2000).
8. One of the activities organized by UNESCO and UNU, attended by the author, was a conference on "Dialogue of Civilizations," held in Tokyo and Kyoto, July 31–August 3, 2001.
9. This is examined in Chandra Muzaffar (2001) "Islamophobia after September 11," *Connect* 5 (Tokyo). See also the Report by Doudou Diene, Special Rapporteur on contemporary forms of racism, racial discrimination, xenophobia, and related intolerance submitted to the Sixty-second session of the Commission on Human Rights on February 13, 2006.
10. For an analysis of negative perceptions of Muslims, see Chandra Muzaffar (2004) "Islamophobia and the War on Terror," *Connect* 8 (4) (Tokyo).
11. An example of this was the conference "Who Speaks for Islam? Who Speaks for the West?" co-organized by an Islam-West dialogue group based in New York and a Malaysian government-linked body in Kuala Lumpur in December 2005.
12. See Chandra Muzaffar (2005) *At the Crossroads* (Petaling Jaya, Malaysia: International Movement for a Just World—JUST).
13. See Mahmood Mamdani (2004) *Good Muslim, Bad Muslim* (New York: Pantheon Books).
14. A comprehensive study of Palestinian resistance is Edward Said's (1995) *Politics of Dispossession* (Britain: Vintage).
15. See Chandra Muzaffar (2006) "Sunni-Shiite Violence," *JUST Commentary* 6 (12) (Petaling Jaya: JUST).
16. The history and growth of Hizbullah is elaborated in Abdar Rahman Koya (2006) *Hizbullah Party of God* (Kuala Lumpur: The Other Press in association with Crescent International).

17. For a detailed account of Western machinations in the "Middle East," see Robert Fisk (2006) *The Great War for Civilisation* (Britain: Harper Perennial).
18. See Chandra Muzaffar (1996) *Dominance of the West over the Rest* (Malaysia: JUST) and (1996) *Human Wrongs* (Malaysia: JUST), on how hegemony has always trumped democracy.
19. Hamas's ideology and politics is the focus of Azzam Tamimi (2007) *Hamas: Unwritten Chapters* (London: Hurst and Company).
20. See "Algeria in the Dock" in Chandra Muzaffar (1993) *Human Rights and the New World Order* (Penang: Just World Trust).
21. This point emerges in several of the dialogues between Noam Chomsky and Gilbert Achcar (2007) *Perilous Power The Middle East and US Foreign Policy* (London: Hamish Hamilton).
22. See Chandra Muzaffar (2007) "Syria: The Target," *Tehran Times* (June 12).
23. The Governor of the Central Bank, the Chairperson of the Securities Commission, and the Director-General of the Inland Revenue Department—three of the most crucial institutions linked to the management of the nation's finances and economy—are all Muslim women.
24. An exception in Western literature on Muslim women from an earlier period would be Charis Waddy (1980) *Women in Muslim History* (London and New York: Longman).
25. This is discussed in "Encounters between Religions and Civilisations: The Power Dimension," in Chandra Muzaffar *Global Ethic*.
26. See Chandra Muzaffar (2007) "Asia, Oil and Hegemony," paper presented at the IX International Conference of Economists on Globalization and Development Problems held on February 5–9 at Havana City, Cuba.
27. Some interesting insights on the weapons of mass destruction issue and the decision to go to war can be found in Bob Woodward (2006) *State of Denial: Bush at War Part III* (New York: Simon and Schuster).
28. This feeling of alienation is captured in Ahmed Yousef (2003) *The Zionist Fingerprint* (Springfield, Virginia: UASR Publishing Group).
29. Few individuals have exposed this bias with greater clarity and honesty than the American journalist Alison Weir. Her Web site address is http://www.ifamericansknew.org
30. See Michael Northcott (2004) *An Angel Directs The Storm* (London-New York: I. B. Tauris). Also, Stephen R Sizer (2004) *Christian Zionists* (Surrey, Britain: Christ Church Publications).
31. There is some discussion on this in Zafar Ishaq Ansari and John L. Esposito (eds.) (2001) *Muslims and the West: Encounter and Dialogue* (Islamabad and Washington, DC: Islamic Research Institute, International Islamic University and Centre for Muslim-Christian Understanding, Georgetown University).

32. This is especially because of the United States's formidable nuclear arsenal. For a comprehensive discussion on the nuclear weapons and hegemony, see Joseph Gerson (2007) *Empire and the Bomb* (London: Pluto Press).
33. See Chandra Muzaffar (2006) "Globalization and Cultural Diversity," *Keynote Address* at a global seminar organized by the Korean National Commission for UNESCO and the UNU at Jeju island, South Korea, July 18.
34. Resistance to hegemony is analyzed in Chandra Muzaffar (2007) "Resisting Hegemony; Raising Dignity," in Corrine Kumar (ed.), *Asking, We Walk* (Bangalore: Streelekha Publications). It has been exhaustively examined in Phyllis Bennis (2006) *Challenging Empire* (Northampton, MA: Olive Branch Press).
35. The popularity of James Petras (2006) *The Power of Israel in the United States* (Atlanta: Clarity Press), which went into a third print within three months of its appearance toward the end of 2007, is testimony to this. The John Mearsheimer and Stephen Walt (2006) essay, "The Israel Lobby and US Foreign Policy" (John. F. Kennedy School of Government, Harvard University, *Working Paper* no. RWP06-011, March 13), also generated a lot of debate. So did the Jimmy Carter (2006) *Palestine: Peace, Not Apartheid* (New York: Simon and Schuster).
36. Among the scholars who have advanced this argument is Chalmers Johnson (2004) *The Sorrows of Empire* (United Kingdom: Verso).
37. The most comprehensive survey yet on global perceptions of George Bush and of the United States was conducted by the Pew Institute and published on June 27, 2007. It revealed that negative sentiments against the US President and his country had increased significantly. 45,239 people in forty-seven nations were polled and the study found "a broad and deepening dislike of American values and a global backlash against the spread of American ideas." See *New Straits Times* (June 29, 2007).
38. The weaknesses and shortcomings of the Muslim community are discussed in "Morality in Public Life: The Challenge Facing Muslims," in Chandra Muzaffar (2003) *Muslims, Dialogue, Terror* (Petaling Jaya, Malaysia: International Movement for a Just World).
39. The imperative importance of emphasizing the "universal" in all religions has been a constant theme in my writings since the mid-seventies. See for instance Chandra Muzaffar (ed.) (1979) *The Universalism of Islam* (Penang: Aliran).

Part IV

Cross-Cultural Dialogue in the Context of Civilizational Encounters

Chapter 11

Openness and the Dialogue of Civilizations—A Chinese Example

Zhang Longxi

> It is completely mistaken to infer that reason is fragmented because there are various languages. Just the opposite is the case. Precisely through our finitude, the particularity of our being, which is evident even in the variety of languages, the infinite dialogue is opened in the direction of the truth that we are.
>
> —H.-G. Gadamer, "The Universality of the Hermeneutical Problem."[1]

Dialogue and conversation are fairly common in people's daily lives, but what we are concerned about here is not the ordinary exchange of ideas and information in our daily routine, but the dialogue among civilizations that helps establish the very condition of the contemporary world in which people live their lives. The particular urgency of such dialogues can be felt as soon as we look around and take notice of the many instances of conflict, violence, and war that threaten the peace and security of our world today. Just a few recent events in different parts of the world would make it abundantly clear that humanity desperately needs dialogue in order to survive.

The publication of twelve cartoons caricaturing Muhammad in the Danish newspaper *Jyllands-Posten* in September 2005 started a firestorm of protest and violent reaction in early 2006 in the Muslim world, not only in the Middle East, but also in parts of South and Southeast Asia. More recently, in a lecture on faith, reason, and violence delivered during his visit to Regensburg University, Germany, in September 2006, Pope Benedict XVI quoted the fourteenth-century Byzantine emperor's sharply critical words on Islam, and that quotation set off an uproar of protest and condemnation from Muslim leaders around the globe. Those cartoons and the quotation might be insensitive and problematic, but the reactions were certainly made possible by globalized networking in a tense atmosphere of animosity and hypersensitivity. Religious toleration is in serious trouble. The strong reactions in the Muslim world must be understood against the background of the US-led "war on terror" following the terrorist attack in New York and Arlington, Virginia, on September 11, 2001. The so-called "war on terror," however, has created more problems than it has solved, and the world has not been any safer, with North Korea embarking on its nuclear tests and Iran following suit. In Iraq, despite the presence of a large number of US troops and the local Iraqi police force, senseless killing and fighting between the Sunnis and the Shiites seem to have no end in sight, even though they are all Muslims. All these have become such common features of daily news that they may lose the shocking effect of real-life violence and atrocities. The world seems to be on edge and people are jittery about any cause for its possibility to create conflict and violence.

More incidents are likely to happen if the international community does not make sustained efforts at genuine dialogues among peoples of different political systems and religious beliefs. Dialogue, in other words, is not just an option, it is a fundamental necessity. Seen from a long-term perspective, as Dallmayr argues, dialogue among civilizations "offers the only viable alternative to military confrontation with its ever-present danger of nuclear holocaust and global self-destruction."[2] With globalization and the increasingly closer contacts of peoples and societies in today's world, we are facing the alternatives of either conflict of civilizations or dialogue of civilizations. The choice is very clear: in the variety of cultures and languages, dialogue is the only opportunity for humanity to speak the truth and to find ways to achieve peaceful coexistence and prosperity.

In this chapter I will argue for a global perspective in which religions and political ideologies are seen as different but equally valid expressions of human life, of which none should have the exclusive claim to absolute truth. To accept our human finitude and be humble in front of some superior being is the core of religiosity, and that should be truly acknowledged by everyone from all faiths. If we recognize our finitude and limited knowledge, it should follow that we may not have the only truth available in all matters, including matters of spiritual life. Therefore, to de-emphasize the exclusive claims of one's own religion over others is a prerequisite for genuine dialogue and for the open-minded readiness to accept the humanity of others and the potential validity of their views. In the context of this line of argument, I turn to Chinese history and cultural tradition. The toleration of different religious beliefs has been a salient feature of Chinese culture, which is traditionally understood as the combination of "three teachings"—those of Confucianism, Taoism, and Buddhism. Despite the violence and conflicts that existed in Chinese history, no war has ever been fought on religious grounds in China, and the cultural concept of identity of what it means to be Chinese may offer some insights for the dialogue of civilizations.

Dangers of Exclusive Claim to Truth and the Acceptance of Human Finitude

The conflict and violence in Palestine, in the Persian Gulf, in South and Southeast Asia all have a complicated history in which political and economic interests and religious confrontations are closely intertwined. It is certainly simplistic, even grossly mistaken, to relate certain behavior to a particular religious belief: for example, Buddhism and its presumed pacifism, or Islam and its alleged relationship with the concept of *jihad* and suicide-bombing. At the same time, however, it is illusory not to recognize the exclusive claim to truth by religious fundamentalists and the fact that religious intolerance creates tension, conflict, and persecution not only in one's own community but also against other faith communities and groups. Religious wars in the medieval and early modern Europe, the horrible treatment of native Americans by European colonizers after Columbus's "discovery of the New World," all offer plenty of examples from which we may draw some lessons.

In 1512, for instance, a set of Spanish laws stipulated that "natives were to be relocated (congregated)" and their old houses burned. They were forbidden, for example, to dance, paint themselves, get drunk, or live in "idleness." They were to be instructed how to clothe themselves in European style. In return, Spaniards would not beat them with whips or clubs or call them "dogs."[3]

These laws were based on the presumption of Spanish superiority over the natives, and religion certainly played a major role in claiming that superiority on the part of the Spaniards. As Kevin Terraciano observes:

> Jurists and other learned Spaniards assumed that God had chosen them to instruct these people in the ways of Christianity, and to do so by force if necessary. This belief was exemplified in the language of a document called the *Requerimiento* (requirement), a speech that Spaniards were supposed to read (in Spanish or Latin) when they initially encountered a group of native peoples.... The requirement was a legal ultimatum for native peoples to submit to the superiority of Christianity and the political authority of Spain or be warred upon.[4]

Be converted to Christianity, the colonizer would read to the natives in Spanish or Latin, otherwise

> with the help of God, I will enter forcefully against you, and I will make war everywhere and however I can, and I will subject you to the yoke and obedience of the church and His Majesty, and I will take your wives and children, and I will make them slaves, and I will take your goods, and I will do to you all the evil and damages that a lord may do to subjects who do not obey or receive him.[5]

In the barbaric acts of colonization, much worse has been done to the natives than just these words of menace and violent intent, but such words served as a prelude to, and were directly linked with, the acts of violence and oppression.

Reimbursement

The language of the *Requerimiento* was the opposite of a dialogue, which is based on the concept of equality, the humble recognition of one's own ignorance and the genuine desire to learn from one's interlocutors. As Gadamer argues in *Truth and Method*, the essence of dialogue is the art of asking the right question and providing the appropriate answer, whereas the failure of conversation is often due to the fact that "people who think they know better cannot even ask the right questions. In order to be able to ask, one must want to know, and that means knowing that one does not know."[6] This self-consciousness of ignorance, which is so clearly demonstrated in the Socratic *Apology* and other dialogues, is not to be put to an end by a definitive answer. In fact, as Gadamer observes, in dialogue the appropriate answer always leaves the question open for further questioning. Thus dialogue as the exchange and development of questions and answers is an open-ended process. "The significance of questioning consists in revealing the questionability of what is questioned," says Gadamer. He continues by asserting that,

> [i]t has to be brought into this state of indeterminacy, so that there is an equilibrium between pro and contra. The sense of every question is realized in passing through this state of indeterminacy, in which it becomes an open question. Every true question requires this openness.[7]

The emphasis on "indeterminacy" and "openness" certainly contrasts sharply with the sense of self-righteousness and the exclusive claim to truth that we often find in the fundamentalist discourse, be it religious or not. How to bring a person with a strong belief in the righteousness and truth-value of their own religion to the realization of their own ignorance, to a sense of "indeterminacy" and "openness," and how to open up the "questionability" of a strong religious belief—these are indeed difficult challenges we must face in the dialogue of civilizations.

It is quite important to recognize, as Dallmayr does, that civilization is not just a benign set of moral and cultural values developed in a long historical process, and that it may have some specific values that identify a group, a community, or a nation, but exclude others from outside that political entity. Because of their different historical sedimentations, says Dallmayr,

> civilization is an intricate, multi-layered fabric composed of different, often tensional layers or strands; moreover, every layer in that fabric is subject to multiple interpretations or readings, and so is the inter-relation of historical strands.[8]

Such a sober-minded recognition of the political nature of traditions or civilizations, of the potential conflict of their "different, often tensional layers or strands," will better prepare us to face the challenge when we come to join a dialogue of civilizations.

Of those potentially conflicting layers or strands, the exclusive claim to truth is probably the most challenging for a genuine dialogue. Here I believe that we need to have a truly global perspective in which religious faiths, moral codes, political systems, and other kinds of convictions and belief systems are all seen as different but essentially equal or equivalent expressions of human life, of which none should have the exclusive claim to absolute truth over others. This may be difficult for someone with a strong religious belief to accept, for a strong belief often means that the person in question believes that theirs' is the true religion, while that of others are not. To open up the rigidity of such a biased view, we may appeal to the sense of humility that is so central to all religions, namely, the idea that each individual believer acknowledges his or her own finitude and ignorance vis-à-vis the omniscience of the divine. God may know all, but each individual believer does not. As the acceptance of human finitude and humility in front of some superior being constitutes the core of religiosity, it is possible to appeal to that sense of humility in all believers, even the strongly committed ones.

There are precedents in the legacy and historical discourse of political prudence and religious toleration. In 1453, for example, when European Christians were horrified by reports of Turkish atrocities following the fall of Constantinople, Nicholas of Cusa wrote his treatise *De pace fidei*, in which he lamented the persecutions of one religion by another and advocated the peaceful harmonization of divergent faiths. The treatise was written in the form of a dream narrative, a typically medieval or early modern form of narration or argumentation, in which, as Cary Nederman summarizes, "God determines to hold a conclave of wise men for the purpose of achieving universal agreement about matters of faith," and these wise men in effect conduct "a dialogue between representatives (although Nicholas does not use that term) of the world religions and spokesmen for Heaven (including Peter, Paul, and the Word)."[9]

This was one of the early advocacies for religious toleration in the European tradition—much earlier than the well-known work by John Locke. Given the historical situation of the fall of Constantinople, Nicholas clearly recognized the necessity for the coexistence of politically and culturally diversified communities and societies—the concept of *natio* in *De pace fidei*, as Nederman argues, though not exactly the same as the modern concept of nation, does contain "a sociopolitical dimension quite distinct from a unified religious conviction that binds together people of diverse heritages"; that is to say, that the concept acknowledges the existence of different communities or "nations" divided by political allegiance, cultural heritage, and linguistic specificities.

What is especially relevant to our purposes here is Nicholas's idea that religious truth may take different forms in its manifestation.

"Although Nicholas consistently maintains that there is only a single ultimate truth in central religious doctrines," as Nederman observes, "he is aware that understandings of that truth are bound to change and diverge due to the fragility of human intelligence and the particular patterns of cultural practice." Thus, for instance, "difference in the manner of speech" produces distinctive confessions and rites, even if the true meaning that each religion intends to convey is identical.[10] The felicitous phrase in Nicholas's treatise, *"religio una in rituum varietate"* or "one religion in a variety of rites," thus acknowledges the diversity—and legitimacy—of religious faiths that are not just one, that is, for Nicholas and his time, not just Christianity.

If we recognize human finitude and the limitedness of human knowledge, it should follow that no human being or group has the monopoly on truth, including spiritual matters. To de-emphasize the exclusive claims to truth by one's own religion over others is a prerequisite for genuine dialogue, which is predicated on the open-minded acceptance of the humanity of others and the potential validity of their views. Once we are open in that sense, the dialogue we join will be led not by our own convictions but by the truth we are trying to pursue together with our interlocutors. Here again, Gadamer provides some useful guidance in understanding the nature of dialogue. "To conduct a conversation means to allow oneself to be conducted by the subject matter to which the partners in the dialogue are oriented," says Gadamer. "It requires that one does not try to argue the other person down but that one really considers the weight of the other's opinion." It is the open-ended questioning that further opens up possibilities of a continual dialogue and leads to a deeper probe of the subject matter under discussion:

> For we have seen that to question means to lay open, to place in the open. As against the fixity of opinions, questioning makes the object and all its possibilities fluid. A person skilled in the "art" of questioning is a person who can prevent questions from being suppressed by the dominant opinion.[11]

The last sentence makes it clear that the engagement in a dialogue, the continuation of a meaningful conversation, depends on the questioning or further inquiry into the nature of things under discussion, on the determination not to be dominated by any one particular view or opinion.

Inclusive and Culturally Defined Nature of Chinese Identity

In traditional Chinese culture, no particular religious faith is dominant because the cultural tradition itself is made of "three teachings"—those of Confucianism, Taoism, and Buddhism. There are of course more than three schools of thought in the Chinese tradition; in fact, in Chinese antiquity there were "a hundred schools of thought" contending with one another, but these "three teachings" are the major ones. Among these, Buddhism is most evidently religious, with a set of scriptures, a system of otherworldly beliefs, an organized structure of monastic life, and sacred temples as places of worship, where religious rituals paying homage to Buddhist deities are regularly performed. With its sutras translated from Sanskrit and a number of exotic-sounding terms assimilated into the Chinese language, however, the Buddhist religion always retains something of its foreign origin and has never become as dominant a faith in China as Christianity in the West or Islam in the Arabic world. Taoism has its philosophical metaphysics and religious tendencies; it is influential among the Chinese literati, but as a popular religion it is active largely in the lower strata of the Chinese society, and it has a limited impact. The most influential of the three is Confucianism, but it is not religious in the sense that it is mainly concerned with family and social relationships; its main concern being the cultivation of polite and cultured individuals with competence and knowledge and, most importantly, with moral virtue and political wisdom.

From the Confucian *Analects*, which give us the earliest and most reliable records of this great Chinese thinker's views, we find Confucius to be a rationalist with little interest in anything beyond the reality of this world. "The topics the Master did not speak of were prodigies, force, disorder and gods," as we read in a significant passage.[12] Concerning the existence of gods and spirits, Confucius held a rather ambiguous view, for he explained that in attending religious rituals, "sacrifice as if present" is taken to mean "sacrifice to the gods as if the gods were present."[13] In other words, he was never unequivocally affirmative of the existence of gods or spirits. Many scholars have noticed this implicitly secular and rational attitude with regard to religious matters. For instance, Feng Youlan, a well-known scholar of Chinese philosophy, singled out Confucius's words quoted above as representing an important aspect of the religious and philosophical thinking in ancient China, arguing that "Confucius already held a sceptical attitude toward the existence of ghosts and spirits."[14] According to Zhou Yutong, another eminent scholar in Chinese classical studies, Confucius did not discard religious rituals completely; though the great thinker was sceptical of the existence of gods and spirits, he was shrewd enough to use religious rituals

> as auxiliaries to his moral philosophy. Thus the ancestor worship and ritual offerings to heaven and earth performed by Confucius and the later Confucians were all outer forms meant to induce inner respect for antiquity and former kings, and to bring individual and social ethics to perfection. Thus Confucius's remarks on rituals had gone beyond old beliefs in ghosts and become a skilful application of the psychology of religion.[15]

Indeed, the rational and largely secular attitude noticed above can also be seen in another passage from the *Analects*. When Ji Lu, one of Confucius's disciples, asked the Master how the gods and the spirits of the dead should be served, Confucius immediately dismissed the whole question, saying, "You are not able even to serve man. How can you serve the spirits?" The student went on, however, with another question: "May I ask about death?" The Master replied, "You do not understand even life. How can you understand death?"[16] It seems that Confucius simply refused to discuss matters of spiritual life or afterlife—precisely those matters that should be at the core of religious thinking. Not that Confucius had no idea about the divine or the transcendental, for he did speak about Heaven (*tian*) several times in the *Analects*, but he was, by and large, more interested in matters that are of this world here and now, rather than things that may lie outside people's social life and their immediate experience of reality.

As mentioned many Sinologists have noted the secular tendency in Confucianism. "The central concern of Confucius was the moral guidance of mankind, and the chief virtue for Confucius was humaneness," as Raymond Dawson remarks. "If his purpose was to restore a paradise on this earth, there was little room for religion."[17] Here the "paradise" Confucius wanted to restore on earth has nothing to do with the biblical Garden of Eden, but the ancient kingdom of Zhou under the reign of King Wen, which Confucius idealized as the model for moral conduct and kingly rule, a model of human perfection rather than divine grace. Therefore, under the influence of Confucianism, no religion can claim to hold all truth and become dominant in the Chinese tradition; the Chinese literati typically move effortlessly among the different positions of the "three teachings," with Confucianism as guidance in social and political life, supplemented by Taoist and Buddhist ideas in their reflections on nature and the world, in the cultivation of aesthetic sensibilities, their literary and artistic creations, and their philosophical and metaphysical contemplations.

Some of the most famous literary pieces in classical Chinese literature beautifully illustrate the ease with which the literati negotiate among the Confucian, the Taoist, and the Buddhist positions when they are in different locations and assume different roles in life. They are unmistakably Confucian as literati-officials dealing with the daily routine of bureaucratic affairs in various offices, but in their leisure time out of office, they may assimilate Taoist and Buddhist ideas in pursuit of a harmonious relationship with nature and all the creatures in it, and in the contemplation of things beyond the reality of their political engagement. "When retired from office in leisure," says Wang Yucheng (954–1001) in a famous work in Chinese literary prose, "I put on a crane-wing robe and a Huayang cap, hold a copy of the *Book of Changes* in my hand, burn some incense and sit in quiet contemplation, enjoying myself far away from all the world's worries."[18] Here we have a vivid image of a Chinese man of letters, sitting at leisure in a pavilion built of bamboos, dressed in Taoist attire and reading one of the Confucian classics. The movement from his life as a magistrate to his private life as a sort of hermit, the change of his person from essentially a Confucian to a Taoist, is absolutely natural and seamless, without any sense of discrepancy. The same is true of another famous piece by the Tang poet and writer, Liu Yuxi (772–843), who describes his own unadorned and elegant study as his personal heaven that provides a place of quiet enjoyment, where, says Liu, "I can tune my plain zither and read Buddhist sutras written in gilded characters. There are no strings or the wind band to disturb my ears, nor documents or letters to trouble me with tedious work at my desk.... As Confucius put it, how can one call it shabby."[19] Again, the mention of Buddhist sutras and Confucius's praise of simple virtue here is without any sense of grating discrepancy, a change or movement totally acceptable in the Chinese literary and cultural tradition.

The integration of Taoist and Buddhist spirit with Confucian moral and political teachings is characteristic of a Chinese syncretism that has made it possible for different ideas, religious and secular, to coexist without serious conflict or clash. A revealing example of this religious toleration is the unusual case of Jews in China—unusual because China is, among the many nations of the world, probably the only one, or at least one of the very few, that does not have an anti-Semitic history. Textual evidence of the presence of the Israelites in China can be traced back to the Tang dynasty in the seventh and the eighth centuries, and in 1163, during the Song dynasty, a synagogue was built in the city of Kaifeng, the capital of China at that time. We can still see stone tablets commemorating the rebuilding of synagogues in Kaifeng, with inscriptions dated 1489 and 1512, and in both inscriptions we see a clear effort to emphasize the affinities between the religion of the Israelites and the teachings of Confucianism. The 1489 inscription, for example, speaks of the fact that all three major religions in China—Confucianism, Taoism, and Buddhism—have their own temples, therefore "a temple of Israel" should also be maintained. The inscription goes on to describe some universal values or principles in a comparison of the religion of Israel with Confucianism:

> The Confucian religion and this religion (*pên chiao*), although they agree on essential points and differ in minor ones, yet the principles of establishing the mind and restraining the conduct (*li-hsin chih-hsing*) are nothing more than honoring the Way of Heaven (*T'ien Tao*), venerating ancestors, giving high regard to the relations between the Prince and his ministers (*Chün ch'ên*), being filial to parents, living in harmony with wife and children, preserving the distinction between superiors and inferiors, and having fraternal relations with friends. In short, their principles do not go beyond the Five Relationships (*Wu Lun*).[20]

It is interesting to note that the language used here is characteristically Confucian, for the Jewish author of this inscription, by the name of Jin Zhong (Chin Chung), was a Confucian scholar and a basic degree holder. Unlike in many other places where Jews were banned from taking government positions or other important occupations, Jews in China were free to practice their religion and, like everybody else in China, free to take the various examinations and join the civil service. It is true that because there was no religious persecution and because of the intermarriage and assimilation over the centuries, the Israelites completely integrated into Chinese society and eventually lost their distinctive identities. But the virtue of religious toleration shone out once again like a lonely star of human decency against a dark sky of violent anti-Semitism and the Holocaust, when Chinese cities, Shanghai in particular, became safe havens for Jewish immigrants and refugees during the Second World War, who were persecuted and murdered by the Nazis in Europe and elsewhere.[21]

There is another important source of religious toleration in the Chinese tradition, namely, the notion of a culturally defined concept of Chinese identity. Although the ancient Chinese, like the ancient Greeks, had a proud sense of their own civilization and thought of others as uncivilized and barbaric, the very idea of Chineseness was defined more culturally than racially or ethnically. "In ancient conceptualization," says Qian Mu, a distinguished scholar of Chinese classical studies, "the barbarians in the four directions and the Chinese at the center had in fact a different sort of criterion, and that criterion was not 'kinship' but 'culture.'" It is an old saying that "when Chinese lords adopt barbarian rituals, one should treat them as barbarians; and when the barbarians bring themselves to behave like the Chinese, one should treat them as Chinese." This may serve as clear evidence that culture was the criterion for differentiating the "Chinese from the barbarian."[22] Such a cultural concept of Chinese identity can be found in many ancient Chinese books, of which I would like to single out the text of Mencius (372–289 BCE), who famously said that

> Shun was an Eastern barbarian; he was born in Chu Feng, moved to Fu Hsia, and died in Ming T'iao. King Wen was a Western barbarian; he was born in Ch'i Chou and died in Pi Ying. Their native places were over a thousand *li* apart, and there were a thousand years between them. Yet when they had their way in the Central Kingdoms, their actions matched like the two halves of a tally. The standards of the two sages, one earlier and one later, were identical.[23]

Now Mencius is the second important figure in the Confucian tradition, which is often called the Confucian-Mencian tradition, so the remark he made above has a tremendously significant impact on the understanding of the relationships between Chinese and barbarian, the centre and the periphery. By identifying their native birthplaces, Mencius pointed out that Shun and King Wen were originally barbarians from the East and the West, outside the Central Kingdoms (China). Now Shun and King Wen were such legendary sage kings at the beginning of Chinese civilization and revered as such paragons of moral virtue and political wisdom in the Confucian classics and the commentary tradition, that it was unthinkable that they are not Chinese. The Western Zhou civilization under the reign of King Wen in particular is Confucius's ideal of a good society and largely defines the positive values of Chinese cultural tradition. The fact that Mencius reminded his contemporaries that Shun and King Wen were originally barbarians indicates that people during his time had already identified them so closely with Chinese culture that they forgot their non-Chinese origin. By reminding his contemporaries (and by extension all of us) that Shun and King Wen were non-Chinese in origin, Mencius emphasized that Chineseness has nothing to do with one's ethnic origin, that Chinese identity is culturally defined rather than ethnically determined, and that culture is not an inborn essence, rather, it is something one adopts, assimilates, and cultivates through learning, experience, and actions.

Conclusions: Chinese's Lessons on Dialogue

This cultural concept of identity is thus essentially open, with its boundaries so porous that the Chinese and the foreign, the civilized and the barbarian, do not form a mutually exclusive opposition. This may explain the coexistence of different teachings in China, particularly the successful integration of Buddhism into the Chinese cultural tradition. Buddhism came to China in the Han dynasty and, since the Tang dynasty, many Buddhist sutras have been translated into Chinese and many Sanskrit terms have found their way into the Chinese language. Though it takes generations to integrate, the spread of Buddhism in China shows the receptiveness of the Chinese tradition in cultural terms. In a discussion of the concepts of nation-state and national consciousness, Yu Ying-shih also argues that

> insofar as Chinese conceptualization is concerned, culture far exceeds nation. Whether we are speaking of "All under Heaven" or the "Central Kingdoms," these were all inclusive cultural notions in antiquity, far transcending purely political or ethnic boundaries.[24]

The point is that Chinese cultural tradition is inclusive rather than exclusive, and that it has assimilated different cultural elements from non-Chinese sources, Buddhist in the past and Western in more recent times, and that the integration or syncretism may offer a constructive alternative to the fundamentalist exclusive claim to truth in dealing with different cultures, traditions, or religious faiths. Despite the violence and conflicts in Chinese history, no war had ever been fought on religious grounds, and the cultural concept of identity, of what it means to be Chinese, may offer some valuable insights for the dialogue of civilizations. The idea of the alternative presented here has nothing to do with a narrow-minded Chinese nationalism that tries to argue that Chinese culture is the best remedy for a world heavily influenced or corrupted by the West, but the point of giving Chinese historical examples is to show a different way of understanding one's own identity and be open to the challenge of engaging others in a serious dialogue of civilizations. Again, as Gadamer points out in the quotation with which this chapter began, the fact that humans speak a variety of languages does not preclude conversation, but rather it constitutes the very reason that "the infinite dialogue is opened in the direction of the truth that we are."

Notes

1. Hans-Georg Gadamer (1976) "The Universality of the Hermeneutical Problem," in David E. Linge (ed. and trans.) *Philosophical Hermeneutics* (Berkeley: University of California Press), 16.
2. Fred Dallmayr (2002) *Dialogue Among Civilizations: Some Exemplary Voices* (New York: Palgrave Macmillan, 2002), 13.
3. Kevin Terraciano (1999) "The Spanish Struggle for Justification in the Conquest of America: Tolerance and Intolerance in Early Writings on Spanish America," in John Christian Laursen (ed.) *Religious Toleration: "The Variety of Rites" from Cyrus to Defoe* (New York: St. Martin's Press), 98.
4. Ibid. Also see Robert A. Williams (1990) *The American Indian in Western Legal Thought: The Discourses of Conquest* (Oxford: Oxford University Press).
5. Ibid., 99.
6. Hans-Georg Gadamer (1989) *Truth and Method*, 2nd rev. ed. by Joel Weinsheimer and Donald G. Marshall (New York: Crossroad), 363.
7. Ibid.
8. Dallmayr, *Dialogue among Civilizations*, 26.
9. Cary J. Nederman, "*Natio* and the 'Variety of Rites': Foundations of Religious Toleration in Nicholas of Cusa," in Laursen (1999), 62.
10. Ibid., 63–64.
11. Gadamer, *Truth and Method*, 367.
12. Confucius, *The Analects*, trans. D. C. Lau (Harmondsworth: Penguin Books, 1979), vii.21, 88.
13. Ibid., iii.12, 69.
14. Feng Youlan (1961) *Zhongguo zhexue shi* [*History of Chinese Philosophy*], 2 vols. (Beijing: Zhonghua), 1:49.
15. Zhou Yutong, *Kongzi* [*Confucius*], in *Zhou Yutong jingxue shi lunzhu xuanji* [*Selected Papers on the History of Classical Studies*], ed. Zhu Weizheng (Shanghai: Shanghai renmin, 1983), 385.

16. Confucius, *The Analects*, xi.12, 107.
17. Raymond Dawson (1981) *Confucius* (Oxford: Oxford University Press), 44.
18. Wang Yucheng (1956) "Huanggang zhulou ji" [The Bamboo Pavilion in Huanggang], in Wu Chucai and Wu Tiaohou (eds.), *Guwen guanzhi* [*The Best of Classical Prose Writings*], 2 vols. (Beijing: Wenxue guji), 2:416.
19. Liu Yuxi, "Loushi ming" [Inscription on My Humble Study], ibid., 2:315.
20. William Charles White (1966), *Chinese Jews: A Compilation of Matters relating to the Jews of K'ai-feng Fu*, 2nd ed. (New York: Paragon Book), 15.
21. I have discussed elsewhere the historical situation of Jews in China. See Zhang Longxi "Toleration, Accommodation, and the East-West Dialogue," in Laursen (1999), 37–57.
22. Qian Mu (1993) *Zhongguo wenhua shi daolun* [*Introduction to the History of Chinese Culture*] (Taipei: Commercial Press), 41.
23. *Mencius*, trans. D. C. Lau (Harmondsworth: Penguin, 1970), IV.B, 128.
24. Yu Ying-shih (1993) *Wenhua pinglun yu Zhongguo qinghuai* [*Cultural Criticism and Chinese Sensibilities*] (Taipei: Yongchen), 18.

CHAPTER 12

FROM TENSION TO DIALOGUE? THE MEDITERRANEAN BETWEEN EUROPEAN CIVILIZATION AND THE MUSLIM WORLD

Armando Salvatore

The Mediterranean Space as a Field of Tension: Beyond the Paradigm of the Clash?

Historically the Mediterranean has always been an area of dense relations and conflict between Europe and the Muslim world. In this chapter I will reconstruct the field of tension where European and Islamic civilizations have interacted—a field where the cultural and the political levels are intersected. It is my goal to link culture to power. The field of tension is given by how power is culturally defined and how culture becomes a yardstick for power politics. Power is not a liquid standard, like money, but is culturally constructed and embedded.

This approach can be compared to the narrative of a clash between civilizations, as proposed by Samuel Huntington.[1] Tension is a concept that can prove to be more balanced if the goal is to make sense of the complex combination of conflict and cooperation that has characterized the history of the Mediterranean space. It also constitutes a more realistic background to a conception of dialogue, often intended today in a variety of civil society forums and academic meetings as an easy access to stability, enduring peace, and mutual cooperation between the two shores of the Mediterranean.

Huntington's conceptual framework, though sharply formulated and highly controversial, has some substantial connection with diagnoses of the tension between the European civilization and the

Muslim world that were formulated by other leading thinkers in the West: from the nineteenth-century scholar of Semitic languages, Ernest Renan, via the early twentieth-century sociologist, Max Weber, up to the historian Henri Pirenne. It is necessary to mention this in order to disperse with the easy condemnation of the controversial theorem of the clash of civilizations as a deviation from the "rational" method of Western political analysis and culture.

The notion of a clash of civilizations and the idea of civilization itself should be reassessed on the basis of their relation to the history of Western Europe and the shaping of its singular political and cultural identity. This is best done not only in comparison with the Muslim world, but via the history of the competition and tension with it. The Huntingtonian theory of the clash should be understood not only in relation to the extent to which Western Europe has emerged as a civilization *sui generis*, but also as a manifestation of this triumph. This analysis requires a double articulation of the notion of civilization: in the singular, as radiating from its European model and from the forms of power it has constituted and exported; and, in the plural, as a set of comparable and interacting, often interlacing, units largely dissociated from the European model, but finally entangled with it, by way of the modern expansion and colonial enterprises of Western European powers.

The Mediterranean as a political and cultural space, as we have known it since the eighteenth century, will then appear as a fertile terrain for analyzing the field of tension between the European civilization and the Muslim world. Yet this is not a simple reflection of the political expansion by European powers, which had begun when the Ottoman Empire recoiled and France first occupied Egypt and Syria with Napoleon and, a few decades later, started a systematic colonial occupation and exploitation of Algeria. The analysis should rather suggest that the two parties, Europe and the Muslim world, are not the representatives of an open and democratic political culture, on one hand, and of a closed and despotic one, on the other. We should instead analyze the divergence between the two conceptions of power, one of which, the European, can be well captured by the Nietzschean idea of the "will to power"[2] as the ultimate engine of expansive civilizing processes originating from the European soil; while the Muslim conception of power will be seen as better aligned with classic notions of the balance between power and culture, and in particular with the Aristotelian notion of *phrónesis* (practical reason).

Such examination facilitates identifying a vital nerve in the body of European subjectivity by suggesting how the emergence of a singular conception of power has shaped a specific cultural identity, suitable to take the form of civilization par excellence, as the unique source of the radiation of civilizing processes worldwide.[3] This singular formation took shape along with the recognition by European scholars, particularly since the Enlightenment, of the existence of other civilizations. This recognition proceeded alongside an emphasis on the alleged disjuncture between the projection of the expansive European civilization and the basically closed "heritage" of the other, non-European civilizations.[4]

Civilizational Analysis

This simultaneous declination of civilization in the singular as well as in the plural allows us to include the Muslim world in our analysis. Seen from the Western viewpoint of civilization in the singular, the Muslim world, whose closest "modern" political formation would be the Ottoman Empire, should be suspected, in the historical civilizing process, of suffering key deficits in the production and deployment of a will power manifested via a capacity of self-critique and self-reform, prior to its succumbing to European hegemony since the late eighteenth century. Confrontation between civilizations becomes, therefore, intertwined with a comparative analysis of the types of subjectivity and related cultural forms. A "civilization" is therefore primarily rooted in a type of worldliness consisting of conceptions of the world and modalities of living in the world, and second, it is enmeshed in a tension with the other sources of civilizing processes with which it interacts and at times clashes.[5] This is why one civilization is not equal to another. Civilizations are, first, rooted in specific models of constructing the worldliness within urban settings, especially in the political centers.

Thus, the roots of this singular, hegemonic (European/Western) civilization are located in the mechanisms through which a certain will to power is constituted both internally and externally. Whilst hegemony unfolds, mechanisms of control are imposed inside and outside the immediate purview of the sovereign power of the European states, at the levels of both domestic and international politics. Hegemony also depends on a capillary conception of power based on knowledge. Key precedents to such a hegemonic vocation can also be detected in the Middle Ages when a European identity was taking shape, as reflected by its cultural elite. Such identity construction also entailed a sense of inferiority toward an Islamic world that was advancing at several levels of the production of knowledge and the accumulation of power.

At the end of the analysis of diverging, yet comparable, and mutually enmeshed, civilizational realms, I will provide an assessment over whether, and to what extent, there are conditions for a dialogue, contact, and coexistence of populations of the two areas largely determined by more recent processes of migration. The desire to engage in dialogues should not only be appreciated by reference to the historic imbalance of power between the two parties, but also in relation to the cultural assumptions supporting the subjectivities and typologies of the actors. Reference to a common Platonic and Aristotelian inheritance—that precedes the divergence between the European civilization and the Muslim world—will facilitate such an assessment.

As much as the field of tension, abstractly seen, between the European civilization and the Muslim world cannot be the object of a naked comparison but should be considered as the outcome of two diverging notions of power and of different, underlying cultures relating to the "world," the Mediterranean appears as something more and something less than a "space" delimiting such a field of tension. Indeed, the idea of the Mediterranean as a strategic space is not as neutral as it appears at first sight, since it is much more deeply embedded in a genuinely European approach to its "world." The *mare nostrum* of the Romans is the *bahr al-Rum* ("sea of the Romans")[6] of the Muslims, even during the most expansive phases of their history. Focusing on the strategic importance of the Mediterranean space amounts to a recognition of the long-term civilizational imbalance between the two realms, and is also a token of the projection of this imbalance backward into antiquity. This idea of the Mediterranean is continuous with a Roman view, while it contrasts with an Islamic perception of the strategic and civilizational importance of this sea.

Nonetheless, it should be noted that in many ways the Ottoman Empire saw itself as both overcoming and incorporating the Eastern Roman Empire. Romanian historian Nicolae Jorga liked to talk about an "Ottoman Rome," namely, of Istanbul as the last hypostasis of Rome engaged in a fierce competition with the self-proclaimed "Third Rome" of the Russian czars.[7] This contrasts sharply with the discontinuity in Western Europe, which transformed Rome of the emperors into Rome of the popes, via Roman Christianity. This metamorphosis of the Roman civilization of Latin Christendom, under the umbrella of a Roman Catholic identity, offers us a first interpretative clue to make sense of the process through which Western Europe was constituted as a singular civilization via the capacity to impose a continuity of identity on the discontinuities of a series of historical upheavals. From such vintage point Western Europe has looked to the Mediterranean as a space where it has found its cultural "sources." These sources happened to be situated at some distance from the "Carolingian" geopolitical hub of the founding members of the European Community/Union, on the last stretch of the long and bumpy road of the European civilization to political unity.

The ambivalent positioning of European-Muslim relations, vis-à-vis the Mediterranean, prefigures the extent to which Western Europe, in the long-term process of its construction as a political entity, happens to find itself outside of the civilizational "axis" that supports the fundaments of its purported politico-cultural legacy. The oscillation between the continental integration of Europe and its expansion toward the Mediterranean can be understood as the systole and diastole of the cumulative pumping up of European civilization as the hegemonic power of the modern world, or even as the civilization par excellence.

The "Roman Road" to European Civilization

The main thread that I will follow consists in a critical reading of Brague's idea of a Roman and Christian (indeed, fundamentally Catholic) character of Western European civilization.[8] His argument is based on the view of the process of formation of a strongly "eccentric" European identity vis-à-vis its two "axial" sources, represented by Greek philosophy and Hebrew prophecy. Brague is a widely read author, whose merit consists in matching a knowledge of the history of Islamic thought with a keen view of the specific character of European civilization. He makes no mystery of his Catholic commitment.

While acknowledging Brague's merits in capturing the essential drama of the historic construction of European identity, I will also highlight some crucial points of his analysis, which are not limited to shedding light on the sensible divergence in the cultural construction of the "Self" and the "Other"—and the attending forms of power—between the European civilization and the Islamic world, but also configure a potentially hegemonic "neo-Catholic" viewpoint on the interpretation of the history of that divergence and a blueprint for managing it in the future by circumscribing the risks of an overt clash. In this sense, Brague's argument is both a piece of analysis and a political bid in the present rival contention between clash and dialogue. I will critically rework Brague's argumentation while suggesting a different diagnosis for constructing a feasible dialogue in the field of tension between the two civilizations that span the Mediterranean space.

Other European authors, of different political and cultural orientation, could also be summoned as representatives of an approach that reaffirms the strong identity of Europe as inherently tied to an expansive civilizing process with a universalist vocation and mission. Yet the originality of Brague consists in his insistent emphasis on the "Roman road" as the pathway to the long-term construction of a European identity under the aegis of a continually reconstructed Catholic guidance. Unlike other comparable analyses, Brague's contribution is particularly valuable since it is not based on a prior inferiorization of the significance of Islamic civilization, and also because his analysis does not take for granted an unbroken genealogy of European civilization from its Greek and Hebrew cultural sources to its global hegemony in the modern world: a continuity that is typically evoked by a host of authors whose intent is to define the simultaneously exceptional imprint and universal slant of European civilization.

In his attempt to penetrate the originality of the Roman road of Western Europe, Brague focuses on the development of an original method for dealing with the civilizational sources instead of defining a set of cultural contents or institutional frameworks that are part of a basically univocal "heritage." In Brague's view, the cultural logic of the construction of Latin Christendom depended on the adoption of a consciously "eccentric" positioning toward its purported sources. Eccentricity here also means that in spite of being perceived as remote and to some extent alien, those sources were eagerly reappropriated via an original method of cultural elaboration.

Before I turn to analyze Brague's argument in depth, let me briefly specify the idea of civilizational source that underlies his reasoning of the "Roman road." It is an idea that we can relate to the theory of an *Achsenzeit* or "axial age," which has been developed over the past fifty years by a school of interpretative reflection situated between philosophy of history and historical comparative sociology, which has also benefited from the decisive contribution of historians and philologists. In its current version, dominated by a theory-oriented, sociological approach to "comparative civilizations," attention is given to a series of functionally equivalent historical-political breakthroughs that unfolded in human history during the period stretching from the first half of the first millennium BCE to the advent of Islam at the beginning of the second half of the first millennium CE: a relatively long, yet also historically circumscribed, period. From the original formulation of Karl Jaspers,[9] up to the current critical debates,[10] this approach has focused on the particular impetus in the production of innovative ideas, practices, and institutions—located at the crucial junctures between the political and cultural levels of social life—within various civilizations of the West and the East, including China and India—and, above all, on the common character of these creative processes.

Jaspers started his reflection from Hegel's dictum that Christ is the beginning and the end of universal history, or rather, its "axis." Jaspers aimed beyond the exclusivism of the post-Christian Hegelian heritage and chose to focus on historical breakthroughs that preceded the advent of Christianity and were common to different civilizations of the West and the East. The idea of Christ as the axis of human history was transformed into the concept of an epochal, "axial" breakthrough or "axial epoch" (*Achsenzeit*), which embraced cultural traditions with widely diverging religious and philosophical premises, and even radically differing in terms of the acceptability of the notion of religion itself. According to the axial approach, in the course of this ongoing process, encompassing this breakthrough, the essential foundations were laid for all subsequent transformations of human societies. The breakthrough marked the rise of notions of societal autonomy, which was supported by an increasingly reflexive collective solidarity. In trying to update the vision of Jaspers in terms of contemporary debates, the result of the "axial perspective" is a revisionist effort vis-à-vis the anachronism of Eurocentrism that singles out the values and institutions of Europe, such as democracy and human rights, as a long-term, exclusive, heritage of Western modernity.

It remains true, nonetheless, that within the specifically Euro-Mediterranean heritage of the wider axial civilizations, we would have to give priority to Greek philosophy, variably tied to the democratic experience, on one hand, and to the "humanizing" monotheism of biblical prophets, on the other. Yet in the post-Jasperian development of the axial approach, during the past two decades, when sociology and social theory advanced within this field of comparative studies, an affiliation with both the Greek and the Hebrew components, and thus an axial pedigree, has also attributed to the last of the Abrahamic religions—inaugurated by Muhammad's prophecy and the advent of Islam.

By reflecting on the work of Islamic studies and by applying to such studies the emerging categories of the axial approach, attention has been devoted to the impact of the growth and expansion of Islamic civilization across a vast geographical area, including the larger Mediterranean space stretching from the Middle East to the Iberian peninsula. Under this approach, Islam appears as the civilization that consolidates and brings to fruition key components, both cultural and institutional, of axial civilizations, and also facilitates the development of intermediate spheres of society bridging the elite and the commoners—a space otherwise regarded as an exclusive preserve of Western European modernity.[11]

In this respect, the advent of Western modernity is no longer to be seen as the result of the coherent development of a homogeneous civilization with a colonial vocation, whose hegemony was challenged in the postcolonial era by rival civilizations whose values diverged from those of Western modernity: the object of contention between Huntington and his critics. Rather, modernity should be articulated in a more plural space, within which its Western version (or prototype) represents not an exceptionalist course but a peculiarly strong development of shared axial civilizational premises, framed in terms of a uniquely hegemonic vocation: indeed, also with the ambition of folding civilization in the plural into the hegemonic singularity of a Western civilization proclaimed as unique.

What remains common to various forms of civilizations and of corresponding patterns of political organization, variably susceptible of modern developments, is the task to articulate a viable balance between individual responsibility and autonomy, on one hand, and the collective aspirations manifested by ideas and practices of justice and of a moral order, on the other. The fundaments of such an order, though immanent to society, are first constructed as transcendent, in order to be subtracted to the arbitrary determination of the rulers. In particular, within various axial civilizations this balance and the corresponding responsibility of the rulers toward the ruled, and of each member of the community toward their brothers and sisters, is guaranteed by the work of intellectual specialists or cultural elites (like scribes, priests, prophets, philosophers, rabbis, "ulama," etc, up to modern intellectuals).

Especially important in the axial perspective are ideas of order based on concepts of justice that transcend the existing political order, and in particular the idea of *nómos* as a superior, transcendent, and divine law that does not depend on the arbitrary goals of the rulers but is administered and interpreted by a class of specialists of the norm. These interpreters became the legislators—and thus a full-fledged intellectual class—in the context of the emergence of modern polities. Yet in the axial perspective, even this latest achievement cannot be considered a monopoly of the West, in spite of the particular strength of the will to power and self-empowering claims manifested by Western intellectuals in the name of the Enlightenment.

Framed in this interpretive context, Europe's relation to its axial roots, the Greek legacy and the Jewish tradition—or Athens and Jerusalem—appears as particularly troubled and far from linear. Brague's analysis of the "Roman road" fits neatly into this framework and attempts to further dynamize it. It has also the merit to relativize the idea of civilization as basically monolithic and singular, and as culminating in Western modernity. At the same time, Brague's argument does not deny, but valorizes, the hypothesis of a cultural divergence between the European civilization and the Muslim world. His thesis is particularly interesting for pointing out, as we will see, that it is not the world of Islam that is different from the norm, when compared to the standards of Western Europe, with its own yardsticks of modernity, but that Europe diverges from the much more linear Islamic path, which reflects a more harmonious and less troubled— albeit original—combination of the double, Greek and Hebrew, axial heritage than Europe does.

The key argument of Brague is that the simultaneously "Latin" and "neo-Carolingian" nucleus of Europe, from which its normative identity still radiates, has been formed not via a cumulative buildup of a civilizational legacy, but via a process evidencing a geopolitical-cultural—as it were—deficiency, which is measured by the distance of this historical nucleus from its axial sources. Brague uses the term "eccentricity" to characterize this distance-*cum*-deficiency. This is not primarily an objective distance, measured by history and geography; it is above all the subjective perception of being located far afield from the centers, from both Athens and Jerusalem. What matters here is the identity of being culturally eccentric to one's own civilizational axes, of rotating eccentrically to those axes. This idea of

Brague cannot be equated to a qualified return to the Eurocentric perspective of Hegel, which Jaspers' idea of *Achsenzeit* intended to make obsolete. There is no possibility to invoke a restoration of a privileged axis of civilization focusing on an exclusively Christian legacy to the detriment of the—by now widely acknowledged—plurality of axial civilizations.

Europe: An Eccentric Civilization?

At the centre of Brague's reflection is the process through which the inescapable eccentricity of Europe has been transformed into a formidable power engine facilitating the formation of its peculiar identity, a process that is inseparably political and cultural. The two main vectors of this process have been Roman Law and Latin Christianity (i.e., Roman Catholicism), both of which have produced original practices of power and institutional configurations that facilitated the affirmation of a European identity—both within that Far Western peninsula of the Eurasian continent, which appropriated the mythical name of "Europe," and with respect to the non-European world, primarily the vast landmasses of Eurasia situated to its East, or "Orient." The cultural crystallizations of this process of constitution of Europe should be seen as the tokens of the long term, expansive universalism of Europe. Let us see how.

The two vectors of the formation of an original European civilization, that is, Roman Law and Roman Catholicism, represent two types of cultural practice with a strong institution-building potential. Increasingly intertwined in the history of Europe, thanks to their common Latin matrix, they secured a method for allowing its political leaders and intellectual elites to selectively draw on the axial sources by magnifying the organizational and regulative potential provided—yet somewhat underutilized—by those sources. The process altered the axial idea of power by rooting it within a unique sense of a historical subjectivity. This sense was nurtured by ideas of individual autonomy and energized by the way this autonomy was not kept free-floating but yoked to the sovereignty of collective bodies (first the church, then the state). The resulting, in no way unambiguous, nexus between autonomy and sovereignty framed the development of overlapping frames of collective solidarity and ideas of subjective rights.

It is not difficult to detect in the theses of Brague, a Catholic scholar, some echoes of the work of other, non-Catholic, key European authors—from Emile Durkheim to Michael Foucault—who theorized about civilization and modernity. Brague's analysis is important precisely because it provides a culturally oriented genealogical perspective to some topics that have been of common concern in the discussion on European identity for a long time within philosophy and the social sciences: autonomy, sovereignty, rights, and solidarity. The specific merit of Brague is to immediately relate these European key-ideas to the analysis of Islamic civilization. The remarkable effect is that the latter appears, in comparison to Europe, more "normal," and hardly eccentric, vis-à-vis its axial sources. Brague also shows how Islamic civilization happened to pivot its own identity, in a much smoother way, on the double tradition—Athens-*cum*-Jerusalem—that is normally claimed by Europe as its own, but which Europe could only appropriate via a suffered process of distancing facilitated by the construction of a subjectively rooted will to power. The formation of this specific notion of subjective will was one with the process of erosion of a classic notion of practical reason (the Aristotelian notion of *phrónesis*), a process that became evident in the Late Middle Ages and came into full visibility with the Scottish Enlightenment.[12]

A paradox becomes visible, on the basis of which I would like to deepen my reasoning, by making more explicit some implications of Brague's thesis. It is the paradox whereby the European civilization, obsessed with an identity drawn from distant sources and therefore built on shaky ground, appears to have been formed via a ceaseless pursuit of significant nexus to remote and inaccessible "axes." This process was later to be substituted by an increasing consciousness of the power that stems from this heroic pursuit. In that sense the idea of Brague may appear as a sophisticated restatement of the thesis of Renan on the uniqueness of Western Europe, a character that emerges with particular clarity if put in comparison with the Muslim world. At Renan's time, not unlike today, the Muslim world was perceived by European cultural elites as hopelessly stagnant and dangerously prisoner to backward-looking ideologies. It is now easier to see how such a perception was, and is, distorted by an obsession for the uniqueness of European identity and in particular by the formidable identitarian engine that has allowed Europe to produce new cultural practices and fresh institutional frameworks precisely because it was impossible for it to rely on a substantial continuity to the axial sources of this construction.

It is also not difficult to discover—as Brague himself admits—that his thesis is indebted to Pirenne's idea according to which it was Islam that broke the unity of the Mediterranean, a unity that could only be conceived and enforced from—politically and culturally—a Roman perspective. For Brague the Roman civilization *is*, historically, the Mediterranean. After the Arab conquest, only on its northern shore, the idea of the Mediterranean as a unitary space, as the platform for launching projects of a universalist, and in this sense "Catholic" type, was then nurtured by a relentless drive toward the reunification of the Mediterranean space—a drive that nowadays lives on in the growth industry of "Mediterranean Studies." In support of this geopolitical idea, we can observe that just a century and a half after being catapulted onto world history, and in spite of its expansion across a vast perimeter of its Western, Southern, and Eastern shores, the Islamic civilization established its political and cultural centre of gravity a bit far off from the Mediterranean, with the founding of Baghdad, a city that soon became not only the new seat of the Abbasid caliphate but also the center of radiation of a new cultural synthesis, looking in particular to the Persian legacy and further to Central and South Asia. However, from a European perspective, the Mediterranean remained originally Roman, even after the break that followed the advent of Islam, as highlighted by Pirenne.

In contrast to this geopolitical appropriation of the Mediterranean by Europe, there is a culturally—and more specifically, philosophically—comprehensive relationship of the Islamic civilization to the Hellenistic legacy. The strength of this heritage had a decisive role in the elaboration of a wider cultural synthesis by a variety of scholars in Baghdad and other Islamic centers of learning, both East and West of Baghdad. Brague cites with approval the German islamologist and friend of Weber, Carl Heinrich Becker, according to whom there would have been no Islamic civilization acting as a bridge between West and East without the previous work of unification—on a political and military level—performed by the conquests of Alexander the Great.[13] For Western Europe, however, the reappropriation of the Greek-Hellenistic axis occurred under the sign of a sharp discontinuity, which contrasts with the greater continuity in the trajectories of the Islamic elaboration on the same civilizational axis. The medieval philosopher, al-Farabi, could boast, unlike his European counterparts, to be the heir to an unbroken chain of affiliations and initiations—imaginary or real—dating back to Aristotle. The continuity of the heritage was palpable in the cultural self-understanding of the pioneers of *falsafa* (Arabic for philosophy). Several branches of Islamic learning—beyond *falsafa*, and also including legal theory—elaborated on the Aristotelian notion of *phrónesis* (practical reason), while this concept was subject to a continuous process of erosion in Western Europe.[14]

Yet Brague shows us that it was exactly the Roman dimension of the wider classical legacy that provided the troubled identity of Europe a powerful engine facilitating its continual reconstruction via a profitable dealing with the axial sources, which were once perceived as distant and even alien. We can assume that if it is true that a Christian and imperial Rome, along with its symbols of identity and power, could be shifted further to the East Roman empire, or to Byzantium, and next to Russia (the Third Rome), the authentic Rome has always remained the original one, on the shore of the Tiber, exactly because only from that location a culture could be produced that was structurally eccentric to its axial sources, be it Greek or Jewish, while claiming a string of continuity with the idea of a "natural" geopolitical rooting in the Mediterranean space. It was precisely this eccentricity that enabled a universal, namely, Catholic, opening to the distant sources. According to Brague, it is the continuity of such eccentricity, starting from Rome, that has facilitated the formation of a European identity. Here lies both its weakness and the root of its historic *dynamis* (power), the recipe for its singular will to power and for the hegemonic vocation of its universal ambitions—formulated from a Roman Catholic perspective.

The Roman identity of Europe becomes the winning formula for the reconstruction of a truly European identity, in the first place via Roman Law, a legal tradition that is at the same time practical and institutional, and second, by means of a religious tradition, its catholicity of faith, whose origin was not Roman but was brought in harmony with the legal tradition within just a few centuries. This combined work allowed for an incessant filtering and reconstruction, and not a simple amalgam, of the axial sources, Hebrew and Greek. The two engines of production of a European identity, the legal and the religious, have worked sometimes in harmony and sometimes in tension with each other, thus ushering in a markedly dualistic institutional configuration inherited and taken over by modernity, based on the relation between the church and the state. Compared with both the Greek Orthodox and the Islamic religious traditions, Roman Catholicism appears as a tradition *sui generis*, the result of a painful and insistent reconstruction furrowed by strong discontinuities and a vocation to institutional innovation. The Roman Catholic Church is thus located at a considerable distance from any axial source. It is the product of a strongly original reconstruction of the idea of the collective body of Christ. We can now better understand the extent to which it might still be acceptable to speak of a Greco-Roman heritage despite the strong Roman eccentricity vis-à-vis Greek civilization. Roman culture selectively appropriated the Hellenistic heritage in a ceaseless pursuit of a source of civilization perceived as superior and therefore as unattainable per se, yet as one that could be pragmatically reconstructed and adapted to specific needs. This is why Roman culture is best depicted, according to Brague, as "essentially a passage: a road, or perhaps an aqueduct."[15]

In short, the inclined plane linking classical culture to barbarism, which the Romans crossed in the dual cycle of the conquests they undertook and in the invasions they suffered, has set in motion the formation of a Roman identity, which has then been transmitted to the making of Europe, thus giving to the latter's identity a sense of perennial incompleteness. European desire for knowledge, conquest, and subjugation of other peoples, up to colonial times, was exacerbated by the lingering inferiority complex toward the original models, a sense reinforced by successive generations of humanists who worked on restituting classical texts to their remote originality. We could say, in trying to bridge Vico with Nietzsche, that the history of Europe looks like an obsessive spiral sustained by an inextinguishable will to power. With this idea in mind, we might issue a first caution concerning the project of singling out the Mediterranean as a unique political space hosting new dialogues. This would signify to absolve the history and identity of the Mediterranean from the geopolitical hubris that marked its formation, and confine the genealogy of modern imperialism to the opening of Atlantic horizons at the dawn of the modern era. If anything, the United States and its imperial ambitions are—both culturally and politically—a continuation of the European enterprise by other means, and is not an entirely new foundation.[16]

Islamic Civilization: The Paradigm of Axial Continuity

The origins of Islam are connected to those post-Jesuan, Abrahamic traditions that resisted the promotion of Jesus to the second person of a divine trinity, via an upgrading of his identity as the "Christ": a move facilitated by folding his messianic mission into the Greek idea of divine incarnation. Through the rejection of this specific twist to the messianic idea of the Christ, which constituted a rupture of the axial prophetic thread, Islam was constituted and legitimized in an open challenge to the idea that the divine incarnation was a solution to the iteration of the tragic spiral of prophetic warnings and recalcitrant responses of peoples, both Jews and Gentiles, to the divine message. For Islam, the way out of the spiral was not an ascent of the inclined plane via a triumphant history of salvation, but a practice of faithful surrender to divine will facilitated by the gift of God's clear speech, the Qur'an, revealed to Muhammad, the seal of the long prophetic chain, via the archangel Gabriel.

Islam recognizes the prophetic and messianic mission of Jesus but refuses the Christ as the second person of the trinity, and therefore the trinity as a whole, in the name of a flexible and inclusive, non-autochthonous appropriation of the Abrahamic heritage. The new faith accepts Jesus as an essential ring in the concatenation of Hebrew prophets, before the chain opens up to the Gentiles with the son of another Semite people, Muhammad, and so fulfils its cycle. Another constitutive characteristic of Islam can be identified in the Qur'an's criticism of the dogmatic closures of Christology as a manifestation of the human insistence to manipulate God's speech for power reasons, as a marker of the human will to build a "scripture," before God spoke a last and unequivocal word, unmediated by human writing, via the Qur'an. This Word is therefore not considered co-essential with the incarnated God but is the ultimate fruit of a prophetic climax that via Muhammad's uttering of Qur'anic speech sets clear all past human misunderstandings of the divine revelation. The Word as manifested in the Qur'an thus becomes a moment of liberation by virtue of its clarifying capacity and normative power, more than via an inherent eschatological dynamic. It is noteworthy that Muslim philosophers interpreted the Qur'anic momentum as the sublime manifestation of the Active Intellect.

Brague has the merit to override the typically "orientalist" ambiguities of the Western view of Islam, so often devalued as an oriental civilization incapable of sharing in the fruits of the progressive ethos of the West, which is considered the exclusive heir of the rationality of the Greek philosophers and of the humanism of the Jewish prophets. Brague's assessment of the historical trajectory of the Islamic world seems to suggest that while Latin Christian Europe made a treasure out of its positional weakness determined by its distance from the axial sources and transformed its eccentricity into a new engine of cultural innovation and institutional strength, Islam suffered, in the long run, from a stronger rooting within the axial sources. Its moderate and inclusive sense of autochthony, inaugurated by the last eruption of prophetic ethos in human history via the preaching by a messenger from the Arab branch of the Semitic peoples, was grafted on the trunk of a rich post-Hellenistic heritage. This constitutive strength prevented that painful sense of alienation from one's civilizational roots that can trigger an unprecedented will to power and a spirit of radical innovation. In this sense, Islam's strength turned, in the long run, into a weakness vis-à-vis Western Europe.[17]

It is also no mere coincidence that the Arabs were febrile translators who developed a consistently rich philosophical school, which was well integrated in a broader cultural production and matched to a formidably well assorted technical expertise and scientific knowledge. Neither East nor West, they worked to harmonize both. Yet their will to power was sedated by the absence of an elaborate theology of salvation that could be transformed into a modern philosophy of history, mediated by a continuous eschatological momentum and, not least, by an enduring inferiority complex toward other civilizations. Fascinated by the Greek disciplines of philosophy, the natural sciences, medicine, and astronomy, they translated little or nothing of the epic and lyric poetry of the Hellenistic world. According to Brague's reasoning, both the Arabs and the other peoples who embraced Islam failed to launch the type of expansive and exclusive cultural project of "renaissance" that could prompt the building—conceived as a restoration—of an historic subjectivity, a process that in Europe led to a competition (nourished by an enduring inferiority complex) of the modern Europeans with the "ancients." In the Muslim view of tradition and history, the "ancients" remained "reputable ancestors" whose unique virtue and knowledge was suitable to be retrieved for revivals and reforms. Yet, any sense of an unbridgeable distance was carefully avoided. Even the Qur'an, which Muslims consider a unique and final revelation delivered in pure Arabic, was celebrated, from a literary point of view, as the culmination of the inherent poetic capacity of the Arabic language, and as the highest expression of a well-rooted tradition.[18]

Conclusion: The "Roman Road" versus the "Meccan Road"—Divergent Approaches to Dialogue?

Compared with the host of discourses, supported by a sometimes patent and more often latent, burgeoning Islamophobia (which was inaugurated long before September 11), some approaches seek to proclaim the cultural deficits of Islamic civilization vis-à-vis the progressive virtues of Europe; the approach of Brague distinguishes itself for a balanced emphasis on the divergence between the two civilizations. This is not constructed by Brague as an essential cultural difference, but is explained in terms of different styles of cultural production and human communication.[19] It is a difference not so much in the "cultural stock" but in the type of "cultural engine" that produces a divergent sense of the Self and the Other. Such an identity difference is the end result and not the remote cause of diverging civilizational processes. The basic components of the original, axial stock were initially shared by the two worlds.

It comes as no surprise that two different approaches to cultural production, two different methods to relate the Self to the Other, the internal to the external worlds, might allow for divergent practices of communication and dialogue. The risk is serious that whenever we might find two well-intentioned dialogue partners in Europe and in the Islamic world, it will be their differing conceptions of dialogue that create a problem, and so hamper the chance of changing the subjectivities of the dialoging parties. This potential change is essential to a classic, Socratic-Platonic, agonic idea of dialogue, integrated by an Aristotelian idea of practical reason (*phrónesis*). Both parties should in principle be able to share in this idea and practice. Yet the historical excesses of the will to power deployed on the European side, especially since the colonial era, and an enduring trust in the resources of tradition on the Islamic side, which has created the risk of a "fundamentalist trap" in the era of the European, colonial, and postcolonial encroachment on Muslim lands, have thus far concurred in occulting this shared potential. Is it eroded for ever? Can it be consigned to the merely academic interest of the archaeologists of civilizations?

For sure, we first need to be realistic as to how deep the divergence in the style of transmission and communication might go. Brague provides us a clue as to how much and in what way the two approaches to communication might differ from each other. He points out that while the Arabs were feverishly engaged in translating manuscripts, Europeans first copied them. The Arabs immediately appropriated the use value of a source as part of a cumulative tradition supported by a chain of translations. Europeans, on the other hand, maintained an obsequious detachment from the source and attributed value to maintaining or restoring its original form. This method became the entry point into a much more tormented process of reappropriation of the sources, which was to become the harbinger of innovative surprises and the stimulator of creativity.[20]

In an essay on Leo Strauss, the well-known German political philosopher of Jewish origin, Brague, has contrasted its "Roman road"—where Athens and Jerusalem remain separate and in tension, while both preserving their essential role within European identity—to a "Meccan," that is, Islamic model, where Athens and Jerusalem are amalgamated into a common tradition. It may seem paradoxical that it was Strauss, considered by many the spiritual father of American neoconservatives, who stressed the unique capacity of Muslim philosophers to reconstruct and appropriate the Greek idea of the *nómos* by making it compatible with the chain of prophecy, culminating with Muhammad.[21]

If we accept this reasoning, we can ask whether it is realistic to invest hopes and energies into a shared practice of dialogue, which could be anchored to institutional forums and yet be largely decentralized, and be based on a sense of translation, exchange, and pragmatic arrangements (inspired by a modern view of *phrónesis*), instead of relying on the imposition of norms unilaterally considered as universal. Value surveys show that Muslims do not value what Westerners do any less than the latter, from democracy to human rights.[22] A shared practice of dialogue should make sure that these values do not become political straitjackets and Trojan horses for neocolonial projects of cultural penetration and political domination (which incidentally still allow Western powers to protect docile dictators in the Muslim world while propagating those values as nonnegotiable norms: nonnegotiable, then, only for those who oppose the dictatorships).

The method of dialogue to be shared cannot be tailored to the hegemonic agenda of Europe and the West if it has to be a dialogue that goes beyond formulaic gestures and takes the necessary risks in order to construct common political spaces where subjectivities can be reformed via the practice of an open, agonic dialogue—and where the European soul can be cured from its inferiority-superiority complex, so deeply ingrained into its "Roman road," and be realigned with its axes. It is hoped that Europe, unlike that singular extension of Europe across the Atlantic, represented by the "American civilization," might gradually exhaust the slant of its historical hubris and recuperate a shared ground of pragmatic orientation to the Other as a neighbor and partner in dialogue.

In conclusion, we should also ask the question whether the variety of sociopolitical movements that proliferate in the contemporary Muslim world in spite of the enduring authoritarian frame of governance that is supported by Europe—in spite of all discourses of democracy-promotion and human rights—might be able to draw energies and inspiration from a time honored tradition of assimilation of the heterogeneous axial legacy via a patient process of translation and piecemeal appropriation. The challenge would be to retrieve an Islamic vocation to a *phrónesis*-oriented, pragmatic dialogue, not thwarted by postcolonial resentments or identity obsessions. The dire alternative would be that these movements will be bound to imitate and reproduce, on the other side of the Mediterranean, the expansionist vocation, the will to power, and finally the imperial hubris that sustained European modernity.[23]

Postscript

Brague's insistence that at the heart of the uniqueness of Latin Europe's eccentric identity lies the culture of Roman Catholic Christianity resonates extraordinarily well with some recent developments. The political perspective that can be gleaned from his benevolent assessment of the "Roman road" is the idea of a universalism "with a human face," and therefore moderately inclusive of the "Muslim Other" as a "brother," which has often the face of the Muslim migrant who has settled in Europe. This Muslim migrant is often painted by European mass media as exposed to a fundamentalist drift. The current message of the Vatican seems to be that the Catholic apostolate, which first articulated human dignity through the incarnation of God via the Christ, can redeem the Muslim from such a drift. The recent, well-publicized ceremony of baptism of a leading Muslim public figure in Italy, Magdi Allam, vice-director of the leading daily *Corriere della Sera*, on the occasion of the 2008 Easter Vigil in the Vatican, is an unmistakable signature under such a program by none other than Pope Benedict XVI. The Bavarian theologian had stirred up an international controversy with his views on Islam during a pastoral visit in Regensburg in September 2006—even more so since the views of Islam as inherently prone to violence, as suggested by the pope in the incriminated speech, were unambiguously spelled out by the catechumen Allam in the open letter where he explained the reasons for his conversion.[24]

For several politicians and intellectuals, within a secular Europe in crisis not only of over its identity but also over its hegemonic loss to its transatlantic Other, this program may appear attractive, as it seems to promise a substantial preservation of Europe's identity and lifestyle while protecting its power and privileges. Such a postsecular compromise might require paying a price considered by many as much more affordable than the risks implied by the feared "Islamic invasion" or "islamization of Europe." For the burgeoning ranks of self-proclaimed "devote atheists" and their more opportunistic allies, this neo-Catholic twist of the "Roman road" might configure a practicable "third way" and thus a better alternative to both the clash of civilizations and the bet on the uncertainties of an agonic dialogue.

Notes

1. Samuel Huntington (1996) *The Clash of Civilizations and the Remaking of the World* Order (New York: Simon and Schuster).
2. Friedrich Nietzsche (1968) *The Will to Power* (New York: Vintage). While this posthumous work by Nietzsche is controversial, the notion of will to power is intimately linked to his more general work on genealogy of Western subjectivity-*cum*-power.
3. Norbert Elias (1976) *Über den Prozess der Zivilisation* (Frankfurt: Suhrkamp).
4. Bruce Mazlish (2004) *Civilization and Its Contents* (Stanford, CA: Stanford University Press).
5. Johann P. Arnason (2001) "Civilizational Patterns and Civilizing Processes," *International Sociology* 16 (3), and (2003) *Civilizations in Dispute. Historical Questions and Theoretical Traditions* (Leiden and Boston: Brill).
6. Here the adjective primarily designated the East Romans, that is, Byzantium.
7. Nicolae Jorga (1935) *Byzantium After Byzantium* (Portland: Center for Romanian Studies).
8. Rémi Brague (2002) *Eccentric Culture: A Theory of Western Civilization* (South Bend: Saint Augustine's Press).
9. Karl Jaspers (1953) *The Origin and Goal of History* (New Haven, NJ and London: Yale University Press).
10. Johann P. Arnason, Shmuel N. Eisenstadt, and Bjorn Wittrock (eds.) (2004) *Axial Civilizations and World History* (Leiden and Boston: Brill).
11. Shmuel N. Eisenstadt, "Concluding Remarks: Public Sphere, Civil Society, and Political Dynamics in Islamic Societies," in Miriam

Hoexter, Shmuel N. Eisenstadt, and Nehemia Levtzion (eds.) (2002) *The Public Sphere in Muslim Societies* (Albany, NY: SUNY Press); Johann P. Arnason "The Emergence of Islam as a Case of Cultural Crystallization: Historical and Comparative Reflections," in Johann P. Arnason, Armando Salvatore, and Georg Stauth (eds.) (2006) *Islam in Process: Historical and Civilizational Perspectives*, vol. 7, *Yearbook of the Sociology of Islam* (Bielefeld: Transcript; New Brunswick, NJ: Transaction), 95–122.
12. Armando Salvatore (2007) *The Public Sphere: Liberal Modernity, Catholicism, Islam* (New York: Palgrave Macmillan), 99–241.
13. Brague, *Eccentric Culture*, 13–15.
14. Salvatore, *The Public Sphere*, 99–131.
15. Brague, *Eccentric Culture*, 40.
16. It is not by chance that the symbolism of Roman power—starting with the Capitols in the federal and state capitals—is quite ubiquitous in the American monumental imagination.
17. Brague, *Eccentric Culture*, 59–62.
18. Brague, *Eccentric Culture*, 116–122.
19. Rémi Brague "Inklusion und Verdauung. Zwei Modelle kultureller Aneignung," in Günter Figal (ed.) (2000) *Hermeneutische Wege. H.-G. Gadamer zum Hundertsten* (Tübingen: Mohr), 203–306.
20. Brague, *Eccentric Culture*, 74–91.
21. Rémi Brague (1998) "Athens, Jerusalem, Mecca: Leo Strauss's Muslim Understanding of Greek Philosophy," *Poetics Today* 19 (2), 235–259; Georges Tamer (2001) *Islamische Philosophie und die Krise der Moderne. Das Verhältnis von Leo Strauss zu Alfarabi, Avicenna und Averroes* (Leiden: Brill). See also Rémi Brague "Is European Culture 'A Tale of Two Cities?,'" in Suzanne Stern-Gillet and Maria Teresa Lunati (eds.) (2000) *Historical, Cultural, Socio-Political and Economic Perspectives on Europe* (Lewiston, NY: The Edwin Mellen Press), 35–50.
22. John L. Esposito and Dalia Mogahed (2008) *Who Speaks for Islam: What a Billion Muslims Really Think* (New York: Gallup Press).
23. See Friedemann (1996) "Büttner Der fundamentalistische Impuls und die Herausforderung der Moderne," *Leviathan. Zeitschrift für Sozialwissenschaft* 24, 469–492; Armando Salvatore (1997) *Islam and the Political Discourse of Modernity* (Reading: Ithaca Press).
24. See Magdi Allam, "Approdo di un lungo cammino Decisivo l'incontro con il Papa" *Corriere della Sera*, March 8, 2008, http://www.corriere.it/cronache/08_marzo_23/conversione_magdi_allam_34d0da06-f8ac-11dc-8874-0003ba99c667.shtml (accessed June 29, 2008).

CHAPTER 13

HISTORY, MEMORY, AND THE DIALOGUE OF CIVILIZATIONS: THE CASE OF NORTHEAST ASIA

Michael T. Seigel

If the purpose of dialogue is to promote reconciliation and harmony, or at least reduce hostility, then clearly dialogue must focus on the very issues that divide. One of the major issues that divide is the way the past is remembered. Differences over history constitute a major aspect of the divisions between peoples, societies, and civilizations. This chapter argues that, in light of the significance it has in the divisions between peoples, dialogue on historical memory must be seen as an important focus area for a dialogue of civilizations.

However, there are numerous factors associated with historical memory that will make this dialogue particularly difficult. The chapter begins by discussing the importance of dialogue on historical memory. It then highlights the factors that make such dialogue difficult by drawing on a comparison with interreligious dialogue. The chapter then focuses on the situation in Northeast Asia, and particularly on Japan's relations with its neighbors. This provides a concrete case study highlighting the need for the kind of dialogue envisioned and shedding light on possible orientations for such a dialogue. The chapter concludes with a few suggestions on how to approach this dialogue.

Why Dialogue?

In order to clarify the goals and orientation of this dialogue, a consideration of why the approach of dialogue has emerged at this particular time in history may be helpful. The idea of dialogue as a means of dealing with differences has been around for a number of decades. Among the Christian churches, which have for centuries proselytized and evangelized, the focus on dialogue dates, for the Catholic Church, to the 1960s, and for the Protestant Churches, to the International Missionary Conference held in Jerusalem in 1928. It appears to have arisen partly in response to the carnage of the two world wars and the perception of the threat to humanity constituted by the ever escalating stockpiles of nuclear weapons.[1] This can be seen in Gordon Kaufman's perception that

> now the threat of nuclear war has irrevocably bound us all together in one common fate.... It is no longer possible, therefore, or desirable, for us to continue living simply and uncritically out of the parochial religious and cultural traditions we have inherited. Entering into dialogue with each other and trying to understand each other...are now demanded of us all.[2]

As a reading of the relevant texts will make clear, another factor was the cumulative experience of missionaries over the years with people of other faiths. While some missionaries remained for many years with people of other faiths without ever overcoming their prejudices, others discovered a richness and depth in other faiths that challenged and changed their perceptions.[3]

The horrors of war and the risk of continued armed conflict, on one hand, and the enormous amount of contact between different peoples, on the other, were undoubtedly instrumental in the broadening of dialogue beyond its original interreligious conception. As our lives and societies intertwine, and with the potential for destruction so great, we can no longer ignore the differences that exist. Added to this is the environmental crisis, the poverty and polarization that mark our world, the ongoing movement of peoples—all issues that require a massive degree of international cooperation—and it is clear that the divisions that inhibit cooperation need to be addressed. To borrow, once again, the words of Kaufman, "the problems with which modernity confronts us...demand that we bring together all the wisdom, devotion, and insight that humanity has accumulated in its long history, as we attempt to find orientation in today's world."[4] The importance of dialogue in such an endeavor is self-evident.

The Fruits of Dialogue

In a dialogical encounter, we discover both difference and commonality. The discovery of difference, and the appreciation of differences, provides us with a different perspective on ourselves, relativizing prior absolutes and revealing new ways of thinking and feeling. Dialogue opens up the possibility not only of appreciating the Other but also of achieving a more profound appreciation of ourselves. At the same time, we achieve a more critical view of ourselves and a view of others less influenced by bias, prejudice, and unquestioned preconceptions.

The discovery of commonality, a common humanness, can also be transforming. This is the discovery that prevents soldiers from killing an enemy when something reminds them of the humanness of the other. Walzer recounts five examples of soldiers being unable or unwilling to fire when something about the enemy reminds them of his humanness: a soldier running along with his arms outstretched in a defenseless and "funny" way; a soldier taking a bath and therefore naked; a soldier half dressed and holding up his trousers with both hands; a soldier forgetful of the war taking a stroll to enjoy the morning sunshine; a soldier lighting a cigarette oblivious to the danger.[5] As Walzer puts it, a soldier in one of these situations "is not a fighting man [sic] but simply a man [sic], and one does not kill men [sic]."[6] Perhaps the most important goal of dialogue is to arrive at that kind of perception of the Other. The discovery of a common humanness in the midst of all differences is perhaps even more transforming than the mutual acceptance of differences. It is probably a necessary condition for the real acceptance of differences. I will come back to the relevance of this for dialogue on historical memory at the conclusion of this chapter.

Historical Memory as a Focus for Dialogue

The Importance of Dialogue on Historical Memory

The way we understand our history has come to have a major place in the way we understand ourselves. "Our histories," says Elazar Barkan, "shape our identities."[7] Both as individuals and groups, perceptions of the past affect the identity of the people. If dialogue aims at reaching mutual understanding, appreciating differences, and discovering commonalities, then it must deal with all the elements that go into forming identity. History, historical memory, or the story of the particular nation or people can comprise one of these elements. History has not always played such a role. Stewart Macintyre points out that "nations once appealed to race or blood as the basis of their nationhood."[8] Religion too has frequently been used as a source of identity. Many ancient cultures based their identity on myth, often myth related to the origins of the people, as the Japanese found their origins in the Sun-Goddess *Ameterasu-Oomikami* and the Gods *Inazagi-no-Makoto* and *Inazami-no-Makoto*. Today, however, many of these traditional sources of identity have been relativized. As these traditional sources of identity have waned, historical memory has emerged as a prominent alternative.

This, in itself, constitutes a problem because historical memory emerges as a source of identity precisely at a time when history itself is no longer perceived as something fixed and permanent. As Barkan points out, "the current heightened prestige and attention given to the historical identity of the nation...arrives at a time when the tentative nature of the historical narrative has become a commonplace and when scepticism regarding a 'true' representation of the past has reached new heights."[9] Or as he describes this phenomenon in another place:

> We used to treat history as an "objective" knowledge of past events that were largely immune from reinterpretation: history was the past, and we could do little about it.... Increasingly, however, we recognize the growing elasticity of history and that it is anything but fixed. More recently, as history has become increasingly malleable, it has simultaneously become more central to our daily life. It informs our identity more intimately today, and being subject to interpretation, it has also become a space for contesting perspectives.[10]

This means that the history that shapes our identity is a history whose content and significance have been shaped by those who interpret it. US historian Sargent Bush points out that "our national memory has created our past, not the other way around."[11] It is not difficult to see how this is so. The present writer has personally noticed that in conversations about the Pacific Theatre of the Second World War, Americans were likely to dwell more on the attack on Pearl Harbor, Australians, on the treatment of prisoners of war, and Japanese, on the firebombings of cities and the atomic bombs. As this shows, our memories of the past are likely to focus on ourselves as victims. Barkan points out that "during the fifties and into the seventies, German memory focused on German suffering during the war and its aftermath"[12] and comments that "there is nothing exceptional about this; every country privileges its own suffering and minimizes the crimes it has inflicted on others."[13]

Otherwise, our memories are likely to focus on great achievements or on certain idealistic elements in our past that are considered to represent our identity. An example of this is the idea in the United States of tracing the ideal of freedom to the Pilgrim Fathers and their quest for religious freedom.[14] This overlooks the many other aspects of America's roots: the colonial origins in the South, the intolerance of the Puritans in Massachusetts, and the practice of slavery—all of which have very little to do with freedom.

The point being made here is that our memories of the past are likely to be arbitrary and selective, and at times may even include elements of fabrication. These factors will of course be reflected in any sense of identity that is grounded in that historical memory. The factors of arbitrariness, selectiveness, and fabrication are likely to result in differences in perceptions of history emerging both within groups and between them. Insofar as this memory is linked with identity, and consequently with issues such as self-esteem and group cohesion, these differences are likely to give rise to or exacerbate tensions. In addition to describing history as "a space for contesting perspectives" Barkan also considers it as "a crucial field for political struggle."[15] Historical memory can be manufactured in such way as to create a desired identity among people, thereby making them susceptible to manipulation. This may be done by people with political power or other forms of influence in order to create a particular ethos, a national identity suited to their goals. As Charles S. Maier points out, "the narrative...is also a political act. It can be an instrument of control."[16]

One goal of a dialogue on historical memory is clearly to achieve mutual understanding, especially in situations where contending interpretations of history are causing or exacerbating tensions or hindering reconciliation in post-conflict peace-building. Gaining the perspective of others, who have a different understanding of the conflict from that of our own, may help us revise our own historical memory, making us less vulnerable to manipulation, and perhaps even helping us to find a grounding for our identity and self-esteem that is less arbitrary and less vulnerable to change.

The Comparison with Interreligious Dialogue

Interreligious dialogue has been around for a number of decades and there appears to be wide consensus on three points. A comparison with these three points in particular will help bring to light the unique aspects of dialogue on historical memory.

One of the three points is the idea that interreligious dialogue must be equitable and on neutral venue. If it is not equitable and the forum is not neutral, then what takes place is more akin to persuasion than dialogue. As Jacques Dupuis puts it, "interreligious dialogue takes place 'between equals'—in their difference."[17] It is therefore divorced from any attempt at persuasion or conversion. It is not a forum for challenge or criticism. As Jakob Kavunkal states, "dialogue is not for changing the other. That is debate."[18] In dialogue, as David Bosch reminds us, "partners in dialogue should be free to 'define themselves.'"[19] In a dialogue of religions, ultimately, each religion is its own authority. It is not consistent with dialogue to try to interpret another faith in a way that makes it consistent with one's own—even when that interpretation is intended to be conciliatory and supportive. While it may be considered desirable that each partner in the dialogue undertake some form of self-criticism, such self-criticism would normally be expected to be carried out within and according to the principles of each particular religion.

The second point is that while interreligious dialogue seeks to achieve mutual understanding and the amelioration of mistrust, prejudice, and bias, it is not task-oriented in the sense of aiming at reaching agreement on particular issues. Again, to use Dupuis's phrasing, "we must say that the encounter and exchange have value in themselves. They are an end in themselves.... Thus the dialogue does not serve as a means to some ulterior end."[20]

Finally, a frequently asserted dimension of interreligious dialogue is that it presumes the commitment of all dialogue partners to their own faith and is therefore divorced from any willingness to compromise or modify that faith. As the World Council of Churches states, "the aim of dialogue is not reduction of living faiths and ideologies to a lowest common denominator,"[21] or as Bosch puts it, "dialogue presupposes commitment. It does not involve sacrificing one's own faith."[22] Since such commitment is expected of all dialogue partners, it requires that there be no attempt to change the other.

These three characteristics—neutrality, dialogue itself being the goal, and commitment to one's own faith with no demand for change—have proven to be essential for interreligious dialogue. As we will see below, there are numerous factors that will make them difficult, if not impossible, to achieve in dialogue on historical memory.

Focussing on Memory and Identity

In regard to historical memory as a focus area for dialogue, what is at issue is not simply a clarification of the facts of history. In so far as this is possible, it can be done by historians. Historical memory is not to be confused with academic history. Historical memory is about the memory that people have of the past. It is distinct from, and may be contradictory to, academic history. It is the story of a people *as they understand it*. It may be unverified or even contradicted by archival documentation, but it is the past as it informs the perceptions and the self-understanding of the people. As such, it informs the identity and psyche of the people.

Norman C. Habel refers to an alleged incident in Elliston, South Australia, in which "a group of aboriginal people were herded by farmers to the edge of a cliff...and forced over the cliff onto the rocks below."[23] Habel notes that this incident is not supported by documentation and has not been verified by academic historians. Nevertheless, as he points out, it forms part of the memory of the Aborigines of that area:

> For Aboriginal people in that country, the story is painfully true and the denial of this truth intensifies the barrier to reconciliation. The voice of the boy who survived that massacre still echoes through the community.[24]

This kind of incident must be included in a dialogue on historical memory. Needless to say, the veracity of the story and historical evidence should also be a part of the dialogue. But even without the story being proven, its persistence in memory requires its inclusion in dialogue. Dialogue on historical memory is at a different level to academic historical research because it focuses on the role of historical memory in forming identity and on the impact of both historical memory and the identity derived from it on relations with other groups. The role of historians in clarifying and highlighting the facts of history is, of course, crucial to the process, but it remains only a part of the dialogical discourse.

An Implicit Demand for Change

The neutrality that characterizes interreligious dialogue will not come naturally, and may even be impossible in a dialogue on historical memory. There are two factors behind this.

One is that, whereas in interreligious dialogue each religion is its own authority, in historical memory there is a certain "external authority" pertaining to facts with which any historical memory must be made consistent. For example, one may debate whether the occupation of Australia by European settlers should properly be called an "invasion." One may debate the meaning of the word "invasion" and it may be possible to argue, for some reason, that this occupation did not constitute an invasion. However, no matter how the debate is carried forward, there are certain undeniable facts (for example, the fact that the occupation took place, that it resulted in a great number of Aborigines being displaced, that the Aborigines were greatly disadvantaged, and that such occupation was uninvited) that must set the parameters for that discussion. No matter how the dialogue develops, these facts cannot be compromised. To restrict oneself to the use of words such as "settlement," which ignores the fact that the land was home to an indigenous population, could hardly be considered as representing the facts of history in a fair and honest way.

In dialogue over historical memory, then, when a particular historical memory can be shown to be inconsistent with known historical facts, or with the preponderance of evidence regarding some event or phenomenon, there is a very real possibility of an implicit, or even explicit, demand for change. This is probably an inevitable aspect of a dialogue on historical memory that sets it apart from such forms of dialogue as interreligious dialogue, and this will clearly make it much more difficult.

The demand to change one's perspective may be particularly difficult in cases in which there has been violent conflict. In such a case, it is likely that all sides in a conflict believe themselves to have been fighting for a good cause. This belief helps provide a positive self-identity, and demands to change this can threaten self-esteem. Furthermore, such belief presumably plays an extremely important role in the way people cope with the death of loved ones in the conflict, and with the fact that they themselves have killed. When the interpretation of the event is challenged, it raises the possibility that one has killed, or that one's loved ones have died, unnecessarily, and possibly even in a cause that was less than just. Japanese, at least those of them who believed that Japan was indeed fighting to free Asia from Western colonialism and to establish a "co-prosperity sphere," must have experienced something along this line following the Second World War, when the interpretation of history that became accepted made them pure aggressors—an interpretation that has become accepted to a significant extent even in Japan. US and Australian soldiers who went to Vietnam, and families who lost loved ones in Vietnam, are likely to have gone through a similar experience.

Shared Experiences, Conflicting Perceptions

The second factor that makes dialogue on historical memory difficult is the fact that the memories of different groups are not mutually independent. In dialogue between religions, except in the case of religions so strongly related to one another as Judaism and Christianity, the specific religions involved in the dialogue are likely to be mutually independent. A Christian in dialogue with a Buddhist can present an interpretation of what Christianity means without challenging the way the Buddhist sees his/her own Buddhism. However an American in dialogue with a Japanese partner cannot discuss the significance of the attack on Pearl Harbor without impinging on the way the Japanese counterpart might understand the same attack. For this reason too, it will be very nearly impossible to carry out a dialogue with others over historical memory without facing the challenge to change and an implicit goal to reach some level of agreement—a demand that, as we have seen, would normally be absent from other forms of dialogue. While perspectives may differ enormously, the events are shared. There will, undoubtedly, always be at least some minimal demand for agreement on the facts of history, and there may frequently be a need for, at the very least, a mutual acceptance of the meaning that the event had for the other. As Barkan points out,

> we have to treat historical identities as negotiated.... Politically,... there are constraints on what a group can legitimately imagine as its history and culture. These limitations become particularly significant when national images and other identities encroach upon one another.[25]

This does not mean that differences of perspectives on the past must always be resolved. Such differences will always exist and they are not necessarily to be deplored. As Maier points out, "trying to 'synthesize' a narrative from diverse sources and voices is a dangerous exercise: reduction of many voices to one coherent story line means valuing some testimonies more than others."[26]

One example of this difficulty would be the different attitudes in Japan and Korea toward the assassination of Itou Hirobumi by An

Jeung-geun in 1909. No amount of factual clarification will alter the fact that, for many Koreans, An is a hero who resisted Japanese occupation, while for Japan, Itou Hirobumi, four times prime minister, is a revered statesman whose assassination was a loss for Korea as well as Japan. For Koreans, he was the first Resident-General of Korea after it was made a Japanese protectorate in 1905 and was a driving force behind the Japanese annexation of Korea in 1910. For the Japanese, he was a pro-Korean, benevolent, and peace oriented leader. It is doubtful that any amount of historical research would resolve the differences in the way that Japanese and Koreans see these two persons and the assassination of one by the other. Such differences need to be appreciated rather than resolved. What Maier says of the historian applies also to the dialogue on historical memory: "The historian must create a narrative that allows for contending voices, that reveals the aspirations of all actors, the hitherto repressed and the hitherto privileged."[27]

The case of Itou Hirobumi and An Jeung-geun highlights one of the major aspects of this interconnectedness of historical memories that is likely to make dialogue on historical memory difficult. That is, the fact that a dialogue on historical memory will sometimes involve coming to grips with the fact that "we" (whoever the "we" might be in a particular case) are the "bad guys" in someone else's memory, that our heroes are someone else's villains. As Barkan points out,

> for a "new" history to become more than a partisan "extremist" story, the narrative often has to persuade not only the members of the group that will "benefit" from the new interpretation but also their "others," those whose own history will presumably be "diminished," or "tainted," by the new stories.[28]

What has been achieved between Germany and Israel over the Holocaust[29] and between Aborigines and at least a number of white Australians over such issues as the Stolen Generations, in spite of lingering opposition in both cases, point to the possibility of a reconciliation that goes beyond simply living with difference and disagreement to one that is grounded in the recognition of truth.

Some Resources for the Dialogue

Much work has been done that can provide background experience and insights for this kind of dialogue. Two obvious examples are the work that has been done in various truth and reconciliation commissions and the work that has been put into producing joint history textbooks by countries that have formerly been in conflict.

There have been numerous programmes to promote forgiveness and mutual understanding after conflict and to resolve issues from the past through truth and reconciliation commissions. From the experiences of countries such as Chile and Guatemala, South Africa and Rwanda, truth and reconciliation processes constitute a kind of precedent for the dialogue envisioned in this chapter, and they are likely to generate important insights. Barkan lists numerous examples, beginning with the process that led to Switzerland selling substantial amounts of gold to aid "Holocaust victims who lost their money in Swiss banks and, further, to amend historical injustice worldwide."[30]

Collaboration in the making of history textbooks could also be considered as constituting a specific form of the dialogue envisioned here. Germany and France produced a joint history textbook that will be used by all students. Additional volumes are due to follow.[31] Germany and Poland have also produced a joint history textbook,[32] and scholars from Japan, China, and Korea have jointly produced a textbook to be used at middle school level. Titled *History to Open the Future*, it is available in Japanese, Chinese, and Korean.[33]

The Task of Dialogue in the Northeast Asian Context
History and Japan's Relations with its Neighbors

Dialogue on historical memory is a matter of particular importance in Northeast Asia, particularly between Japan and its neighbors. Failure to address the problem of history is a significant contributing factor to the current tensions in the area. It is associated with the tensions that arose over the visits of the Japanese prime minister to Yasukuni Shrine, with the overall distancing of Japan from its neighbors, and with the apprehensions about the reemergence of Japanese militarism. It is a factor that impedes the resolution of issues such as the abduction of Japanese citizens by North Korea, North Korea's nuclear programme, and so on.

From the early Meiji Period (1868–1912), Japan set itself on a course that would alienate it from its neighbors. As early as the fourth year of the Meiji Period (1871) the Japanese government seriously considered invading Korea. By the latter half of the Meiji Period, Japan had adopted a policy of "leaving Asia and joining Europe," and Japan was seen by other Asian countries as having gone over to the West. By the latter half of the 1890s, Japan had already had a war with China and had been responsible for the assassination of Queen Min of Korea. By the end of the Meiji era it had defeated Russia, annexed Korea, and taken effective control of the Manchurian Railroad. Japan subsequently took advantage of the First World War to expand its interests in China, and dealt with the effects of the World Depression of 1929 by effectively colonizing Manchuria through the establishment of a puppet government (1931), and subsequently by an expansion into China that led to all out war in 1937. In 1940, it marched into Indochina, provoking sanctions from the United States, including an oil boycott, which, in turn, is what provoked Japan to attack Pearl Harbor.

This period of Japanese history was marked by numerous atrocities, from forced labor and forced prostitution to the killing of civilians in Manchuria, the medical experiments by Unit 731, the massacre that was perpetrated in Nanking, and the brutal treatment of prisoners of war. The memories of these events constitute a significant portion of the attitude of Asians and others toward Japan to this day. A search on the Internet regarding these incidents will show the extent to which these memories are kept alive amongst many peoples.

Whitewashing the Past

Japan is severely criticized in Asia for the way it deals with this history. As Barkan points out, "by the late nineties Japan's refusal to apologise for its war crimes had become a significant regional marker of a lack of goodwill."[34]

There have been some moves at an official level to recognize Japan's war crimes. Prime Minister Hashimoto Ryutaro, in the mid-nineties, made a personal apology for the "comfort women" but "avoided using the words *government* and *Japan*"[35]—a strategy similar to the one used by Prime Minister John Howard of Australia, in relation to the "Stolen Generations," of offering his own personal apology but refusing to allow an apology by parliament.[36] Beginning with a statement of regret by the Japanese emperor on a visit to China in 1992, there have been similar gestures of acknowledgement by prime ministers ever since. However, these gestures have not amounted to an apology. As Barkan describes it, "Japan is embroiled in its very specific, ritual-like diplomatic dance that provides only for remorse, not for apology."[37] As Barkan notes, these "partial apologies were viewed as hollow when set against the Japanese commemorations of the war atrocities and Japanese militarism, particularly at the controversial Yasukuni Shrine."[38]

Attempts to whitewash Japan's past, in revisionist textbooks, movies such as *Puraido: Unmei no Shunkan* (Pride: a Moment of Destiny),[39] or through the displays in the museum at Yasukuni Shrine,[40] indicate that there is a trend to rewrite history. This understandably creates negative responses from overseas. However, it is important to note that this is not the dominant approach of the Japanese to the history of aggression. The more prevailing Japanese attitude toward this period of history may be described as planned amnesia. The primary goal is not to rewrite, but to forget.

Planned Amnesia

A recent scandal associated with high schools helps bring this trend into focus. It was discovered in October 2006 that a number of high schools in Japan had not been teaching all the subjects required for graduation. Often, schools gave students credit for courses that they never took. A report by the Ministry of Education, Culture, Sports, Science and Technology found that out of a total number of 5,408 high schools in Japan, 540 (approximately 10 percent) failed to offer the courses required by law to the students due to graduate in March 2007. In terms of the numbers of students, from a total of 1,161,925 students in the final year of high school, 83,743 (roughly 7 percent) had not taken the courses required for graduation.[41]

Behind this is the fact that with the declining number of students (due to the decline in birthrate), schools found themselves more and more in competition with one another. To attract students, they needed to have a good record of getting their students through the university entrance exams. Therefore, subjects less important for these exams were likely to be dropped—even subjects officially required for graduation. The schools themselves are reported to have argued that they were responding to requests from students to limit the courses to those necessary for the university entrance exams.[42]

What is significant for our discussion is that there is an absolute consistency throughout the country in the subjects that were dropped. The subject always dropped was history—and primarily world history. Japanese history has also been dropped in some schools.

In Japanese media, discussion on this issue focussed on the question of fairness, particularly on the difficulty of dealing with the problem in a way that would not punish students for the failure of their schools to provide the required courses and, at the same time, would not disadvantage students at the schools that taught these courses. What has been lacking in Japan is a discussion over what this incident reveals about the place of history in Japanese education.

What the above incident reveals is that university entry has greater impact on what is taught in schools than official education policy. Obviously, these examinations will have an even greater impact on what students actually study, even when the required courses are taught at schools. The fact that the courses dropped are history courses indicates that history has been a subject that has been relatively unimportant for the entrance examinations, and therefore it is reasonable to conclude that it has not received a lot of attention for some time. In fact, the ignorance of some university students in regard to relatively recent Japanese history can sometimes be staggering. When correcting students' papers for a course on war and peace in the autumn semester of 2006, I found one student to have given the name of the wrong emperor (the Taisho Emperor—emperor from 1912 to 1925—instead of the Showa Emperor) as the wartime emperor.

In George Orwell's *1984*, the policy of "the Party" is described as "who controls the past controls the future: who controls the present controls the past."[43] In *1984*, the control of memory is an essential means of controlling the people. For Japan, the failure to teach history may well be a means of avoiding confronting the past, at the expense of disconnecting younger Japanese from their history. Such disconnection, consistent with Orwellian typology, may well be creating a more malleable generation of young Japanese.

Japanese Perspectives on History and the Need for a Broader Approach to the Past

It is probably fair to say that the Japanese do not have, at least at present, a coherent collective historical memory. This is presumably partly because of the lack of emphasis on history in education, but also because of the different perspectives that people have. There is, in Japan, something similar to what Macintyre calls the "History Wars."[44]

Perhaps the most fundamental difference is between seeing Japan as an aggressor or a victim in the Second World War. Barkan argues that "Japan has always presented itself as the victim of the war and has consistently ignored and repressed any attempts to focus on its aggression and war crimes. The campaign has largely been successful at instilling these lies domestically and around the world."[45] While this may reflect the official stance and also a good deal of popular consciousness, the real historical memory of the people is more variegated. Ideas that tend to justify Japan's past are more characteristic of people ideologically associated with the political Right—whilst those who deny Japan's justification are associated with the Left. Probably the majority of Japanese see a good deal of truth on both sides. That Japan's militarization evolved as a response to Western colonialism and racism, that Japan was, to some extent, provoked into attacking Pearl Harbor by the oil embargo, and that there were both unfairness and cultural misunderstanding in the war crimes trials, are views held by many who also condemn the military government of Japan and the exploitative activities of Japan on the Asian mainland. This suggests that, in terms of Japan's reconciliation with its neighbors, it may be possible to achieve more by promoting dialogue over historical memory between Japan and its neighbors at a popular level than by seeking apologies at an official level.[46]

At this point, it would be well to take cognition of what is being demanded of Japan in terms of acknowledging history. The issues that repeatedly provoke debate are the textbook issue, official visits to Yasukuni Shrine, and the Nanking massacre. In all these situations Japan is being asked to recognize its own wrongs.

There is certain unfairness in demanding Japan to apologize for its wrongs without there also being a recognition that not all the fault lies with Japan. Japan had good reason to feel threatened by the Western powers. The 1919 Paris Peace Conference did take place at the height of social Darwinism and fears of a "Yellow Peril" onslaught.[47] The oil embargo pushed Japan into a corner, and there is evidence that the "Hull Note"—the US response to Japan's proposed solution to the oil embargo, and the immediate cause of the attack on Pearl Harbor—was in fact written with the intention of provoking a Japanese attack.[48] Outside Japan, ambiguities such as these are recognized almost exclusively by historians. Aside from such experts, public perception has Japan as the sole aggressor. It is reasonable to consider that if there was a fairer acknowledgement of the responsibility of other parties in the lead-up to the war, it might be easier for Japan to acknowledge its own responsibility in relation to Asia.

The Role of Social Darwinism and the Importance of De-racializing History

There has been a tendency to interpret Japan's aggressiveness as indicative of something about the Japanese national character. In the years immediately following the war, commensurate with the racialist thinking of the time, the atrocities carried out by Japan were attributed to the very nature of their race. Christopher Thorne's description of attitudes toward Japan during and after the war reveals the extent to which discussions regarding Japan were replete with references to the idea of race, referring, for example, to "the innate cruelty of the Japanese."[49] He reports that, at least for a while after the war, Franklin D. Roosevelt considered the total isolation of the Japanese "in order that their congenital delinquency should not contaminate the process of bringing about more stable and peaceful conditions in the East through a programme of racial inter-breeding."[50]

The impact of social Darwinism and eugenics (and with these the quest for racial purity and racial superiority) on world opinion of that time should be considered. It was not merely Adolf Hitler who was driven by this. It was relevant to the Armenian Genocide,[51] to Joseph Stalin's ethnic purges,[52] as well as to Australia's "Stolen Generations."[53] Social Darwinism had been promoted in Japan by a number of thinkers, particularly Tokutomi Soho—an important Japanese thinker from the late Meiji Period until the end of the Second World War. Tokutomi introduced social Darwinism in his seminal work *Shorai no Nihon* (The Future Japan), published in 1886. Tokutomi was perhaps the single most influential thinker in the emergence of Japanese militarism. After the war, he was placed under house arrest for promoting militarism, but was exempted from trial due to his advanced age.

Coming, as they did, in a period characterized by atrocities of a similar or even greater scale around the globe (the Armenian Massacre, the Holocaust, Stalin's purges), it may well be more accurate to see Japan's atrocities as an expression of the same mentality that was behind so many of the other atrocities, rather than something inherent in the nature of the Japanese people. This does not diminish the responsibility or reduce the need for later generations to resolve the problems that still remain (failure to do this could even be considered a form of complicity), but it does substantially change what these events mean for identity formation.

The tendency to attribute atrocities of the past to some underlying characteristic of the people, as if there were some kind of genetic basis for these acts, rather than as seeing them as a result, for example, of the mentality of the times, may in fact indicate a residual presence of that racialist mentality in our own worldview today.

It can be argued that the same residual thinking can be seen, for example, in the attitudes that some take in Australia toward the issue of the Stolen Generations, the stories of frontier conflict, and of massacres of Aborigines. These allegations are abhorred by some because they are taken to associate Australian identity with racism or bigotry. Macintyre gives much evidence of these kinds of reactions, such as the expression of Ron Brunton, saying that the Stolen Generations report, *Bringing Them Home*, had been welcomed by people "who know in the depth of their bowels that Australia is bad."[54] This associates admission of past wrongdoing with "bad" identity.

When the suggestion of facing the wrongdoings carried out in the past is taken to show something evil about the very nature of the people, about the national character, it certainly seems like a carryover of the mentality that associated behavior and culture with racial makeup. Recognition of past injustices has not always been dealt with in such a way. During the Enlightenment, memories of the century of wars that followed the Reformation did not lead commentators to attribute some evil characteristic to their own national character. It was religion—or at least the combination of religion with politics—that caused the wars. Rather than feeling shame over this period of brutality, Enlightenment thinkers felt proud of having distanced themselves from these former fallacies.

Given that the rationale behind so many of the atrocities of the first half of the twentieth century has consistently been associated with social Darwinism and the concept of eugenics, it is likely that the atrocities should be more associated with a way of thinking than with national character or national identity. One of the tasks of dialogue on historical memory, then, would be to understand those ideas and their relation to the harm that was done, and become perceptive of any residual presence of such ideas in our own thinking. We probably should not consider that past atrocities reflect some evil dimension of our own nature as a people, nor that the atrocities of others represent something about their fundamental nature.

Conclusion

As I have noted, there are numerous unresolved issues of history in Northeast Asia—particularly issues relating to Japan's past aggression. The region is also confronting serious problems today that are not necessarily related to the past. The issue of abductions of Japanese and South Koreans by North Korea and the North Korean nuclear issue are prominent examples. While these two issues appear more related to the Cold War than to Japan's past aggression, it is likely that a resolution of the differences over historical memory in Northeast Asia, especially in regard to Japanese aggression, would be very helpful in resolving these issues. In fact, it may well be that such a resolution is essential, because, insofar as a resolution is not achieved, there will continue to be lingering problems and tensions in the region.

It should also be clear, from what has been said, that Japan's aggression did not take place in a vacuum. As has been noted, at least to some extent it came about in response to Western expansionism, and may have been affected by such things as ideas related to the "Yellow Peril" and social Darwinism. It may be very difficult for Japan's policy-makers to make formal apologies for Japan's past wrongdoings when there is little done to promote awareness of the factors external to Japan that drove Japan in that direction. A broader dialogue, which would include not just Japan and its neighbors, but the United States, Britain, and Australia, would deal with the whole background to the problems more comprehensively and may make a resolution of differences over historical memory more feasible. This means that dialogue in Northeast Asia should not take place in isolation. Rather it should include, for example, such countries as the United States, Britain, and Australia, along with Japan and its immediate neighbors.[55] This would make possible the more comprehensive approach envisioned here.

It must be reemphasized that the dialogue on historical memory that is advocated is not simply the task of historians. Among historians, dialogue is already being conducted at a multitude of academic fora around the world. Unless some effort is made to address the issue of historical memory at a popular level, glorifications and whitewashing of the past, dwelling on past victimization and vilification of others, will persist. As Maier points out, "just as a trial must produce some verdict...a national public demands some overall assessment. If historians shun doing it carefully, there will be no shortage of calculating or naively apologetic versions."[56] One might add that these same "calculating or naively apologetic versions" will arise if the work of the historian is not transmitted to the general public.

Earlier, the chapter argued for a form of dialogue that is not task-oriented, and that is therefore distinct from negotiation. However, the understanding of the dialogue on historical memory has been quite task-oriented. It has been clearly aimed at resolving differences, either through acceptance of differences or by reaching a consensus on the facts of history and their interpretation. What has been argued is, in a sense, similar to what Barkan describes as "a space to negotiate identities and a mechanism to mediate between national histories...and a negotiation regarding whose story and what versions of the national narratives can be legitimated, not only by supporters but also by adversaries and 'impartial' outsiders."[57]

It might be well to reconsider the experience of interreligious dialogue, in which not having goals other than the dialogue itself has proved crucial. While this will clearly not come naturally, there may be a need for, or at least a strong desirability for, a preliminary stage that is not task-oriented, which is not immediately targeted at correcting or modifying viewpoints. The focus of this earlier stage would be on learning the human experience of the Other. If we take memories of war as an example, the issue would not be what the war meant to the country, but what it meant to the people as human beings. The loss of loved ones, the loss of life and limb, and the experience of having killed are tragedies in the lives of people. Concerning interreligious dialogue, Dupuis argues that "each partner in the dialogue must enter into the experience of the other, in an effort to grasp that experience from within."[58] Something similar may be the starting point for a dialogue on historical memory. With a mutual appreciation of these experiences, people can proceed, even when there is no resolution to the complex issues of the rights and wrongs, with the truths and falsehoods of history. This kind of dialogue would hopefully lead to the discovery, referred to earlier, of a common humanity—a discovery that would make possible an acceptance of the Other and of the Self, and this would enormously help the dialogue envisioned in this chapter.

Notes

1. It would be a mistake to see the emergence of an approach of dialogue in the Christian churches as simply a result of the failure of mission. Neither in 1928 nor in the early 1960s was there any widespread sense that the mission had "failed." The International Missionary Conference held in Edinburgh in 1910 took as its theme "the conversion of the world in this generation." See Kim Caroline Sanecki (2006) "Protestant Christian Missions, Race and Empire: The World Missionary Conference of 1910, Edinburgh, Scotland," MA Thesis, George State University, 22 ff. The difference between this and the theme of dialogue in the 1928 conference is enormous. It is clear that the major event that occurred between these two conferences was the First World War, and this must be seen as a major factor in the transformation of consciousness.
2. Gordon D. Kaufman (1987) "Religious Diversity, Historical Consciousness, and Christian Theology," in John Hick and Paul Knitter (eds.), *The Myth of Christian Uniqueness* (Maryknoll, NY: Orbis Books), 14.
3. See, for example, Wilfred Cantwell Smith's account of how he himself came to this awareness. Wilfred Cantwell Smith (1987) "Idolatry: In Comparative Perspective," in Hick and Knitter, *The Myth of Christian Uniqueness*, 55.
4. Kaufman "Religious Diversity, Historical Consciousness, and Christian Theology," 13.
5. Michael Walzer (1977) *Just and Unjust Wars: A Moral Argument with Historical Illustrations* (New York: Basic Books), 138–143.
6. Walzer *Just and Unjust Wars*, 139.
7. Elazar Barkan (2000) *The Guilt of Nations: Restitution and Negotiating Historical Injustices* (New York: W. W. Norton and Company), x.
8. Stuart Macintyre and Anna Clark (2003) *The History Wars* (Melbourne: Melbourne University Press), 201.
9. Barkan *The Guilt of Nations*, xxi.
10. Ibid., x.
11. Sargent Bush (2000) "America's Origin Myth: Remembering Plymouth Rock," *American Literary History* 12 (4), 746.
12. Barkan *The Guilt of Nations*, 10.
13. Ibid., 11.
14. For a good summation of the various ways in which the Pilgrim Fathers have been interpreted to suit various ideals and causes, see Bush *America's Origin Myth*.

15. Barkan *The Guilt of Nations*, x.
16. Charles S. Maier (2000) "Doing History, Doing Justice: The Narratives of the Historian and of the Truth Commission," in Robert I. Rotberg and Dennis Thompson (eds.), *Truth v. Justice: The Morality of Truth Commissions* (Princeton: Princeton University Press), 272.
17. Jacques Dupuis (1991) *Jesus Christ at the Encounter of the World Religions* (Maryknoll, NY: Orbis Books), 233.
18. Jakob Kavunkal (1989) "Dialogue: On Conversion," in Leonardo N. Mercado and James J. Knight (eds.) *Mission and Dialogue: Theory and Practice* (Manila: Divine Word Publications), 122.
19. World Council of Churches (1998) *Guidelines on Dialogue with People of Living Faiths and Ideologies*, para III. 4, http://www.wcc-coe.org/wcc/what/interreligious/77glines-e.html (accessed October 9, 2007).
20. Dupuis *Jesus Christ at the Encounter*, 241.
21. World Council of Churches *Guidelines on Dialogue*, para II, 22.
22. David J. Bosch (1993) *Transforming Mission: Paradigm Shifts in Theology of Mission* (Maryknoll, NY: Orbis Books), 484.
23. Norman C. Habel (1999) *Reconciliation: Searching for Australia's Soul* (Sydney: HarperCollins Publishers), 34. A brief description of the story of this massacre can be found on the Flinders University homepage at http://www.flinders.edu.au/news/articles/?fj14v12s03 (accessed April 23, 2008).
24. Habel *Reconciliation*, 34.
25. Barkan *The Guilt of Nations*, xxi.
26. Maier "Doing History, Doing Justice," 272.
27. Ibid., 274.
28. Barkan *The Guilt of Nations*, x.
29. See Barkan *The Guilt of Nations*, Chapter 1.
30. Barkan *The Guilt of Nations*, xv.
31. See Mélina Gazsi, "France and Germany make history together," available on the homepage of the French Ministry of Foreign Affairs, http://www.diplomatie.gouv.fr/en/article-imprim.php3?id_article=4573 (accessed October 8, 2007).
32. For information on both the German-French textbooks and the German-Polish textbooks, see the homepage of the Goethe-Institut at http://www.goethe.de/ins/jp/lp/prj/wza/enindex.htm (accessed October 10, 2007).
33. In Japanese, *Mirai wo Hiraku Rekishi*. Kyoubunkan, 2005.
34. Barkan *The Guilt of Nations*, 62.
35. Ibid., 61.
36. See Macintyre and Clark *The History Wars*, 155.
37. Barkan *The Guilt of Nations*, 62.
38. Ibid., 62.

39. Released on May 23, 1998 by Toei Company, it presents Tojo Hideki as carrying out a struggle to resist the interpretation of the victors at the Tokyo War Crimes Tribunal and was controversial inside and outside Japan.
40. The Yasukuni Shrine has its own home page, including an English section. An online presentation of the war museum exhibits is available at http://www.yasukuni.or.jp/english/ (accessed June 7, 2007).
41. *Asahi Shinbun*, evening edition, November 2, 2006, 3. Accommodation has been made for these students to take special courses and write papers to make up for the failure of the schools to teach these courses—although there are complaints that the solution is unfair to the students at the schools who did keep the law and study the required courses.
42. *Ruuru Mushi no Sekinin Juudai*, *Asahi Shinbun*, October 26, 2006, 1.
43. George Orwell (1950, orig. published 1949), *1984: A Novel by George Orwell,* (New York: Penguin), 35.
44. Macintyre and Clark *The History Wars.*
45. Barkan *The Guilt of Nations*, 50.
46. For a good overview of the distance between the official views and the way most ordinary Japanese think with regard to history, see Alexander Bukh, "Japan through the Looking Glass," *Asia Times Online*, May 20, 2005, http://www.atimes.com/atimes/Japan/GE20Dh02.html.
47. See, for example, Naoko Shimazu (1998) *Japan, Race, and Equality: The Racial Equality Proposal of 1919* (London: Routledge).
48. The NHK (Japan Broadcasting Corporation) programme *Sono Toki Rekishi ga Ugoita* presented evidence that Roosevelt had consulted with both Churchill and Chiang Kai-shek who pressured him into producing a response to Japan's proposals for an end to the oil embargo that would provoke Japan to open hostilities. *Nichibei Kaisen wo Kaihi Seyo: Shinshiryou ga Akasu Saigo no Heiwa Koushou. Sono Toki Rekishi ga Ugoita* 160, December 4, 2003.
49. Christopher Thorne (1985) *The Issue of War: States, Societies and the Far Eastern Conflict of 1941–1945* (New York: Oxford University Press), 127.
50. Ibid., 135.
51. See Mustafa Akyol (2005) "A Sultan with Swat: Remembering Abdul Hamid II, a Pro-American Caliph," *The Weekly Standard* (15) (December 26). Akyol's source is Princeton scholar Sukru Hanioglu.
52. Niall Ferguson (2006) *The War of the World: Twentieth-Century and the Descent of the West* (New York: The Penguin Press), 212–220.
53. See Robert Manne (1998) "The Stolen Generation," *Quadrant* 42 (1/2), 53–63.
54. Macintyre and Clark *The History Wars*, 156.

55. Note that there are numerous activities being carried out to promote this dialogue within Northeast Asia, including particularly Japan, China, and Korea. See, for example, *Asian Network for History Education, Japan*, http://www.jca.apc.org/asia-net/english/index.shtml (accessed October 11, 2007).
56. Maier "Doing History, Doing Justice," 275.
57. Barkan *The Guilt of Nations*, xxi.
58. Dupuis *Jesus Christ at the Encounter of the World Religions*, 231.

Bibliography

Abu-Nimer, Mohammad (2003) *Nonviolence and Peacebuilding in Islam: Theory and Practice* (Gainesville: University Press of Florida).
Aguiton, Christophe (2001) *Le monde nous appartient* (Paris: Plon).
Ali, Tariq (2002) *The Clash of Fundamentalisms* (London: Verso).
Amartya Sen (2006) *Identity and Violence: The Illusion of Destiny* (New York: W. W. Norton).
Anderson, Sarah (ed.) (2000) *Views from the South* (Oakland, CA: Food First).
Andrea Riccardi (2004) *La pace preventiva. Speranze e ragioni in un mondo di conflitti* (Cinisello Balsamo, Edizioni San Paolo).
Andretta, Massimiliano (2005) "Il framing del movimento contro la globalizzazione neoliberista," *Rassegna italiana di sociologia* XLVI (2), 249–274.
An-Na'im, Abdullahi Ahmed (ed.) (1992) *Human Rights in Cross-cultural Perspectives: A Quest for Consensus* (Philadelphia: University of Pennsylvania Press).
Ansari, Zafar Ishaq and John L. Esposito (eds.) (2001) *Muslims and the West: Encounter and Dialogue* (Islamabad and Washington, DC: Islamic Research Institute, International Islamic University and Center for Muslim-Christian Understanding, Georgetown University).
Arendt, Hannah (1972) "On Violence," in *Crises of the Republic* (New York: Harcourt Brace Jovanovich).
Ariyaratne, R. R. (2004) "Global Defiance of Globalisation? The World Social Forum at Mumbai, January 16–21, 2004," *Regional Centre for Strategic Studies Newsletter* (Colombo) 10/2, April.
Arnason, Johann P. (2001) "Civilizational Patterns and Civilizing Processes," *International Sociology* 16 (3), 387–405.
Arnason, Johann P. (2003) *Civilizations in Dispute. Historical Questions and Theoretical Traditions* (Leiden and Boston: Brill).
——— (2006) "The Emergence of Islam as a Case of Cultural Crystallization: Historical and Comparative Reflections," in Johann P. Arnason, Armando Salvatore, and Georg Stauth (eds.), *Islam in Process: Historical and Civilizational Perspectives*, vol. 7, *Yearbook of the Sociology of Islam* (Bielefeld: Transcript; New Brunswick, NJ: Transaction), 95–122.
Arnason, Johann P., Shmuel N. Eisenstadt, and Bjorn Wittrock (eds.) (2004) *Axial Civilizations and World History* (Leiden and Boston: Brill).
Aron, Raymond (1973) *Imperial Republic* (London: Weidenfeld and Nicholson).

Arts, Bas, Math Noortmann, and Bob Reinalda (eds.) (2001) *Non-State Actors in International Relations* (Aldershot: Ashgate).

Azra, Azyumardi (2006) *Indonesia, Islam, and Democracy: Dynamics in a Global Context* (Jakarta: Solstice Publishing).

Badie, Bertrand, and Marie-Claude Smouts (eds.) (1996) *L'International sans Territoire* [the international without territory] (Paris: L'Harmattan).

Banawiratma, Johannes B. (2002) "Contextual Theology and the Dialogical Building Blocks of Democracy," in Alan Race and Ingrid Shafer (eds.), *Religions in Dialogue: From Theocracy to Democracy* (Aldershot: Ashgate), 51–62.

Banerjee, Mukulika (2000) *The Pathan Unarmed: Opposition and Memory in the North West Frontier* (Oxford: James Currey).

Bardos, A. A. (2001) "'Public Diplomacy': An Old Art, a New Profession," *The Virginia Quarterly Review* 77 (3), 424–437.

Barkan, Elazar (2000) *The Guilt of Nations: Restitution and Negotiating Historical Injustices* (New York: W. W. Norton and Company).

Barkawi, Tarak and Mark Laffey (2002) "Retrieving the Imperial: Empire and International Relations," *Millennium: Journal of International Studies* 31 (1), 109–127.

Barnavi, Elie (2006) *Les religions meurtrières* (Paris: Flammarion).

Barry, Brian (1989) *Theories of Justice: A Treatise on Social Justice* vol. 1 (Hemel Hempstead: Harvester-Wheatsheaf).

Barry, Brian (1999) "International Society from a Cosmopolitan Perspective," in D. Maple and T. Nardin (eds.), *International Society* (Princeton, NJ: Princeton University Press), 144–163.

—— (1999) "Statism and Nationalism: A Cosmopolitan Critique," in I. Shapiro and L. Brilmaye (eds.), *Global Justice: NOMOS vol. XLI* (New York: New York University Press), 12–66.

Barry, Tom, and Jim Lobe (2003) "The People," in John Feffer (ed.) *Power Trip: U. S. Unilateralism and Global Strategy after September 11* (New York: Seven Story Press), 39–49.

Bartoli, Andrea (2001) "Catholic Peacemaking: The Experience of the Community of Sant'Egidio" (SantEgidio Community and Columbia University) presented at a U.S. Institute of Peace workshop, Washington, DC, February 5.

Becker, Carl L. (1958) *Modern History* (Morristown, NJ: Silver Burdett).

Beers, Charlotte (2002) "Funding for Public Diplomacy," Statement before the Subcommittee on Commerce, Justice, and State of the House Appropriations Committee, April 24. www.state.gov/r/us/9778.htm (accessed April 15, 2005).

—— (2002) "U.S. Public Diplomacy in the Arab and Muslim Worlds," remarks at the Washington Institute for Near East Policy, Washington, DC, May 7. www.state.gove/r/us/10424.htm (accessed May 10, 2002).

Beitz, Charles (1979) *Political Theory and International Relations* (Princeton: Princeton University Press).

—— (1999) "Social and Cosmopolitan Liberalism," *International Affairs* 75 (3), 512–599.
Bello, Walden (2004) *De-Globalization: Ideas for a New World Economy* (London: Zed).
Benford, Robert D. and David A. Snow (2000) "Framing Processes and Social Movements: An Overview and Assessment," *Annual Review of Sociology* (26), 611–639.
Bennis, Phyllis (2006) *Challenging Empire* (Northampton, MA: Olive Branch Press).
Berger, Peter (ed.) (1999) *The Desecularization of the World: Resurgent Religion and World Politics* (Grand Rapids, WI: Wm. B. Eerdmans/Ethics and Public Policy Center).
Bernard, J. F. (1973) *Talleyrand: A Biography* (New York: Putnam).
Bharucha, Rustom (2000) *The Politics of Cultural Practice: Thinking Through Theatre in the Age of Globalisation* (London: Athlone Press).
—— (2003) *Rajasthan: An Oral History—Converstaions with Komal Kathari* (Delhi: Penguin Books).
Birringer, Johannes (1991) *Theatre, Theory, Postmodernism* (Bloomington and Indianapolis: Indiana University Press).
Blaut, James M. (1993) *The Colonizer's Model of the World: Geographic Diffusionism and Eurocentric History* (New York: Guilford Press).
Blinken, Antony J. (2002) "Winning the War of Ideas," *The Washington Quarterly* 25 (2), 101–114.
Bloom, Irene, J. Paul Martin, and Wayne L. Proudfoot (eds.) (1998) *Religious Diversity and Human Rights* (New York: Columbia University Press).
Bobbio, Noberto (1979) *Il problema della guerra e le vie della pace* (Bologna: Il Mulino).
Bond, Patrick (2004) *Talk Left, Walk Right: South Africa's Frustrated Global Reforms* (Scottsville: University of KwaZulu-Natal Press).
—— (2007) "Reformist Reforms, Non-Reformist Reforms and Global Justice: Activist, NGO and Intellectual Challenges in the World Social Forum," *Societies Without Borders* 3, 4–19.
Bonhoeffer, Dietrich (1995) *The Cost of Discipleship* (New York: Touchstone).
Booth, Ken and Tim Dunne (eds.) (2002) *Worlds in Collision: Terror and the Future of Global Order* (New York: Palgrave).
Bosch, David J. (1993) *Transforming Mission: Paradigm Shifts in Theology of Mission* (Maryknoll, NY: Orbis Books).
Brague, Rémi (1998) "Athens, Jerusalem, Mecca: Leo Strauss's Muslim Understanding of Greek Philosophy," *Poetics Today* 19 (2), 235–259.
—— (2000) "Inklusion und Verdauung. Zwei Modelle kultureller Aneignung," in Günter Figal (ed.) *Hermeneutische Wege. H.-G. Gadamer zum Hundertsten* (Tübingen: Mohr), 203–306.
—— (2000) "Is European Culture 'A Tale of Two Cities?,'" in Suzanne Stern-Gillet and Maria Teresa Lunati (eds.), *Historical, Cultural, Socio-Political*

and *Economic Perspectives on Europe* (Lewiston, NY: The Edwin Mellen Press), 35–50.

Brague, Rémi (2002) *Eccentric Culture: A Theory of Western Civilization* (South Bend: Saint Augustine's Press).

Braybrooke, Marcus (1998) *Faith and Interfaith in a Global Age* (Oxford: Braybrooke).

Brecher, Jeremy, Tim Costello, and Brandon Smith (2002) *Globalization from Below* (Cambridge: South End).

Brennan, Frank (2003) *Tampering with Asylum: A Universal Humanitarian Problem* (Sta. Lucia: University of Queensland Press).

Brown, Chris (1992) *International Relations Theory: New Normative Approaches* (Hemel Hempstead: Harvester Wheatsheaf).

Brzezinski, Zbigniev (1997) *The Grand Chessboard: American Primacy and Its Geostrategic Imperatives* (New York: Basic Books).

Buber, Martin (1986) *I and Thou*, trans. Ronald G. Smith (New York: Scribner).

Buchanan, A. (1989) "Assessing the Communitarian Critique of Liberalism," *Ethics* 99 (4), 852–882.

Bull, Hedley (1977) *The Anarchical Society: A Study of Order in World Politics* (London: Macmillan).

Bull, Hedley and Adam Watson (eds.) (1984) *The Expansion of International Society* (Oxford: Clarendon Press).

Burch, Mark A. (2000) *Stepping Lightly* (Gabriola Island: New Society).

Burton, John W. (1969) *Conflict and Communication: The Use of Controlled Communication in International Relations* (London: Macmillan).

Bush, George W. (2001) "Remarks in the National Cathedral," Washington, DC, September 14, www.whitehouse.gov/news/releases/2001/09.html (accessed May 21, 2007).

Bush, Sargent (2000) "America's Origin Myth: Remembering Plymouth Rock," *American Literary History* 12 (4), 745–756.

Butler, Judith (2003) *Precarious Life: The Powers of Mourning and Violence* (London and New York: Verso).

Caldicott, Helen (2002) *The New Nuclear Danger* (New York: New Press).

Callinicos, Alex (2002) "The Actuality of Imperialism," *Millennium: Journal of International Studies* 31 (2), 319–326.

Camilleri, Joseph A. (2004) "Citizenship in a Globalising World: The Role of Civilizational Dialogue," paper presented at the "Islamic-Western Dialogue on Governance Values: Rights and Religious Pluralism" Workshop, Canberra, February 15–18.

—— (2004) "Rights and Pluralism in a Globalising World: The Role of Civilizational Dialogue," paper presented at the "Islamic-Western Dialogue on Governance Values: Rights and Religious Pluralism" Workshop, Canberra. February 15–18.

Camilleri, Joseph A., Kamal Malhotra, and Majid Tehranian (2000) *Reimagining the Future: Towards Democratic Governance* (Melbourne: La Trobe University).

Caney, Simon (2005) *Justice Beyond Borders: A Global Political Theory* (Oxford: Oxford University Press).
Carment, David and Albrecht Schnabel (eds.) (2003) *Conflict Prevention— Path to Peace or Grand Illusion* (Tokyo: United Nations University Press).
Carr, Edward Hallett (1939) *The Twenty Years Crisis, 1919–1939* (London: Macmillan).
Carter, Jimmy (2006) *Palestine: Peace, Not Apartheid* (New York: Simon and Schuster).
Cassano, Franco and Danilo Zolo (eds.) (2007) *L'alternativa mediterranea* (Milano: Feltrinelli).
Chambers, Iain (2001) *Culture After Humanism: History, Culture, Subjectivity* (London: Routledge).
Chappell, David W. (ed.) (1999) *Buddhist Peacework: Creating Cultures of Peace* (Boston: Wisdom Publications with Boston Research Center for the 21st Century).
Charlene Spretnak (1991) *States of Grace* (New York: Harper Collins).
Chomsky, Noam and Gilbert Achcar (2007) *Perilous Power: The Middle East and US Foreign Policy* (London: Hamish Hamilton).
Clark, Ian (1997) *Globalization and Fragmentation: International Relations in the Twentieth Century* (Oxford: Oxford University Press).
—— (2007) *International Legitimacy and World Society* (Oxford: Oxford University Press).
Confucius (1979) *The Analects*, trans. D. C. Lau (Harmondsworth: Penguin Books).
Coward, Harold and Gordon S. Smith (2003) *Religion and Peacebuilding* (Albany: SUNY).
Cox, Michael (2003) "Empire's Back in Town: Or America's Imperial Temptation—Again," *Millennium* 23 (1), 1–27.
—— (2004) "Empire by Denial? Debating US Power," *Security Dialogue* 35 (2), 228–236.
—— (2005) "Empire by Denial: The Strange Case of the United States," *International Affairs* 81 (1), 15–30.
Czempiel, Ernst Otto and James N. Rosenau (1992) *Governance without Government: Order and Change in World Politics* (Cambridge: Cambridge University Press).
Dallmayr, Fred (1996) *Beyond Orientalism: Essays on Cross-Cultural Encounter* (New York: State University of New York Press).
—— (2001) "Dialogue of Civilizations: A Gadamerian Perspective," *Global Dialogue* 3, 67–75.
—— (2002) *Dialogue among Civilizations: Some Exemplary Voices* (New York: Palgrave).
—— (2004) "Beyond Monologue: For a Comparative Political Theory," *Perspectives on Politics* 2 (2), 249–257.
—— (2004) *Peace Talks—Who Will Listen?* (Notre Dame, IN: University of Notre Dame Press).

Dallmayr, Fred and Abbas Manoochehri (eds.) (2008) *Civilizational Dialogue and Political Thought: Tehran Papers* (Lanham, MD: Lexington Book).

D'Ambra, Sebastiano (2006) "Silsilah Dialogue: A Movement for Muslims and Christians and People of other Faiths," in S. H. Toh and V. F. Cawagas (eds.), *Cultivating Wisdom, Harvesting Peace* (Brisbane: Multi-Faith Centre, Griffith University), 187–192.

Daniel, E. Valentine (1996) *Charred Lullabies: Chapters in an Anthropography of Violence* (Princeton: Princeton University Press).

Darby, John and Robert MacGinty (eds.) (2003) *Contemporary Peacemaking: Conflict, Violence and Peace Processes* (New York: Palgrave MacMillan).

Darby, Phillip (2003) "Reconfiguring 'the International': Knowledge Machines, Boundaries and Exclusions," *Alternatives* 28, 141–166.

—— (ed.) (2006) *Postcolonizing the International: Working to Change the Way We Are* (Honolulu: University of Hawai'i Press).

Das, Veena (1995) *Critical Events: An Anthropological Perspective on Contemporary India* (Delhi: Oxford University Press).

—— (2002) "Violence and Translation," in *Sarai Reader 02: The Cities of Everyday Life* (Delhi: Centre for the Study of Developing Societies), 205–209.

Dawson, Raymond (1981) *Confucius* (Oxford: Oxford University Press).

Dear, John (2004) *The Question of Jesus* (New York: Image Books).

Dehejia, Harsha, Prem Shankar Jha, and Ranjit Hoskote (2000) *Despair and Modernity: Reflections from Modern Indian Paintings* (Delhi: Motilal Banarsidass).

Djerejian, Edward (2004) Chair of the Congressional Advisory Group on Public Diplomacy, "Statement to the House Committee on Appropriations," February 4, www.appropriations.house.gov (accessed February 7, 2004).

Doob, Leonard W. (ed.) (1970) *Resolving Conflict in Africa: The Fermeda Workshop* (New Haven and London: Yale University Press).

Doob, Leonard W. and William J. Foltz (1973) "The Belfast Workshop: An Application of Group Techniques to a Destructive Conflict," *The Journal of Conflict Resolution* 17 (3), 489–512.

Doran, Michael S. (2002) "Somebody Else's Civil War," *Foreign Affairs* 81 (1), 22–42.

Doyle, Michael W. (1997) *Ways of War and Peace* (New York: W. W. Norton).

Dupuis, Jacques (1991) *Jesus Christ at the Encounter of the World Religions* (Maryknoll, NY: Orbis Books).

Dussel, Enrique (1998) "Beyond Eurocentrism: The World System and the Limits of Modernity," in Frederic Jameson and Masao Miyoshi (eds.), *The Cultures of Globalization* (Durham: Duke University Press), 3–31.

Edwards, Dennis (2006) *Ecology at the Heart of Faith* (Maryknoll: Orbis Books).

Edwards, J. W. and Louis de Rose (2002) *United We Stand* (Ann Arbor, MI: Mundus).

Eisenstadt, Shmuel N. (2000) "The Civilizational Dimension in Sociological Analysis," *Thesis Eleven* 62 (1), 1–21.
—— (2002) "Concluding Remarks: Public Sphere, Civil Society, and Political Dynamics in Islamic Societies," in Miriam Hoexter, Shmuel N. Eisenstadt, and Nehemia Levtzion (eds.), *The Public Sphere in Muslim Societies* (Albany, NY: SUNY Press), 139–161.
——(2003) *Comparative Civilizations and Multiple Modernities* (Leiden: Brill).
Elias, Norbert (1976) *Über den Prozess der Zivilisation* (Frankfurt: Suhrkamp).
Elshtain, Jean Bethke (1999) "Really Existing Communities," *Review of International Studies* 25 (1), 141–146.
Elwood, Wayne (2001) *The No-nonsense Guide to Globalization* (Oxford: New Internationalist).
Erdheim, Stuart G. (1997) "Could the Allies Have Bombed Auschwitz-Birkenau?," *Holocaust Genocide Studies* 11(2), 129–170.
Escobar, Arturo (2004) "Other Worlds Are (Already) Possible: Self-organisation, Complexity and Post-Capitalist Cultures," in Jai Sen, Anita Anad, Arturo Escobar, and Peter Waterman (eds.), *The World Social Forum: Challenging Empires* (New Delhi: Viveka Foundation), 349–358.
Esposito, John L. and Dalia Mogahed (2008) *Who Speaks for Islam: What a Billion Muslims Really Think* (New York: Gallup Press).
Etzioni, Amitai (2004) *From Empire to Community: A New Approach to International Relations* (New York: Palgrave).
EuroMeSCo Report (2006) "Getting It Right: Inclusion within Diversity— Lessons of the Cartoons Crisis and Beyond" (European Commission MED-2005/109-063, November).
European Centre for Conflict Prevention (1999) *People Building Peace* (Utrecht: ECCP with IFOR and Coexistence Initiative of State of the World Forum).
European Commission (2004) *Dialogue between Peoples and Cultures in the Euro-Mediterranean Area*, Report by the High-Level Advisory Group established at the Initiative of the President of the European Commission (Brussels: European Commission).
Falk, Richard (2001) "The Religious Foundations of Humane Global Governance," in Mische, Patricia M. and Melissa Merkling (eds.), *Toward a Global Civilization? The Contribution of Religions* (New York: Peter Lang), 41–59.
Feinberg, J. (1984) *Harm to Others: The Moral Limits of the Criminal Law* (Oxford: Oxford University Press).
Feng Youlan (1961) *Zhongguo zhexue shi* [*History of Chinese Philosophy*], 2 vols. (Beijing: Zhonghua).
Ferguson, Niall (2006) *The War of the World: Twentieth-Century and the Descent of the West* (New York: The Penguin Press).
Finnemore, Martha and Kathryn Sikkink (1998) "International Norms Dynamics and Political Change," *International Organization* 52 (4), 887–917.

Fisher, Kim (1997) "Locating Frames in the Discursive Universe," *Sociological Research Online* 2 (3), http://www.socresonline.org.uk/socresonline/2/3/4.html (accessed February 02, 2008).
Fisher, William and Tomas Ponniah (eds.) (2003) *Another World is Possible* (London: Zed Books).
Fisk, Robert (2006) *The Great War for Civilisation* (Britain: Harper Perennial).
Foreign Affairs (1996) *Samuel P. Huntington's The Clash of Civilizations? The Debate* (New York: Foreign Affairs/W. W. Norton).
Fousek, John (2000) *To Lead the Free World: American Nationalism & the Cultural Roots of the Cold War* (Chapel Hill, NC: University of North Carolina Press).
Fox, Jonathan and Shmuel Sandler (2004) *Bringing Religion into International Relations* (New York: Palgrave Macmillan).
Freire, Paulo (1985) *The Politics of Education* (New York: MacMillan).
Friedemann (1996) "Büttner Der fundamentalistische Impuls und die Herausforderung der Moderne," *Leviathan. Zeitschrift für Sozialwissenschaft*, 24, 469–492.
Fukuyama, Francis (1989) "The End of History," *The National Interest* 16, 3–16.
——— (1992) *The End of History and the Last Man* (New York: Free Press).
Gadamer, Hans-Georg (1975) *Truth and Method* (New York: The Seabury Press).
——— (1976) "The Universality of the Hermeneutical Problem," in David E. Linge (ed. and tran.), *Philosophical Hermeneutics* (Berkeley: University of California Press), 3–17.
Gaddis, John Lewis (1987) *The Long Peace: Inquiries Into the History of the Cold War* (New York and Oxford: Oxford University Press).
Gandhi, Leela (2006) *Affective Communities: Anticolonial Thought, Fin-de-Siècle Radicalism and the Politics of Friendship* (Durham and London: Duke University Press).
Garcia, Ed (ed.) (1994) *Pilgrim Voices: Citizens as Peacemakers* (Quezon City: International Alert, GZO Peace Institute, and Ateneo Center for Social Policy and Public Affairs).
Gardner, Gary T. (2006) *Inspiring Progress: Religions' Contributions to Sustainable Development* (New York: W. W. Norton).
Gerring, John (1997) "Ideology: A Definitional Analysis," *Political Research Quarterly* 50 (4), 957–994.
Gerson, Joseph (2007) *Empire and the Bomb* (London: Pluto Press).
Goffman, Ervin (1974) *Frame Analysis: An Essay on the Organisation of the Experience* (New York: Harper Colophon).
Gottlieb, Roger S. (ed.) (1996) *This Sacred Earth* (New York: Routledge).
Habel, Norman C. (1999) *Reconciliation: Searching for Australia's Soul* (Sydney: HarperCollins Publishers).
Habermas, Jürgen (1979) *Communication and the Evolution of Society*, trans. Thomas McCarthy (Boston, MA: Beacon Press).

—— (1984–1987, originally 1981) *The Theory of Communicative Action*, tran. Thomas McCarthy (Boston: Beacon Press).

—— (1994) "On the Pragmatic, the Ethical, and the Moral Employments of Practical Reason," in *Justification and Application: Remarks on Discourse Ethics*, trans. Ciaran P. Cronin (Cambridge, MA: MIT Press), 1–17.

Hall, Martin and Patrick Thaddeus Jackson (eds.) (2007) *Civilizational Identity: The Production and Reproduction of "Civilizations" in International Relations* (New York: Palgrave).

Ham, Peter van (2003) "War, Lies, and Videotape: Public Diplomacy and the USA's War on Terrorism," *Security Dialogue* 34 (4), 427–444.

Hamilton, Clive and Richard Denniss (2005) *Affluenza: When too Much is Never Enough* (Crows Nest, NSW: Allen and Unwin).

Hanh, Thich Nhat (2005) *Calming the Fearful Mind: A Zen Response to Terrorism* (Berkeley: Parallax).

Hardt, Michael and Antonio Negri (2000) *Empire* (Cambridge, MA: Harvard University Press).

Hasenclever, Andreas and Volker Rittberger (2003) "Does Religion Make a Difference? Theoretical Approaches to the Impact of Faith on Political Conflict," in Hatzopoulos, Pavlos and Fabio Petito (eds.), *Religion in International Relations: The Return from Exile* (New York: Palgrave), 107–45.

Hatzopoulos, Pavlos and Fabio Petito (eds.) (2003) *Religion in International Relations: The Return from Exile* (New York: Palgrave).

Haufler, Virginia (2001) *A Public Role for the Private Sector: Industry Self-Regulation in a Global Economy* (Washington, DC: Carnegie Endowment for International Peace).

Heidegger, Martin (1962) *Being and Time*, trans. John Macquarrie and Edward Robinson (New York: Harper and Row).

—— (1971) *The Way to Language*, trans. Peter D. Hertz (San Francisco: Harper and Row).

Held, David and Anthony McGrew (eds.) (2000) *The Global Transformations Reader: An Introduction to the Globalization Debate* (Cambridge: Polity).

—— (2002) *Globalization/Anti-Globalization* (Cambridge: Polity).

—— (eds.) (2002) *Governing Globalization: Power, Authority and Global Governance* (Cambridge: Polity).

Held, David, Anthony McGrew, D. Goldblatt, and J. Perraton (1999) *Global Transformations: Politics, Economics and Culture* (Cambridge: Polity).

Hick, John and Paul Knitter (eds.) (1987) *The Myth of Christian Uniqueness* (Maryknoll, NY: Orbis Books).

Higgott, Richard A., Geoffrey R. D. Underhill, and Andreas Bieler (eds.) (2000) *Non-State Actors and Authority in the Global System* (New York: Routledge).

Hoexter, Miriam, Shmuel N. Eisenstadt, and Nehemia Levtzion (eds.) (2002) *The Public Sphere in Muslim Societies* (Albany, NY: SUNY Press).
Hoffmann, Stanley (1977) "An American Social Science: International Relations," *Dædalus* 3, 41–60.
Howard, Michael (2000) *The Invention of Peace: Reflections on War and International Order* (London: Profile Books).
Howarth, David, Aletta Norval, and Yannis Stavrakakis (eds.) (2000) *Discourse Theory and Political Analysis* (Manchester: Manchester University Press).
Hu Jintao (2006) "Speech delivered at Yale University" (New Haven, April 21).
—— (2008) "Continuing Reform and Opening-up and Advancing Win-Win Cooperation," Speech delivered at the Opening Ceremony of the Boao Forum for Asia Annual Conference (Boao, Hainan, April 12).
Huntington, Samuel P. (1993) "Clash of Civilizations?," *Foreign Affairs* 72 (3), 22–49.
—— (1996) *The Clash of Civilizations and the Remaking of World Order* (New York: Simon and Shuster).
—— (1999) "The Lonely Superpower," *Foreign Affairs* 78 (2), 35–49.
Hutchinson, Robert (2004) *Weapons of Mass Destruction* (London: Cassell).
Ignatieff, Michael (2003) "Empire Lite," *Prospect* 83, 36–43.
Ikenberry, John G. (2002) "America's Imperial Ambition," *Foreign Affairs* 81 (5), 44–60.
Inayatullah, Sohail and Gail Boxwell (eds.) (2004) *Islam, Postmodernism and Other Futures: A. Ziauddin Sardar Reader* (London: Pluto Press).
ISESCO (2001) *White Book on Dialogue among Civilizations* (Rabat: Islamic Educational, Scientific and Cultural Organization-ISESCO).
—— (2004) *Islamic Declaration on Cultural Diversity*, adopted by the 4th Islamic Conference of Culture Ministers (Algiers: Islamic Educational, Scientific and Cultural Organization-ISESCO).
Jackson, Robert (2000) *The Global Covenant* (Oxford: Oxford University Press).
Jaspers, Karl (1953) *The Origin and Goal of History* (New Haven, NJ; and London: Yale University Press).
Johnson, Chalmers (2004) *The Sorrows of Empire: Militarism, Secrecy, and the End of the Republic* (New York: Metropolitan Books).
Johnston, Douglas and Cynthia Sampson (eds.) (1994) *Religion, the Missing Dimension of Statecraft* (Oxford: Oxford University Press).
Jones, Charles (1999) *Global Justice: Defending Cosmopolitanism* (Oxford: Oxford University Press).
Jones, Ken (2003) *The New Social Face of Buddhism* (Boston: Wisdom Publications).
Jorga, Nicolae (1935) *Byzantium After Byzantium* (Portland: Center for Romanian Studies).
Juergensmeyer, Mark (2000) *Terror in the Mind of God: The Global Rise of Religious Violence* (Berkeley, CA: University of California Press).

Kagan, Robert (1998) "The Benevolent Empire," *Foreign Policy*, 111, 24–34.
Kaldor, Mary (1999) *New and Old Wars: Organised Violence in a Global Era* (Cambridge: Polity Press).
Kant, Immanuel (1970) *Kant's Political Writings*, ed. Hans Reiss, trans. H. B. Nisbet (Cambridge: Cambridge University Press).
Karagiannis, Nathalie and Peter Wagner (eds.) (2007) *Varieties of World-Making: Beyond Globalization* (Liverpool: Liverpool University Press).
Kavunkal, Jakob (1989) "Dialogue: On Conversion," in Leonardo N. Mercado and James J. Knight (eds.), *Mission and Dialogue: Theory and Practice* (Manila: Divine Word Publications), 117–129.
Kelsen, Hans (1944) *Peace Through Law* (Chapel Hill: The University of North Carolina Press).
Kennedy, Paul (1987) *The Rise and Fall of Great Powers: Economic Change and Military Conflict from 1500 to 2000* (New York: Random House).
Keohane, Robert and Joseph Nye (1972) *Transnational Relations and World Politics* (Cambridge, MA: Harvard University Press).
Khatami, Mohammad (1998) *Islam, Liberty, and Development* (Binghamton, NY: Binghamton University).
—— (2000) *Islam, Dialogue, and Civil Society* (Canberra: The Centre for Arabic and Islamic Studies, the Middle East and Central Asia-ANU).
—— (2001) *Dialogue Among Civilizations* [in Persian] (Teheran: Tarh-e-No Publication).
Kimball, Charles (2003) *When Religion Becomes Evil* (New York: HarperCollins).
Kleinman, Arthur, Veena Das, and Margaret Lock (eds.) (1998) *Social Suffering* (Delhi: Oxford University Press).
Knudtson, Peter and David Suzuki (eds.) (1992) *Wisdom of the Elders* (Toronto: Stoddart).
Korten, David (1999) *The Post Corporate World* (West Hartfort, CT: Kumarian).
Koya, Abdar Rahman (2006) *Hizbullah Party of God* (Kuala Lumpur: The Other Press in association with Crescent International).
Krauthammer, Charles (1991) "The Unipolar Moment," *Foreign Affairs* 1, 23–33.
Kristeva, Julia (1991) *Strangers to Ourselves*, trans. Leon S. Roudiez (New York: Columbia University Press).
Kumar, Corrine (ed.) (2007) *Asking, We Walk* (Bangalore: Streelekha Publications).
Küng, Hans and Karl-Josef Kuschel (eds.) (1995) *A Global Ethic: The Declaration of the Parliament of the World's Religions* (London: Continuum).
Kurtz, Stanley (2002) "The Future of History," *Policy Review* 112, 43–58.
Laclau, Ernesto (1996) "The Death and Resurrection of the Theory of Ideology," *Journal of Political Ideologies* (1), 201–220.
Lantieri, Linda and Janet Patti (1996) *Waging Peace in our Schools* (Boston: Beacon).

Bibliography

Lao Tsu - Tao Te Ching (1991) (London: Wildwood House), trans. Gia-Fu Feng and Jane English.

Lapid, Yosef and Friedrich Kratochwil (eds.) (1996) *The Return of Culture and Identity in International Relations Theory* (London: Lynne Rienner).

Laraña, Enrique, Hank Johnston, and Joseph Gusfield (eds.) (1994) *New Social Movements: From Ideology to Identity* (Philadelphia, PA: Temple University Press).

Larson Gerald James, and Eliot Deutsch (eds.) (1988) *Interpreting Across Boundaries: New Essays in Comparative Philosophy* (Princeton: Princeton University Press).

Laursen, John Christian (ed.) (1999) *Religious Toleration: "The Variety of Rites" from Cyrus to Defoe* (New York: St. Martin's Press).

Layne, Christopher (1993) "The Unipolar Illusion: Why New Great Powers Will Rise," *International Security* 17 (4), 5–51.

Lederach, John Paul (2004) *The Moral Imagination* (Oxford: Oxford University Press).

Lee, Donna (2005) "The Dehumanisation of the Other: Genocide, Film and the Ethical," PhD thesis (Deakin University).

Lessing, Doris (1973, originally 1952) *This was the Old Chief's Country* (London: Michael Joseph).

Lessing, Gotthold Ephraim (1780) *Die Erziehung des Menschengeschlechts* (Berlin: Voss and Sohn).

Linklater, Andrew (1990) *Men and Citizens in the Theory of International Relations* (London: Macmillan).

——— (2001) "Citizenship, Humanity and Cosmopolitan Harm," *International Political Science Review* 22 (3), 261–277.

——— (2002) "Cosmopolitan Communities in International Relations," *International Relations* 16 (1), 135–150.

——— (2006) "The Harm Principle and Global Ethics," *Global Society* 20 (3), 329–343.

Lipset, Seymour Martin (1997) *American Exceptionalism: A Double Edged Sword* (New York: Norton).

Little, David (ed.) (2007) *Peacemakers in Action: Profiles of Religion in Conflict Resolution* (Cambridge: Cambridge University Press).

Lord, Carnes (2006) *Losing Hearts and Minds? Public Diplomacy and Strategic Influence in the Age of Terror* (Westport: Praeger).

Loy, David R. (2003) *The Great Awakening: A Buddhist Social Theory* (Boston: Wisdom).

Lundestad, Gier (1986) "Empire by Invitation? The United States and Western Europe, 1945–1952," *Journal of Peace Research* 23 (3), 263–277.

Lynch, Marc (2000) "The Dialogue of Civilizations and International Public Spheres," *Millennium: Journal of International Studies* 29 (2), 307–330.

MacIntyre, Alasdair C. (1985) *After Virtue: A Study in Moral Theory* (London: Duckworth).

Macintyre, Stuart and Anna Clark (2003) *The History Wars* (Melbourne: Melbourne University Press).
Maddison, Angus (2003) *The World Economy: Historical Statistics* (Paris: OECD Development Centre Studies).
Maier, Charles S. (2000) "Doing History, Doing Justice: The Narratives of the Historian and of the Truth Commission," in Robert I. Rotberg and Dennis Thompson (eds.) *Truth v. Justice: The Morality of Truth Commissions* (Princeton: Princeton University Press), 261–278.
Mamdani, Mahmood (2004) *Good Muslim, Bad Muslim* (New York: Pantheon Books).
Mandelbaum, Michael (2002) *The Ideas that Conquered the World: Peace, Democracy and Free Markets in the Twenty-First Century* (Washington, DC: Public Affairs).
Manheim, Jarol B. (1994) *Strategic Public Diplomacy and American Foreign Policy: The Evolution of Influence* (New York: Oxford University Press).
Manonelles, Manuel (2007) "Building an Alliance of Civilizations," *Pace diritti umani* IV (1), 41–50.
Manoochehri, Abbas (2003) "Enrique Dussel and Ali Shari'ati on Cultural Imperialism," *Intercultural Studies* (1), http://www.intercultural-studies.org/ICS1/Manoocheri.html (accessed July 30, 2008).
Mansergh, Nicholas (1949) *The Coming of the First World War: A Study in the European Balance 1878–1914* (London: Longmans, Green and Coy).
Marcel, Galbriel (1962) *Homo Viator: Introduction to a Metaphysics of Hope*, trans. Emma Craufurd (New York: Harper and Row).
Marchetti, Raffaele (2005) "Interaction-Dependent Justice and the Problem of International Exclusion," *Constellations* 12 (4), 487–501.
—— (2008) *Global Democracy: For and Against Ethical Theory, Institutional Design, and Social Struggles* (London and New York: Routledge).
Mazlish, Bruce (2004) *Civilization and Its Contents* (Stanford, CA: Stanford University Press).
McAdam, Doug, John D McCarthy, and Mayer N. Zald (eds.) (1996) *Comparative Perspectives on Social Movements: Political Opportunities, Mobilizing Structures, and Cultural Framings* (Cambridge: Cambridge University Press).
McEvoy-Levy, Siobhan (2001) *American Exceptionalism and US Foreign Policy: Public Diplomacy at the End of the Cold War* (New York: Palgrave).
McIntosh, Ian S. (2000) *Aboriginal Reconciliation and the Dreaming: Warromiri Yolngu and the Quest for Equality* (Needham Heights, MA: Allyn and Bacon for Cultural Survival).
Mearsheimer, John and Stephen Walt (2006) "The Israel Lobby and US Foreign Policy" (John. F. Kennedy School of Government, Harvard University, Working Paper no. RWP06-011, March 13).
Mencius, trans. D. C. Lau (Harmondsworth: Penguin, 1970).
Mendelssohn, Moses (1783) *Jerusalem, oder über religiöse Macht und Judentum* (Berlin: Maurer).

Mertes, Tom (ed.) (2004) *A Movement of Movements: Is Another World Really Possible?* (London: Verso).
Miller, David (2004) "Holding Nations Responsible," *Ethics* 114, 240–268.
Mische, Patricia M. and Melissa Merkling (eds.) (2001) *Toward a Global Civilization? The Contribution of Religions* (New York: Peter Lang).
Moellendorf, Darrel (2002) *Cosmopolitan Justice* (Boulder: Westview).
Morgenthau, Hans (1948) *Politics among Nations* (New York: Knopf).
Mouffe, Chantal (2007) "Carl Schmitt's Warnings on the Dangers of a Multipolar World," in Odysseos, Louiza and Fabio Petito (eds.), *The International Political Thought of Carl Schmitt: Terror, Liberal War and the Crisis of Global Order* (London: Routledge), 147–153.
Mulhall, Stephen and Adam Swift (1996) *Liberals and Communitarians*, rev. edn. (Oxford: Blackwells).
Muzaffar, Chandra (ed.) (1979) *The Universalism of Islam* (Penang: Aliran).
—— (1993) *Human Rights and the New World Order* (Penang: Just World Trust).
—— (1996) *Dominance of the West over the Rest* (Malaysia: JUST)
—— (1996) *Human Wrongs* (Malaysia: JUST).
—— (2003) *Muslims, Dialogue, Terror* (Petaling Jaya, Malaysia: International Movement for a Just World).
—— (2004) "Islamophobia and the War on Terror," *Connect* 8 (4) (Tokyo).
—— (2005) *At the Crossroads* (Petaling Jaya, Malaysia: International Movement for a Just World—JUST).
—— (2005) *Global Ethic or Global Hegemony: Reflections on Religion, Human Dignity and Civilizational Interaction* (London: Asean Academic Press).
—— (2006) "Globalization and Cultural Diversity," *Keynote Address* at a global seminar organized by the Korean National Commission for UNESCO and the UNU at Jeju island, South Korea, July 18.
—— (2007) "Asia, Oil and Hegemony," paper presented at the IX International Conference of Economists on Globalization and Development Problems held on February 5–9 at Havana City, Cuba.
Nagel, Thomas (2005) "The Problem of Global Justice," *Philosophy and Public Affairs* 33 (2), 112–147.
Nandy, Ashis (1998) "Defining a New Cosmopolitanism: Towards a Dialogue of Asian Civilizations," in Kuan-Hsing Chen (ed.) *Trajectories: Inter-Asia Cultural Studies* (London: Routledge), 142–149.
—— (2003) "The Twilight on Certitudes: Secularism, Hindu Nationalism and Other Masks of Deculturation," *The Romance of the State and the Fate of Dissent in the Tropics* (New Delhi: Oxford University Press), 61–82.
Nandy, Ashis, Shikha Trivedi, Achyut Yagnik, and Shail Mayaram (1995) *Creating a Nationality: The Ramjanmabhumi Movement and Fear of the Self* (New Delhi: Oxford University Press).
Nederman, Cary J. (1999) "*Natio* and the 'Variety of Rites': Foundations of Religious Toleration in Nicholas of Cusa," in John Christian Laursen

(ed.), *Religious Toleration: "The Variety of Rites" from Cyrus to Defoe* (New York: St. Martin's Press), 59–74.
Nietzsche, Friedrich (1968) *The Will to Power* (New York: Vintage).
Nisbet, Erik C., Matthew C. Nisbet, Dietram A. Scheufele, and James E. Shanahan (2004) "Public Diplomacy, Television News, and Muslim Opinion," *Harvard International Journal of Press/Politics* 9 (2), 11–37.
Northcott, Michael (2004) *An Angel Directs The Storm* (London and New York: I. B. Tauris).
Nussbaum, Martha (ed.) (1966) *For Love of Country: Debating the Limits of Patriotism* (Boston: Beacon Press).
Nye, Joseph S. (2004) "The Decline of America's Soft Power: Why Washington Should Worry," *Foreign Affairs* 83 (3), 16–20.
―――― (2004) *Soft Power: The Means to Success in World Politics* (New York: Public Affairs).
Odysseos, Louiza and Fabio Petito (eds.) (2007) *The International Political Thought of Carl Schmitt: Terror, Liberal War and the Crisis of Global Order* (London: Routledge).
Oliver, Pamela and Hank Johnston (2000) "What A Good Idea! Ideology and Frames in Social Movement Research," *Mobilization* 5 (1), 37–54.
Orwell, George (1950, originally 1949) *1984: A Novel by George Orwell* (New York: Penguin).
Pantham, Thomas (1992) "Some Dimensions of Universality of Philosophical Hermeneutics: A Conversation with Hans–Georg Gadamer," *Journal of Indian Council of Philosophical Research* 9 (3), 123–135.
Pape, Robert A. (2005) *Dying To Win: The Strategic Logic of Suicide Terrorism* (New York: Random House).
Parekh, Bhikhu (1989) "Dialogue with the Terrorists," in *Colonialism, Tradition and Reform: An Analysis of Gandhi's Political Discourse* (New Delhi: Sage), 139–171.
―――― (2000) *Rethinking Multicultumlism: Cultural Diversity and Political Theory* (Basingstoke: Macmillan Palgrave).
Parliament of the World's Religions (1993) *Declaration Toward a Global Ethic* (Chicago: Parliament of the World's Religions).
Patomäki, Heikki and Teivo Teivainen (2004) "The World Social Forum: An Open Space or a Movement of Movements?," *Theory, Culture and Society* 21 (6), 145–154.
Payne, Robert (1969) *The Life and Death of Mahatma Gandhi* (London: Bodley Head).
Petersen, Peter G. (2002) "Public Diplomacy and the War on Terrorism," *Foreign Affairs* 81 (5), 74–94.
Petito, Fabio (2007) "The Global Political Discourse of the Dialogue among Civilizations: Mohammad Khatami and Vaclav Havel," *Global Change, Peace & Security* 19 (2), 103–126.
Petras, James (2006) *The Power of Israel in the United States* (Atlanta: Clarity Press).

Pianta, Mario and Federico Silva (2003) *Globalisers from Below. A Survey on Global Civil Society Organisations* (Roma: Globi Research Report), 235–238.
Picco, Giandomenico (ed.) (2001) *Crossing the Divide: Dialogue among Civilizations* (South Orange, NJ: Seton Hall University).
Pieterse, Jan Nederveen (2004) *Globalization or Empire?* (New York: Routledge).
Pogge, Thomas (1989) Realizing Rawls (Ithaca, NY: Cornell University Press).
Pope John Paul II (2005) *Non uccidere in nome di Dio* ed. Natale Benazzi (Casale Monferrato: Edizioni Piemme).
Power, Jonathan (2001) "For the Arrogance of Power-America Now Pays a Terrible Price," TFF Press Info 127, Transnational Foundation (September 13).
Price, Richard (2003) "Transnational Civil Society and Advocacy," *World Politics* 55 (4), 579–607.
Purdy, Jedediah (2003) "Liberal Empire: Assessing the Arguments," *Ethics and International Affairs* 17 (12), 51–64.
Putin, Vladimir (2005), Speech delivered at the High-Level Plenary Meeting of the 60th UN General Assembly, New York.
Qian Mu (1993) *Zhongguo wenhua shi daolun* [Introduction to the History of Chinese Culture] (Taipei: Commercial Press).
Queen, Christopher S. (ed.) (2000) *Engaged Buddhism in the West* (Boston: Wisdom).
Qureshi, Arshad (2005) "11 September 1906: Ek Nazar," Unpublished paper circulated by Swarajpeeth and Nonviolent Peaceforce (New Delhi).
Raiser, Konrad (2003) "Spirituality of Resistance," Paper presented at the World Council of Churches Internal Encounter of Churches, Agencies and other Partners on the World Bank and IMF, Geneva, September 12.
Raju, P. T. (1997) *Introduction to Comparative Philosophy* (Delhi: Motilal Banarsidass).
Rawls, John (1972) *A Theory of Justice* (Oxford: Oxford University Press).
Rawls, John (1999) *The Law of Peoples* (Cambridge, MA: Harvard University Press).
Religions for Peace (2006) *The Kyoto Declaration on Confronting Violence and Advancing Shared Security* (Religions for Peace Eighth World Assembly, August).
Riccardim, Andrea (2006) *Convivere* (Bari: Edizioni Laterza). For an English translation (by Francesca Simmons) of its Introduction, see http://www.resetdoc.org/EN/Coexistence.php (accessed June 1, 2007).
Rosenau, James (2003) *Distant Proximities: Dynamics Beyond Globalization* (Princeton University Press).
Ross, Christopher (2002) "Public Diplomacy Comes of Age," *The Washington Quarterly* 25 (2), 75–83.
Ruether, Rosemary Radford (1992) *Gaia and God* (San Francisco: Harper).

Ruggie, John G. (2004) "Reconstituting the Global Public Domain—Issues, Actors, and Practices," *European Journal of International Relations* 10 (4), 499–531.
Ryn, Claes G. (2003) "The Ideology of American Empire," *Orbis* 47 (2), 383–397.
Said, Edward (1978) *Orientalism* (New York: Vintage).
—— (1995) *Politics of Dispossession* (Britain: Vintage).
Salvatore, Armando (1997) *Islam and the Political Discourse of Modernity* (Reading: Ithaca Press).
—— (2007) *The Public Sphere: Liberal Modernity, Catholicism, Islam* (New York: Palgrave Macmillan).
Samadder, Ranabir (2000) "State in the Revision of Space and History Today," in Ranabir Samadder (ed.), *Space, Territory and the State: New Readings in International Politics* (Hyderabad: Orient Longman), 166–183.
Sanecki, Kim Caroline (2006) "Protestant Christian Missions, Race and Empire: The World Missionary Conference of 1910, Edinburgh, Scotland," MA Thesis, George State University.
Schlesinger, Arthur M. (1986) *The Cycle of American History* (Boston: Houghton Mifflin).
Schmitt, Carl (2003) *The Nomos of the Earth in the International Law of the Jus Publicum Europaeum*, trans. G. L. Ulmen (New York: Telos Press).
Schote, Jan Aart (2004) *Democratizing the Global Economy: The Role of Civil Society* (Warwick: Centre for the Study of Globalisation and Regionalisation).
Sefa Dei, George J. (1997) *Anti-racism Education and Practice* (Halifax: Fernwood).
Shapcott, Richard (2001) *Justice, Community and Dialogue in International Relations* (Cambridge: Cambridge University Press).
Shaw, Martin (2002) "Post-Imperial and Quasi-Imperial: State and Empire in a Global Era," *Millennium: Journal of International Studies* 31 (2), 327–336.
Shimazu, Naoko (1998) *Japan, Race, and Equality: The Racial Equality Proposal of 1919* (London: Routledge).
Singer, Peter (1972) "Famine, Affluence and Morality," *Philosophy and Public Affairs* 1 (1), 229–243.
Sivaraksa, Sulak (2005) *Socially Engaged Buddhism* (Delhi: B. R. Publishing).
Sizer, Stephen R. (2004) *Christian Zionists* (Surrey, Britain: Christ Church Publications).
Smith, Brian (1990) *More than Altruism: The Politics of Private Foreign Aid* (Princeton: Princeton University Press).
Smith-Christopher, Daniel L. (ed.) (1998) *Subverting Hatred: The Challenge of Nonviolence in Religious Traditions* (Maryknoll: Orbis Books).
Smock, David R. (ed.) (2002) *Interfaith Dialogue and Peacebuilding* (Washington, DC: U.S. Institute of Peace).

Smyth, Rosaleen (2001) "Mapping US Public Diplomacy in the 21st Century," *Australian Journal of International Affairs* 55 (3), 421–444.
Snow, David A. and Robert D. Benford (2000) "Clarifying the Relationship between Framing and Ideology," *Mobilization* 5 (1), 55–60.
Steger, Manfred B. (2003) *Globalization: A Very Short Introduction* (Oxford: Oxford University Press).
——(2005) "Ideologies of Globalization," *Journal of Political Ideologies* 10 (1), 11–30;
—— (2005) *Globalism: Market Ideology Meets Terrorism*, 2nd ed. (Lanham, MD: Rowman and Littlefield).
Steger, Manfred B. (2008) *The Rise of the Global Imaginary: Political Ideologies from the French Revolution to the Global War on Terror* (Oxford: Oxford University Press).
Sturmer, John von (2006) *"Gunbanjng, sorry to say these words…" An Occasional Performance Piece for Many Voices* (Melbourne: Institute of Postcolonial Studies), August 19, 4. available at www.ipcs.org.au.
Suganami, Hidemi (1989) *The Domestic Analogy and World Order Proposals* (Cambridge: Cambridge University Press).
Sweig, Julia E. (2006) *Friendly Fire: Losing Friends and Making Enemies in the Anti-American Century* (New York: Public Affairs).
Tacey, David (2003) *The Spirituality Revolution* (Sydney: Harper Collins).
Tamer, Georges (2001) *Islamische Philosophie und die Krise der Moderne. Das Verhältnis von Leo Strauss zu Alfarabi, Avicenna und Averroes* (Leiden: Brill).
Tamimi, Azzam (2007) *Hamas: Unwritten Chapters* (London: Hurst and Company).
Taylor, Charles (1989) *Sources of the Self: The Making of the Modern Identity* (Cambridge, MA: Harvard University Press).
—— (1994) "The Politics of Recognition," in Amy Gutmann (ed.) *Multiculturalism: Examining the Politics of Recognition* (Princeton: Princeton University Press), 25–74.
Tehranian, Majid and David W. Chappell (eds.) (2002) *Dialogue of Civilizations: A New Peace Agenda for a New Millennium* (London: I. B. Tauris).
Thich, Nhat Hanh (1991) *Peace is Every Step* (New York: Bantam).
Thomas, Scott (2005) *The Global Resurgence of Religion and the Transformation of International Relations* (New York: Palgrave).
Thorne, Christopher (1985) *The Issue of War: States, Societies and the Far Eastern Conflict of 1941–1945* (New York: Oxford University Press).
Tiryakian, Edward A. (2001) "Introduction: The Civilization of Modernity and the Modernity of Civilizations," *International Sociology* 16 (3), 277–292.
Todorov, Tzvetan (1984) *The Conquest of America: The Question of Other* (New York: Harper and Row, translated from the French by Richard Howard, first published 1982).

Toh Swee-Hin (ed.) (2000) "Education for a Culture of Peace," Special Issue, *International Journal of Curriculum & Instruction* 2 (1).
Tutu, Desmond and Douglas Adams (2004) *God Has a Dream: A Vision of Hope for Our Time* (New York: Doubleday).
United Nations (2001) "Report of the Secretary-General on the United Nations Year of Dialogue among Civilizations," (New York: UN) (A/56/523).
—— (2001) *Global Agenda for Dialogue among Civilizations* (New York: UN General Assembly), (A/RES/56/6).
—— (2006) *Alliance of Civilizations: Report of the High-Level Group*, November 13.
United Nations Development Program (1999) *Human Development Report 1999—Globalization* (Oxford: Oxford University Press).
Volf, Miroslav (2000) "Forgiveness, Reconciliation, and Justice: A Theological Contribution to a More Peaceful Social Environment," *Millennium: Journal of International Studies* (29) 3, 861–877.
Volkan, Vamik D. (1988) *The Need to Have Enemies and Allies* (New York: Jason Aronson).
Vora, Rajiv (2005) "11 September: Kaun si aur Kiyun," Unpublished Hindi paper circulated by Swarajpeeth and Nonviolent Peaceforce (New Delhi).
Waddy, Charis (1980) *Women in Muslim History* (London and New York: Longman)
Wæver, Ole (2004) "Peace and Security: Two Concepts and Their Relationship," in Stefano Guzzini and Dietrich Jung (eds.), *Contemporary Security Analysis and Copenhagen Peace Research* (London: Routledge): 94–116.
Wagner, Peter (2006) "Social Theory and Political Philosophy," in Gerard Delanty (ed.), *Social Theory and Political Philosophy* (London: Routledge), 25–36.
Walker, R. B. J. (2002) "On the Immanence/Imminence of Empire," *Millennium: Journal of International Studies* 31 (2), 337–345.
Waltz, Kenneth (1979) *Theory of International Politics* (Reading: Addison-Wesley).
—— (2000) "Structural Realism after the Cold War," *International Security* 25 (1), 5–41.
Walzer, Michael (1977) *Just and Unjust Wars: A Moral Argument with Historical Illustrations* (New York: Basic Books).
—— (1994) *Thick and Thin: Moral Argument at Home and Abroad* (Notre Dame, IN: University of Notre Dame Press).
Wang Yucheng (1956) "Huanggang zhulou ji" [The Bamboo Pavilion in Huanggang], in Wu Chucai and Wu Tiaohou (eds.), *Guwen guanzhi* [*The Best of Classical Prose Writings*], 2 vols. (Beijing: Wenxue guji).
Wendt, Alexander (1995) "Constructing International Politics," *International Security* 20 (1), 71–81.

Wendt, Alexander (2003) "Why a World State is Inevitable," *European Journal of International Relations* 9 (4), 491–542.

White, William Charles (1966) *Chinese Jews: A Compilation of Matters relating to the Jews of K'ai-feng Fu*, 2nd ed. (New York: Paragon Book).

Wight, Martin (1991) *International Theory: The Three Traditions* (Leicester: Leicester University Press).

Williams, Appleman William (1980) *Empire As a Way of Life* (Oxford: Oxford University Press).

Williams, Robert A. (1990) *The American Indian in Western Legal Thought: The Discourses of Conquest* (Oxford: Oxford University Press).

Wittgenstein, Ludwig (1968) *Philosophical Investigations*, trans. G. E. M. Anscombe (Oxford: Blackwell).

Wohlforth, William C. (1999) "The Stability of a Unipolar World," *International Security* 24 (1), 5–41.

Woodward, Bob (2006) *State of Denial: Bush at War Part III* (New York: Simon and Schuster).

World Commission on the Social Dimension of Globalization (2004) *A Fair Globalization—Creating Opportunities for All* (Geneva: ILO).

Index

Abizaid, John (US General) 147
Aborigines (Australian) 244, 246, 248, 255
absolute/ism 30
abstention rule 55
Active Intellect 231
Afghanistan 176, 184–5, 192
Africa 8, 33, 132, 134
  Horn of 136
  North 158, 189, 194
  see also South Africa
agonal (agonistic) dialogue 38–9
Aguiton, Chrisophe 98
Alexius II (Patriarch of Moscow) 105
al-Farabi, Abu Nasr 229
Algeria 187
Allam, Magdi 235
Alliance of Civilizations 21 n, 60, 79, 105
Al-Qaeda 147, 149, 171, 184
amnesia 251
An Jeung-geun 247–8
Analects (Confucius) 31, 208–9
An-Nai'im, Abdullahi Ahmed 78
Annan, Kofi 75
anthropology 4, 52, 133
anti-Americanism 8, 150, 154, 159
antithesis 4, 195
Antonio Negri 144
  see also Michael Hardt
apodiotic (truth) 30
Arab 79, 157, 232–4
  countries 60, 188
  League 60
  world 187
Arendt, Hannah 38

Aristotle 12, 31, 37, 112, 220, 228
Arnason, Johann P. 9
Aron, Raymond 8
Asia-Pacific 71, 79
Athens 225, 227, 234
Australia 71, 78, 134, 255–6
  European occupation 246
  indigenous 15 n, 129
  northern 135
  soldiers 247
  South 24
axis of evil 8
Azra, Azyumardi 74

Baghdad 228
Banawiratma, Johannes B. 70
Bandyopadhyaya, Jayantanuja 133
barbarians 131, 212, 213
Barkan, Elazar 241–3, 247–51, 253, 257
Baudrillard, Jean 167
Becker, Carl Heinrich 228
Beers, Charlotte 154–7, 159–61
Beitz, Charles 113, 118, 121
Bharucha, Rustom 140, 144 n
bipolar system 3, 53
Birringer, Johannes 140
Bismarck, Otto von 129, 132
Blaut, James 158
Bond, Patrick 97, 98
Bonhoeffer, Dietrich 83
Bosch, David 244
Brague, Rémi 18, 221–2, 225–31, 233–5
"Brand USA" 150, 156, 159
  see also United States of America
Bringing Them Home (Report, 1997) 255

Index

Britain 158, 256
  empire 7, 176
  India 175–6
  Iraq 187, 189
  leadership 159
  Suez 184
Brunton, Ron 255
Buber, Martin 33
Buddhism 18, 76, 81, 174, 203, 208, 211, 213, 247
Bull, Hedley 9, 56
Burton, John W. 144 n
Bush, George H.W. 153
Bush, George W. 23 n, 149, 154, 190
  administration 16, 147–50, 158, 162, 192
Bush, Sargent 242
Butler, Judith 138
Byzantium 229, 236 n

Camilleri, Joseph viii, 22 n
capitalism 22 n, 98, 153
categorical imperative 41, 111
Central Intelligence Agency (CIA) 168
Centre for Dialogue (La Trobe University) vii, 44 n
Chambers, Iain 130
China 6, 53, 106, 208–14
  civilization 212
  culture 18, 203, 213
  dialogue 213–14
  history 18, 203, 213–14, 249
  identity 208–13
  and Japan 250
  Jews 210–11
Christ, Jesus 223, 230–1, 235
Christianity 32, 190, 204, 223
  see also Roman Catholicism
Christian-Muslim
  dialogue 70, 74
  violence, Maluku 74
Churchill, Winston 129, 170, 260 n
Cicero 31

civil society,
  global 29, 43, 192
  groups 93, 99, 102
  NGOs 76
civilizational
  debate 4, 19
  dialogue 5–6, 10–14, 17–19, 59–60, 62, 185
  encounters 11, 18
  "Clash of Civilizations" (1983) 105
  see also Huntington
Clinton, Bill 153
Cold War 3, 8, 61, 69, 132, 152, 256
  end 7, 47, 66 n
  post- 6, 9, 11–12, 25 n, 53, 73
collective action framing 95
colonialism 133, 184, 204, 246, 253
  de- 132
Committee on Public Information (US) 151
commonalities 15, 19, 55, 134, 241
communitarian 6, 13, 14, 22 n, 24 n, 112, 114
  Beitz 118
  critique 123
  see also cosmopolitan/ism
conflict 18, 49, 62, 63 n, 73–4, 79, 103–4, 249
  armed 36, 240
  Chinese 213
  ethnic 39
  Europe and Islam 217
  identity 140
  intervention 55
  Israeli-Palestinian 190, 194, 203
  perception 247
  post- 61, 243
  resolution 61, 63 n, 71, 73–5, 131, 136–7, 140
  unresolved 19
  violent 58, 69, 72, 79, 83, 84, 201–3, 246
Confucius 31, 37, 208–10, 212
  see also Analects
connectivities 10
Constantinople 206

Index

constructivism, social 64n, 105
consumerism 22n, 80, 168, 177
conversation 201, 204, 207, 214
Cosmopolitan Harm Principle
  (CHP) 111–12, 114–19, 122–3
cosmopolitan/ism 6, 14, 22n, 24n,
  43, 51, 56, 61, 94–102,
  111–20, 124–5
  anti- 111–20, 123–4
  constitution 42
  liberalism 50, 56, 123
  stoic 36
  model 98–102
  "thick" 13
  see also Cosmopolitan Harm
    Principle
Cox, Michael 8
cross-cultural 12, 15, 61, 119
  dialogue 18, 29, 31, 34, 37, 51,
    149–50, 161
  jus gentium 13, 52, 56, 58,
    59–62, 78
culturalist 9, 59, 62
  enclosure 60, 62
  Huntingtonian 21n
  -orientalist 5
Cusa, Nicholas of 206

Dallmayr, Fred R. 7–8, 12, 56, 105,
  202, 205
Darby, Phillip 14, 15
Darebin Town Hall 3
Darwinism (social) 253–6
Das, Veena 138, 139
Dawson, Raymond 209
Dean Edmund Guillon 151
Dehejia, Harsha 172
Descartes 31
development, sustainable 71, 80–1
dialogue
  alternative model 12, 13, 63–3,
    94, 106
  approaches 5, 11, 19
  civilizational 5–6, 10–14, 17–19,
    59–60, 62, 187

civilizations, of 4–6, 10–11, 12–13,
  17, 47–63, 105, 182, 195, 202,
  205, 214, 239
communication, as 12, 29–30,
  32–6, 131, 140
cross-cultural 12, 18, 31, 34–7, 51,
  78, 149–50, 161–2
cultures, religions and
  civilizations 11, 15, 19, 134
dia-lógos 12, 30–1
dimension 39, 101
discourse 14, 48–52, 56, 61, 63, 78,
  85, 245
encounter 3, 10, 18, 39, 55, 58,
  240, 244
global 63n, 161, 124
idea of 19, 52, 63, 233, 239
Platonic 31, 233
plurality 60, 62
politics of 6, 10, 55, 60, 62, 95
process 14–15, 134, 136
strategy 84–5
theory of 5, 8, 33, 49, 51–3, 57–9
see also interfaith, interreligious
  dialogue
Dialogue among Civilizations, UN
  Year of 4, 47, 62, 79
Dietrich Fischer 172
diversity 99, 104, 152, 157, 159
  cultural 78, 112, 195
  linguistic 152
  unity in 6, 51, 79
Doob, Leonard W. 136
Dupuis, Jacques 244, 257
Durkheim, Emile 227
Dussel, Enrique 9

Earth 13, 73
  Charter 81
  harmony 80
ecology, crisis 69, 80–1, 172
empire 3, 7, 8, 15, 30, 147–8
  East Roman (Byzantium) 229
  evil 8, 147, 153
  geography of 133

empire—*Continued*
  "lite" 7
  neoliberal 148, 155
  Ottoman 218–20
  politics of 85
  Roman 163, 220
  see also United States of America, empire; imperialism; monologue of empire
"End of History" 9, 48–50
Enlightenment 6, 10, 40, 219, 225, 227, 255
Erikson, Erik 175
Escobar, Arturo 136
ethos 19, 37, 231–2, 243
Etzioni, Amitai 50, 57
Eurasia 226
Euro-Mediterranean Dialogue 105
Europe 6, 17, 60, 132–3, 175, 203, 218–36
  centre, as 9
  Christianity 206
  civilization 218–20, 226–36
  Concert of 44 n, 132
  and dialogue 141
  experience 51, 134
  identity 18, 190, 219, 222
  integration 60
  model 218
  modernity 224
  and Muslim world 60, 190, 217–21
  nation-states 32
  non- 15, 130, 132, 159
  Western 218–19, 225
  see also European Union
European Union (EU) 33, 60, 105–6, 186, 191
evangelical Christians 190
evil 43, 72, 116, 152, 167, 171, 255

falsafa (philosophy) 228
First World War 132, 151, 250, 258
foreignness within 138
Foster, E. M. 133
Foucault, Michael 227

Franco-Prussian War (1871) 132
Franklin, Benjamin 151
free market 75, 98, 152–3, 158
Freire, Paulo 76, 85
Fukuyama, Francis 9, 51, 153
Fulbright, J. William 151
fundamentalism 17, 79, 153, 175

Gadamer, Hans-Georg 6, 33, 51, 55, 201, 204–7, 214
Gaddis, John Lewis 132
Galtung, Johan 172
Gandhi, Mahatma 131, 175–6, 179 n
Gani, Abdul 175
Gardner, Gary T. 81
Geneva Convention 36
Genocide Convention 117
geopolitics 133
  arguments 5, 228
  Caroligian 221
  -cultural 225
  discourse 9
  Mediterranean 228–90
global distributive justice (GDJ) 113–14, 118, 120, 123–4
global transformations 96, 100, 102–4
globalization 7–9, 14–15, 18, 75–7, 93–106, 134, 141, 147–9, 160, 202
  alter- 5
  "below", from 76, 81
  civilization 104
  economic 102, 153
  liberalism, of 4, 12, 48–9, 62, 98
  and modernization 16, 158
  neoliberal 104–6, 130
  process 60, 162
goodwill 104
great depression (1929) 9, 250
Great War (1914–18) 3
  see also First World War
Greece
  city-state 32
  civilization 230

culture 223–4
democracy 158
dialogue 30
and Hebrew 222, 225, 229, 231
nómos 234
Orthodoxy 229
philosophy 223, 232
sources 225, 229
green
justice 81
theology 81
greenhouse 80
Großraum 54
Grotius, Hugo 36

Habel, Norman C. 24
Habermas, Jürgen 22 n, 34
Habib, Haji 175
Hahn, Thich Nhat 74, 77
Hamas 186, 192
Hardt, Michael 144
 see also Antonio Negri
Hashimoto Ryutaro (PM Japan) 250
Havel, Václav 56, 62, 63 n
Heaven 206, 209, 211, 213
Hebrew
culture 223–4
and Greek 225–9
prophecy 221, 231
Hedley, Bull 9, 56
Hegel, Georg Wilhelm Friedrich 112, 226
hegemony 6, 17, 30, 34, 51, 167, 184–7, 189, 219, 224
Blaut 158
counter- 15, 106
European 219, 221, 234–6
framework 7
global 17, 222
and occupation 184–5
system 167
resistance to 184
US 8, 15, 53, 153, 179 n, 184, 186, 191–5
Heidegger, Martin 33
Held, David 97, 98

hermeneutics 6, 22 n 104–5, 201
ethical 12, 34, 37, 39
method 104
 see also Gadamer
Hinduism 174
Hirobumi, Itou 247–8
history 3, 24 n, 41, 103, 181–2, 222–32, 239–49
American in 133, 149, 152
Chinese 18, 203, 213
European 226, 230
Japanese 18, 249–57
Mediterranean 217
memory 18–19, 252–7
Muslim 17, 220–1
national 80
philosophy 51–2, 222
textbooks 249–53
universal 223, 228
Western 31, 218
 see also "End of History"; memory
History of the Peloponnesian Wars (Thucydides) 19 n
History to Open the Future (2005) 249
Hizbullah 185, 192
Holbrooke, Richard 151
holism 84
Holocaust 9, 211, 248, 249, 254
nuclear 202
Hoodbhoy, Pervez 172
Howard, John 250
humaneness 209
Huntington, Samuel P. 4, 9, 49, 54–5, 59, 134, 196 n, 224
approach 21 n
clash of civilizations 9, 49, 59, 79, 181, 217–18
"lonely superpower" 53
model 59, 62
Hussein, Saddam 160, 189
hyper-power 147, 150

idealism 5, 64 n
identity 18, 80, 94, 103–4, 114, 123, 221, 241–4

identity—*Continued*
  conflicting 140
  cultural 80, 103, 203, 218–19
  groups 79, 118
  and memory 245
  national 59, 255
  politics of 10
  religious 50, 79, 195
imperial globalism 147–8, 150, 152, 164 n
imperial monologue 7–8, 15–16, 157
imperialism 7, 148, 230
  American 8, 159
  modern 230
  neo- 98, 147
  theory 22 n
  see also empire
inclusive 76, 161, 195, 213 n, 232, 235
indeterminacy 205
India 6, 53, 71, 170–1, 176, 223
  British 175–6
  nuclear 173
  partition 138
Indonesia 187, 188
industrial revolution 6
Institute of Postcolonial Studies (Melbourne) 130, 137, 144 n
inter-civilization 17
  dialogue 55, 62
  empathy 191–2
  and mutual understanding 10, 17, 59
  politics 51
  see also civilizational dialogue
interfaith
  dialogue 3, 13, 37, 69–76, 78, 81, 84
  initiatives 71, 74
  learning 70
  movements 70
international economic order (IEO) 121
International Missionary Conference
  (1910) 258
  (1928) 240
international relations 4–5, 8, 11–14, 47–9, 52, 59, 105–6, 168
  and dialogue 182
  model 133
  realists 55
  theory 96
interreligious dialogue 243–4, 246, 257
Inter-Services Intelligence (ISI) 176
Iran 53, 105, 106, 184, 186, 194, 202
  hostages (1980) 152
  Islamic Revolution (1978) 20 n
  Khatami 4, 47, 105, 161, 181
  Mossadegh 184, 187
  oil 187
  youth 149
Ireland 171
  Northern 74, 136
ISESCO's (Islamic Educational, Scientific and Cultural Organization) 22 n
Islamic Salvation Front 187
Islamic studies 224
Islamism 150
Islamophobia 183, 232

James Rosenau 162
Japan 53, 246, 249–56
  history 18, 250
  and Korea 247–9
  militarism 249–51, 254
  and neighbours 19, 239, 249–55
  and WWII 242, 246
Jaspers, Karl 223, 226
jihad 75, 203
  globalism 160
  greater 83
  and suicide bombing 203
Jintao, Hu 105
John Paul II (Pope) 61, 81
Johnson, Chalmers 147–8, 149, 163
Jorga, Nicolae 220
Judaism 247
jus (natural) gentium 56–60
  cross-cultural 13, 52, 62, 55–6, 57–60
JUST (International Movement for a Just World) 22 n

Index

justice 3, 12, 13, 29–31, 37, 61, 71–2,
    75–7, 81, 84, 112–15, 120–1, 224–5
  economic 71
  environmental 70, 81
  distributive 113, 115, 120, 123, 169
  as fairness 49
  global 30, 77, 97, 124
  restoration 39
  social 71, 83
  and truth 39

kamikaje 171
Kant, Immanuel 36, 40–3, 45 n, 111
Kashmir 169, 171
Kaufman, Gordon 240
Kavunkal, Jakob 244
Khatami, Mohammad 4, 6, 17, 20 n,
    47–8, 105, 181–2, 195
  and Havel 62–3 n
  and "Other" 50, 57
Khudai Khidmatgars (God's
    servants) 176
  see also Pathan
Kiehl, William 155
Kimball, Charles 72
King 3
  Asoka 70
  see also Wen
Kipling, Rudyard 133
Klein, Naomi 159
Korea 247–50
  North 185, 202, 249, 256
  South 256
Kristeva, Julia 138
Kuwait 160, 185

Laden, Osama bin 159, 176, 183
Langton, Marcia 135, 141
Latin America 8, 33
League of Nations 33, 40
Lederach, John Paul 71
legitimacy 38, 97, 169
Lessing, Doris 137
Leviathan 34, 38, 66 n
liberal 6, 49, 56–8, 112–15, 120

assumptions 50, 56, 58
colonial 175
cosmopolitan 51, 56, 112, 114, 123
democracy 61, 169
global order 13, 51, 112
/idealist debate 7
internationalism 98
neo- 98
non- 11
solution 112, 120
Western 10, 50
world 6, 13, 15, 47, 52
Linklater, Andrew 116, 117, 124
lógos (word) 12, 30, 31, 32, 33
Lord, Carnes 151, 162
Lu, Ji 209

MacIntyre, Alasdair 10
Macintyre, Stewart 241, 253, 255
Maier, Charles S. 243, 247, 257
Manchuria 250
Mandelbaum, Michael 158–9
Marcel, Gabriel 33
Marchetti, Raffaele 14
marketing 148, 159–60
McEvoy-Levy, Siobhan 152
McGrew, Anthony 97, 98
Meccan Road 234
mediation 74, 133
  joint 55
  peer 73
Medina, Charter 195
Mediterranean 60, 217–35
  euro- 223
  Islam 228
  societies 158
  South 228
  space 217–18, 221–2, 224–30
  studies 228
  Western Europe 221
Meiji Period (1868–1912) 249, 254
Melian 3
  dialogue 19
memory 3, 239, 243, 245–9
  and dialogue 245

Index

memory—*Continued*
  historical 18–19, 239, 241–8, 252–6
  and identity 243, 245
Mencius 37, 212–13
Mendelssohn, Moses 50–1
Middle Ages 31, 32, 219
  late 227
Middle East 60, 74, 150, 156, 159–60
middle-ism 13
millennialism 17, 175
Miller, David 116, 122
Mische, Patricia N. 81
modernity 9–10, 36, 94, 229, 235, 240
  Christianity 32
  end 9
  Western 223–4
modernization 16, 49, 75, 104, 158
Moellendorf, Darrel 113, 121
monologue 6, 12, 30, 32, 34
  see also monologue of empire
monologue of empire 4, 16, 147–8, 150, 155, 157, 159–3
Morgenthau, Hans 112
Mossadegh, Mohamed 184, 187
Mouffe, Chantal *see* Zolo
Mu, Qian 212
Muhammad 201, 231, 234
multiculturalism 6, 13, 16, 60, 168–9, 174
  dialogical 59, 62, 168–9
  global society 48
  politics of 60
multilateralism 30, 65, 98, 149
multipolarity 9, 13, 24 n, 52–5, 59–62
  world 53–4, 104, 106
  see also unipolarity
Muslim 79, 181–91, 220, 234–6
  non- 185, 188, 195
  "Other" 190, 235
  preoccupation with 183–4
  social justice 83
  West 181, 189–91
  women 188–9

world 17, 60, 150, 155–7, 159, 185, 187–8, 190–1, 194, 201–2, 217–20, 225, 234–5
World League 71
  see also ummah
Muzzafar, Chandra 16, 17

Nandy, Ashis 16, 50, 130, 134, 141 n, 142 n
Nanking massacre 250, 253
nationalism 98
  Chinese 214
  European 44 n
  fallacy 40
  mystique 3
  South 98
  Taliban 18
Nedeman, Cary 206–7
neutrality 3
New World Order 47, 153
Nietzsche, Friedrich 172–3, 218, 230
nonalignment 132
normative 49, 50–61, 94–5, 104
  critique 52
  identity 225
  order 51, 59, 62
  pluralism 113
  politics 4, 94
  power 231
  rejection 5
  structure 10, 12, 48, 50–7
  systems 177
  theory 40
Northeast Asia 19, 239, 256
nuclear
  arms race 73, 160
  disarmament 74
  holocaust 202
  North Korea 202, 249, 256
  weapons 9, 73, 198, 240
Nye, Joseph S 161

Obama, Barack 150, 161
Office of Public Diplomacy (US) 153
openness 71, 80, 205

Orient 226
-Occident 10
orientalist 5, 57
  ambiguities 19, 231
  models 15, 158
Orwell, George (*1984*) 252
Ottoman Empire 218-20

Pakistan 160, 194
Palestine 184-5, 186, 189-91
  conflict 160, 190, 194
  youth 178
Pape, Robert A. 175
Parekh, Bhikhu 57
Paris Peace Conference (1919) 253
Parliament of the World's
  Religions 37, 70, 74
  (1893) 104
  (1993) 105
Pathan 176-7
Pearl Harbor 152, 242, 247, 250, 253
Petito, Fabio 12, 13
Pew Charitable Trust Poll 150, 198 n
Pflicht (moral duty) 42
phrónesis (practical reason) 18-19, 218,
  227, 229, 233-5
Pianta, Mario 98
Pieterse, Jan Nederveen 147-8, 155
Pirenne, Henru 218, 227, 228
Plato 31, 220, 233
pluralism 14, 48-9, 56, 99, 102-4,
  111-14, 118, 148
Pogge, Thomas 113, 115-16, 120-1
Pope Benedict XVI 202, 235
positivism
  language 65 n
  legal 56, 57, 61
  post- 4
Powell, Colin 154-5
power 3, 19, 30, 53-4, 79, 167-8, 185,
  193, 217-35
  balance 53-4
  culture 217
  and dialogue 38-40
  distribution 53

dynamis 229
em- 71, 73, 76, 84-5, 225
hegemonic 185-6, 193, 195, 221
hyper- 150-1
institutional 97, 139
-less 38, 84
Muslim perception 18
political 30, 98-103, 107
politics 52, 117, 162, 217
relations 76, 133
soft- 153, 165 n
state 130
struggle 49
super- 7, 53, 162, 181, 185, 191, 243
see also imperialism
pragmatism 3
praxis 58, 60
  political 56, 83, 169
Prodi, Romano 105
propaganda 148, 151, 154, 156
public diplomacy (DP) 151
public sphere 29, 37, 139
Puraido: Unmei no Shunkan (Pride: a
  Moment of Destiny) 251
Putin, Vladimir 105

Queen Min (Korea) 250
Qur'an 81, 84, 189, 195, 231, 232

Rajiv Vora 175
rational choice theory 35
Rawls, John 56, 113
  Rawlsianism 112-13, 118, 120-1
Reagan, Ronald 8, 153
Recep Tayyip Erdoğan 60, 105
reconciliation 13, 19, 39, 43, 61,
  70-3, 84, 131, 137, 239, 245,
  248-9, 253
Reformation 255
relativism 30
Religions for Peace 70
  Kyoto Declaration 70, 74
renaissance 232, 188, 208
Renan, Ernest 218, 227
Requerimiento (requirement) 204

respect 70, 77, 99, 104, 191
  culture of 72, 118
  inner 209
  intercultural 13, 72, 79
  Kantian 124
  mutual 12, 17, 34, 37, 39, 70, 149, 182
revivalism 17, 172, 175
Riccardi, Andrea 59, 61
Robespierre, Maximilien 169, 170
Roman 2, 220–2, 228–30
  Catholicism 226, 229, 235
  East 229
  empire 7, 163, 220
  Greco- 230
  identity 229–301
  Law 226
  Road 221–2, 225, 232–6
  view 220, 228
Roosevelt, Franklin D. (US President) 254, 260 n
RSL (Returned and Services League of Australia) 3
Rumsfeld, Donald (US Secretary of Defence) 8, 154

Said, Edward 58
Salvatore, Armando 18, 19
Satyagraha 175
Saudi Arabia 160, 184, 186, 188
Sawa, Radio and TV 156
Schlesinger, Arthur M. 24 n
secularization 49
security 15–16, 71, 83, 112, 129–32, 138–41
  "fence" 162
  human 15, 140
  in- 7, 55, 130, 137, 139, 154
  Iraq 53
  national 35, 112, 161
  studies 66 n, 131, 140
  UN Council 104
  US national 8, 148, 154, 161–2
Seigel, Michael T. 18, 19, 67 n
Self 221, 233
Sen, Amartya 5

September 11, 30–7, 47, 79, 105, 130, 169
  Dialogue among Civilizations 4, 47, 58, 62
  globalization 148
  and Islam/Muslims 17, 181–7, 191, 233
  post- 15–16, 51, 58, 69, 77, 131, 147, 168
  US public policy 148–60
Shapcott, Richard 5, 14
Shorai no Nihon (The Future Japan, 1886) 254
Shue, Henry 116–17
Silva, Federico 98
Singer, Peter 113
Sivaraksa, Sulak 74, 77
social movement/s 5, 93, 99, 102
social theory 21 n, 100, 224
Song dynasty 211
South 137, 175
  global 6
  and North 10, 129, 141
South Africa 175, 249
South Asia 129, 179 n, 201, 203, 228
Southeast Asia 185, 201, 203
sovereignty 32, 114, 147, 226
  national 117
  state 32, 34–5
Soviet Union 8, 153
  Afghanistan 184
  anti- 176
Spain 21 n, 204
Sri Lanka 138, 170
  Tamil Tigers 171
State Department (US) 150, 154, 160, 162
Steger, Manfred B. 16
Stolen Generations (Australia) 248, 250, 255
Strauss, Leo 234
suffering 76, 83, 121, 138–41, 174, 178, 190, 242
Sufism 62, 195
suicide 82

bombing 16–17, 170–2, 175, 178, 179 n, 191, 203
  terrorism 175–6
Sweig, Julia E. 153

Tacey, David 83
Taliban 176, 185
Talleyrand, Abbé 38
Taoism 18, 203, 208, 211
telos 182
Terraciano, Kevin 204
terrorism 15, 73–4, 161, 169–70, 172, 177, 184
  global 149
  Islamic 174
  Network of 156
  suicide 175
  see also war on terror
theology 16, 67 n, 168, 170
  arguments 4, 75
  "green" 81
  movement 76
  salvation 232
Third Rome (Russia) 220, 229
Third World 132–3
Thorne, Christopher 254
three teachings (Confucianism, Taoism, and Buddhism) 18, 203, 208, 210
Todorov, Tzvetan 133
Toh, Swee-Hin (S.H. Toh) 12, 13
Tokutomi Soho 254
trinity (holy) 230–1
truth and reconciliation commissions 39, 249
  South Africa 39, 61
Turkey 21 n, 60, 187, 188, 191
Tutu, Desmond (Bishop) 39, 61
Tzu, Lao 82

ummah 18, 183–4, 188, 189
UN *see* United Nations
UNESCO (United Nations Educational, Scientific and Cultural Organization) 72, 182

unilateralism 12, 30, 34, 37
  hard 65 n
  militant 150
unipolarity 9, 24 n, 53, 65 n
  era 53
  moment 147
  trend 106
  world order 52, 181–2
United Nations (UN) 33, 47, 149
  Alliance of Civilizations 105
  Charter 57
  Khatami 181
  see also Dialogue among Civilizations
United Nations University (UNU) 182, 196 n, 198 n
United States of America
  century, new 50
  empire 7, 8, 15, 22 n, 147–8, 191, 193
  exceptionalism 152, 161
  Grand Strategy 7, 65 n
  power 8, 147, 149
  public diplomacy 148, 157, 159, 162
  values 16, 147–8, 150, 152–3, 155–61, 198 n
Universal Declaration of Human Rights 36, 77
universal morality 55, 56, 111, 113
universalism 9, 14, 35, 50, 56, 62, 78, 99, 104, 111–13, 118, 120, 124, 195, 222, 235
  dialogue 124
  of Europe 226
  moral 12, 34–6, 55, 111, 113
  tools 101–2
US Information Agency (USIA) 151–2, 154
utilitarian 12, 34, 112

van Ham, Peter 151, 153, 156
Vico, Giambattista 56, 230
Vietnam (war) 152, 247
Von Sturmer, John 137–8 n, 141

Wahabism 17, 160
Wallerstein, Immanuel 136
Walzer, Michael 57, 112, 127 n, 241
war 36, 43, 72–6, 129, 148–9, 150–5,
    184, 204, 240–1
  absence of 72, 75
  crimes 36, 250–3
  culture of 13, 72–5
  global 149–50, 160
  just 75, 150
  new 25 n
  preventive 61
  propaganda 148, 154
  prisoners of 242, 250
  see also war on terror
war on terror 8, 79, 130, 148–50,
    160, 202
Weber, Max 218, 228
Weeramantry, Christopher G. 133
Wen (King) 209, 212–13
West 6–7, 9, 15–17, 19, 49–51, 103,
    130–4, 158, 186, 208, 218–34,
    250, 253
  centricity 4–5, 10, 12–13, 50–1, 56
  and China 212–14
  civilization 50, 103, 168, 219–24
  dominance 9, 35, 56–7, 246, 256
  modernity 223–5
  and Muslim 17, 19, 79, 183–5,
    187–91, 231
  non- 5, 11, 49–50
  revolt against 9, 15
  thought 5–6, 31–2, 131, 218
  US-cenetred 6, 13, 15, 47, 52, 194

Westphalia (1648) 130
  paradigm 98
  system 97
White House 154, 162
Wittgenstein, Ludwig 33
women 70, 78
  comfort 250
  Muslim 184, 188–9, 194
Word, The 206, 231
World Congress of Faiths 71
    (1936) 104
World Council of Churches 74,
    81, 224
  Office on Interreligious
    Relations 71
World Court (International Court of
    Justice) 162
World Public Forum "Dialogue of
    Civilizations" viii, 22 n, 37, 105
World Social Forum 37, 76, 134, 136

Yasukuni Shrine 249, 251, 253, 260 n
"Yellow Peril" 256
Ying-shih, Yu 213
Youlan, Feng 208
Yucheng, Wang 209
Yutong, Zhou 209
Yuxi, Liu 209

Zapatero, Jose Luis Rodriguez 105
Zhang Longxi 18
Zhong, Jin (Chin Chung) 211
Zhou, kingdom 209, 212
Zolo, Danilo 53–4, 59, 66 n